THIS BOOK WAS STOLEN
under the guise of borrowing
From THOMAS E. FARRELL

" They borrow books they will not buy,
They have no ethics or religions;
I wish some kind Burbankian guy
Could cross my books with homing pigeons"

HAIL, CAESAR!

HAIL, CAESAR!

BY

FLETCHER PRATT

WITH ILLUSTRATIONS BY DA OSIMO
AND RELIEF MAPS BY THE AUTHOR

MCMXXXVI · HARRISON SMITH
AND ROBERT HAAS · NEW YORK

To

Marie and her Leica

PREFATORY NOTE

Thanks are especially due to Mr. Alfred Best, for help in photographing several of the maps and for advice and counsel in their construction; to Mr. Arthur Glass for much assistance in looking up obscure references to Caesar among minor Latin authors; to Mr. Laurence Manning for information on the bow-woods of Numidia; to Mr. Wilton Cole for information and references on Roman law; and to anyone who may have been inadvertently forgotten in compiling the above list.

The ordinary quotation marks (" ") have been used to indicate direct quotations wherever they have been set down by the ancient authors. In many cases they have used the indirect quotation or summations of remarks. Where these have been transformed to direct quotations or excerpted, the Continental quotation marks (—— ——) have been used to indicate the difference. Many of the quotations have been somewhat abbreviated.

F. P.

CONTENTS

MAPS AND ILLUSTRATIONS

HAIL, CAESAR!

A CASE IN CANON LAW

Vive l'Amour—Pompeia was a misunderstood wife, with a grievance and a mother-in-law, the latter a hook-nosed dowager of impressive but uninteresting respectability, with a vinegar tongue and a conviction that a young wife's interests should be co-terminous with her domestic responsibilities. The mother-in-law's name was Aurelia, and her presence formed but part of Pompeia's woe. The rest was due to her husband, who neglected society to dabble in politics, kept the atrium of his house filled with ward-heelers and quite overlooked the pleasures inherent in jewelry and trips to watering places.

A strawberry blonde, tall and willowy, Pompeia looked back at her teens as a period when she had somehow missed the ideal young love that was her due as a swan in a world of dark-haired women. Existence in her husband's home had become nearly intolerable when a young man named Publius Clodius Pulcher swam over the horizon—a small-boned youth in his twenties, with an exquisitely turned ankle and a flood of scandalous tales that barely escaped indecency. He was much *à la mode* that summer, with the whole town chuckling over the story of his "campaign in Armenia."

Publius Clodius had gone out to that inhospitable country for a spot of military service as aide to the Proconsul Lucullus, who was commanding an army against King Mithridates of Pontus. The young man was not ambitious for military renown, but wished to please his sister, who had made a May-December marriage with the Proconsul and was determined to see her brother well started in life. Besides, Clodius had reached the stage in his education where he would have to go on a military campaign or else visit some Greek island and hear an old man with fleas in his beard discourse philosophy.

The campaign would be both more exciting and more profitable. Those eastern nations are weak fighters but regular ants for piling up gold, and every time a town is sacked the general and his staff have first choice of the spoil. Proconsul Lucullus had made simply pots of money already; his last report had been accompanied by such magnificent presents for the senators that they had voted him the gratitude of the Republic and declared the honor of Rome demanded that he continue the war.

Clodius felt he could be a success under such a leader. He remembered Lucullus rather vaguely through the haze of idealism with which boyhood surrounds the rich relative (it was six years now since the Proconsul left to take the Armenian command)—a kind of living statue, a figure of cold and boundless generosities, like Jupiter the Benevolent, in whose train the world moved through an iridescent glamour of magnificence.

Alas for illusion!—in Armenia he found a grumpy, unshaven old martinet, living in a skin tent on a hillside. The country was pestilentially cold, the army subsisting on gruel and glory around fires of camels' dung. The lootable cities had been taken long before, the slave-dealers had gone home out of the muck like sensible men, so even prisoners were valueless.

As the general's brother-in-law and ranking staff officer, Clodius had exceptional opportunities for airing his grievances among men and officers. He found both in much the same humor as himself. Their time had expired, there was no more profit in the war, and they wanted to go home and spend their money, whereas Lucullus had promised them only another unappetizing winter campaign among the iron mountains of Lake Van. The gilded youth suggested a novel and pranksome method of protest—a soldiers' strike. Not mutiny, you understand—that would be a crime and legally punishable. Following out his idea they fell into ranks, as usual, at the word of command, but instead of marching toward the enemy, turned around and headed back for the coast. Old Lucullus' face ran the gamut of the rainbow and Publius Clodius nearly fell off his horse with suppressed merriment. It ruined the campaign, of course; the barbarians followed up the retreating army and captured most of the Asian Province. The Senate had to recall Lucullus, who arrived in Rome to find society laughing itself into hysterics over Clodius' account of his joke and his funny mimicry of the general's indignation.

The incident put a period to Clodius' military career—no other commander would have had him in camp for the wealth of King Midas—but what did he care? he would rather play politics. Lucullus was a leader in the Conservative party, so the young man naturally accepted an invitation to a political dinner given by the Radical boss, Caius Julius Caesar. This Caesar was a curious character; like Clodius a politically tarnished aristocrat, he was often quoted as a horrible example for young men contemplating a plunge into socialism. In younger years his prospects had been brilliant, but he had taken the wrong, or leftward turn, and was now in his thirty-ninth year with no possessions but some fame as a neat dresser and an overwhelming load of debt. The svelte Pompeia was his wife; at the dinner she and Clodius met for the first time.

The two were attracted as though by a magnetic current. Each was flattered by the other's attention; Clodius because she was the daughter of one grandee and wife of another, a woman of the most exalted society; she, because she had defied the advancing years to capture the most fashionable young rake in Rome. The knowledge that Pompeia's husband held the office of Pontifex Maximus, which made him a kind of lay Pope of the state religion and official superintendent of Roman morality, undoubtedly added a certain fillip to Clodius' enjoyment of the liaison. Pompeia found it pleasantly difficult, the difficulty being Aurelia, the hawk-beak dowager with whom we commenced. She was a regular Gorgon, but unlike Medusa, sleepless. The household slaves were so much afraid of her that Pompeia dared not risk a rendezvous.

Communications were nevertheless established through Pompeia's personal slave, Abra. By her intermediacy the lovers worked out a plan in the most antic Clodian humor for deceiving Caius Julius under his own roof-tree. There was a festival due soon, the fête of the Bona Dea, one of those queer Eastern goddesses imported at the time of the Punic wars. She was a women's goddess exclusively,

having something to do with fertility—the Greeks called her
Gynaeca. Naturally men were not allowed in any building where
her rites were taking place. Pompeia, being wife of the high pontiff,
was ex-officio chief priestress of the Bona Dea, and the celebration
would be in her house, but as she did not know the ritual, Aurelia
would be in charge of the actual ceremonies. They would last

P. Clodius Pulcher

through the day, held behind drawn curtains; and Pompeia counted
on slipping away while they were in progress to a room where
Clodius (dressed as a woman, trusting to his un-masculine features
and graceful ankle) would have been introduced by the faithful
Abra.

The plan was a mirror of Clodius' mind, too ingeniously bold; it
creaked i' the joints. Instead of being just a woman he decked himself out in a gaudy collection of bangles and ornaments as a singing
girl. Abra let him in and installed him in one of the sleeping cham-
bers, but just then Pompeia was close under Aurelia's eye, dedicating
a consecrated serpent, the most sacred part of the ritual. Clodius
became bored with waiting and began to wander through the dark

corridors; spied a girl in a slave's dress and stage-whispered "Abra!" after her. The girl started round; her name was Abra, but she was another Abra, not Pompeia's maid. In the dimness she could only make out that an attractive singing girl was trying to get her attention. The Bona Dea (as mentioned) was an Oriental deity; wordlessly the wrong Abra pulled Clodius into the alcove they were passing. He tried to push her away but she got close enough to discover that he was no woman, gave a scream, and when he tried to choke her, wrenched loose and ran shrieking through the house.

The women boiled out like so many hornets and when Clodius got involved in the passages of a strange house, tracked him down. They began to beat him; might even have killed him had not Aurelia intervened to keep the building from being profaned by death. He escaped over a wall sans dignity or clothing and the next day the dining tables of Rome were ringing with the scandal. It was called "Clodius' campaign in Juliana" to go with his "campaign in Armenia."

2

Imperturbe—The matter demanded official cognizance; it affected the state religion. Most of the senators could, indeed, recall a time when they had sown a few wild oats of their own. They were willing to let the young man amuse himself, and consoling misunderstood wives was not so unheard-of a method of recreation that he should be made to pay through the nose for it. As a matter of fact Caius Julius himself had so often been guilty in the same fashion that there was a good deal of quiet pleasure among the aristocracy in seeing him thus paid in his own coin. Nor did the offense to the Bona Dea agitate many people in a society convinced that death was an oblivion and that Fate supervised the activities of gods and men.

No—it was neither morality nor reverence that made them prepare to deal hardly with him, nor even the fact that he was a renegade to the Conservative party in which Lucullus was a powerful voice. No—it was rather the curious atmosphere of shame, not for himself, but for the whole Roman people, that hung around Clodius Pulcher's little jokes. He laughed—and every honest man hung his head over a permanent smirch on something ancient and lordly.

This was the third time it had happened now. The famous campaign in Armenia, with its disreputable entail of mutiny and defeat by mere barbarians, had been the second, and it was decidedly more serious than appeared on the surface. The gay society that drifted timelessly under the blue skies of Baiae might find that Pontic business a comedy, but for the Senate it had been a nightmare. The credit of the Roman army was involved; when Lucullus went flooding back to the coast with his troops in revolt and the triumphant King Mithridates on his heels, all the petty dynasts of the Near East looked upon the event as a portent. The Roman conquest (they perceived) was no more permanent than any other in this land of mushroom empires. The Jews rebelled; the Arab sheiks raided into Syria and cut off the spice caravans; the King of Egypt had the Roman tribute collectors drowned; there was an outburst of piracy in the Dodecanese, and something like a financial panic at Rome, with the shares of the big firms that had Oriental connections tumbling out of sight and grain prices soaring on the news from Alexandria.

A delegation of outraged financiers had demanded action from the Senate, and as they had heavy call loans out with many of the senators, the demand had teeth. Unfortunately, the only cure they could suggest was the appointment of Gnaeus Pompey to supreme command of the eastern armies, a remedy which struck the Senate as curing the patient's headache by decapitation. Pompey was unquestionably a brilliant soldier and attracted so intense a devotion from the rank and file that the mere news of his appointment would automatically end the mutiny. He was already near the seat of trouble, with the rank of High Admiral of Rome, commanding a fleet which would be adequate to establish a close blockade of Mithridates' kingdom, and a force of troops which would make him irresistible. His success, in short, was certain; but that success would bring him back to Rome one day at the head of forty or fifty thousand triumphant veterans.

An event to which the Senate looked forward with no pleasure whatever. Pompey's political and economic views had a faint touch of radicalism and a strong infusion of personal ambition. He had signalized a victorious return from an earlier campaign by breaching the sacred constitution in the interests of himself and his soldiers. It was more than likely that with the additional prestige of completing an Oriental conquest in which the Senate's own nominee had failed, he would return in a mood to demand a sharp revision toward

Catiline

monarchy in the scheme of government, and toward socialism in the economic structure. Nobody could think of an adequate answer should he do so, for it is difficult to conceive arguments that will stand against 50,000 sword-blades.

Still, the emergency provoked by Clodius' campaign in Armenia was too grave to be treated with a palliative. The Senate, with a wry grimace, swallowed its dose of the infallible nostrum and passed a bill entrusting Gnaeus Pompey with the command against King Mithridates.

Thus Clodius' harebrained prank had caught the government of Rome in a dilemma; and the worst of it was that it came while the memory of an earlier and more appalling humoresque was yet so fresh that one of the reasons he had gone east was to escape from a city where his social pleasures were hampered by general disapproval.

That first jest started back in the days when Lucius Sergius

Catiline was electioneering for the consulate on a platform of bleed-ing the rich. He was known for a vicious rat; there were whispers afloat that he meant to bleed them in more than a metaphorical sense. As one of his proposals was a general cancellation of debts—extremely attractive to a debt-ridden proletariat indifferent to or ignorant of his character—it seemed possible that he would carry the election. In the narrow ring of high society where they knew so much about Catiline that the subject of his doings was avoided as not quite fit for conversation, the prospect of having such a man as chief magistrate of the state made people's hair stand on end.

Catiline belonged to the topmost crust of the old aristocracy, so the ordinary process of having him blackjacked and dumped in the Tiber would not do. On the other hand it would have a bad effect on the popular mind (so easily stirred to thoughtless violence against its masters) if a high-born lord of his rank were brought to trial for the murders of which he was really guilty and dragged down the Wailing Stairs with the executioner's hook under his chin. Besides, the legal evidence for murder was weak—he might be acquitted, and what then?

Catiline had, however, been administrator of the African province during the previous year and had taxed the provincials rather severely. The Conservative leaders held a quiet meeting at which it was agreed that a peculation-in-office charge could be made to stick, especially as the juries before which such cases were tried were drawn from the Senate list. The penalty was exile, which would keep Lucius Sergius out of mischief while preserving the good moral reputation of the aristocracy, since a larceny conviction carried no such disgrace as one for irreverence or taking fees for legal service. It was simply a step in the normal course of public honors—serve a year as judge of the high court—then a year in a provincial governorship, making money—stand trial, be convicted and exiled—spend a couple years doing the Grand Tour of the Greek Islands—then come back for another election to a judgeship or a consulate.

Young Clodius probably heard of the plan at his father's table. He had just abandoned his *toga praetexta* for the white robe of manhood, and he conceived the impish idea of announcing in the Forum that he would impeach Catiline before the assembly of the whole people. Legally, he had every right to do it; he was a man and a citizen and as his announcement was made first, it took precedence over the senatorial prosecution. Actually, the joke ruined the Senate's plan. Instead of a grave consultation before a few jurors, the trial became a bawdy open-air comedy with all Rome for the judge—this perfumed boy, not out of his teens, appearing as public prosecutor of the strong and sinister politician who had been juggling at empires before his accuser was born. Clodius took full advantage of the comic values in the situation by accentuating the natural femininity of his appearance; blushed, stammered, giggled, lisped and left people with the impression that his real complaint against Catiline was personal and epicene.

The magistrate in charge of the elections tried to save something out of this mess by ruling that since Catiline was under indictment he could not be permitted to run for the consulate. It cost Lucius Sergius the chance of election, but also provided him with an unanswerable argument; after his acquittal he spread the story that the prosecution was a piece of vindictive jobbery to keep him, the people's friend, from pushing through his cancellation-of-debts proposal. The lower orders stopped laughing as this version went round. There was enough truth in it to make it seem all true. They angrily accepted Catiline's deduction that the only way to escape financial slavery was to break their chains by force. Catiline used their fury as a mainspring of the conspiracy he organized; and as his acquittal on Clodius' fraud charge was a bar to further prosecutions, the Senate had to sit aside till Catiline's machinations reached the stage of actual armed rebellion.

Publius Clodius' practical jokes had thus brought him to a kind of zany's apotheosis. He had turned the Republic upside down and proven both the legal and military systems impotent in the face of certain emergencies. The Romans, a people devoted to order, felt life not worth living in such an idiot's paradise, where the wisdom of the fathers was incompetent to provide institutions that could not be wrecked by any dissolute buffoon with a neat ankle and a good list of ancestors.

Thus more than anything else it was in a spirit of stern self-protection that the Senate prepared to deal with the young man's third escapade. But even had these rather philosophical considerations been lacking there was plenty of reason for the Senate to wish Publius Clodius flayed alive. The incident was rich in political possibilities. A stiff punishment for Clodius Pulcher, following not many years on Catiline's miserable death would remind other aristocratic youths of what lay in store for them if they forgot their origins so far as to take the Radical side. Better yet, the trial on such a charge would announce in the most public terms that Clodius had been carrying on an affair with Julius Caesar's wife, and the announcement could hardly fail to split the Radical party wide open. Caius Julius would break with the man who had shamed him. The veterans constituted a powerful political bloc with a slight reddish tinge; they had regarded Clodius as their peculiar friend since the Armenian business, and if he split with Caesar the Radicals would not be able to elect a candidate for years to come.

There were good heads in the Senate; they ran down these ideas in less time than it takes to relate them and the morning after the abortive "campaign in Juliana" the machinery was already at work. An old senator named Cornificus rose to inform the house that an event gravely comprising the Republic's relations with the immortal gods had taken place. He moved that public business be suspended until the college of priests had met under presidency of the Pontifex Maximus to consider the matter. The rest of the Senate wagged solemn agreement with their tongues in their cheeks—for the Pontifex Maximus was, of course, Julius Caesar, and the college of priests was another name for the elder statesmen of the Senate in their religious capacity.

The meeting was a great success. The Vestal Virgins, who were present—naturally, it being a religious cause—described the shocking scene they had witnessed in Pompeia's house. One of the older senators put a motion that gross sacrilege had been committed and the rest rose, in dreary iteration, to deplore the immoral spirit of the age and the anti-religious influence of radical doctrine on Roman youth.

Caius Julius, who must have been frying inwardly, had to sit there and hear himself and his lieutenant Clodius pounded without offering a word of defence. Considering the circumstances he bore it amazingly well. A long peninsula of baldness extended back from the median of his forehead at this time; the only sign of emotion he gave was to reach up with his right forefinger now and then and carefully to adjust one or two of the hairs that had been combed across this

Pompeia

central desert. When he took the vote on the motion he was low-voiced, impersonal—for all he appeared to care the senators might have been discussing the adultery of Trojan Helen instead of that of Pompeia, Caesar's wife.

When the motion had been passed he remarked easily that the matter appeared to call for action, but for his part he was ignorant of any law applying to such a case—perhaps one of his more learned colleagues could help him? The senators gazed at each other, suddenly nonplussed. It was true; the only laws on the books provided fines for minor cases of impiety. No one in the history of the Republic had committed so outrageous a crime. Bringing a prosecution under these statutes would have the piquant ineffectiveness of slapping a man on the wrist for murder. There was more discussion; the college of priests voted to refer the matter to the Senate for action and

Caesar closed the session by announcing that he had divorced his wife lest he be suspected of condoning impiety. It was not until his persecutors were leaving the temple that they realized the Pontifex Maximus had adroitly sidetracked the adultery question by assuming that the religious issue was the only one on which the college of priests had the right to act.

3

Hail the Conquering Hero—At this point the sacrilege case became curiously complicated by reason of involvement with the justice-to-veterans movement. While the senators were debating the report from the pontifical college the argosy they had dreaded for six years swam into harbor. Pompey the Great returned from the East, surrounded by a halo of military renown quite beyond hyperbole. In his triumphal procession were borne tablets setting forth the names of the nine hundred cities he had taken; they were followed by pictures of his glorious naval victories and the trophies of eight hundred enemy warships. Seven captive kings walked in chains behind his car; unfamiliar beasts and wild men from regions whose very names the Romans had never before heard testified to the fact that he had carried the eagles to the Caspian Sea. He distributed a largesse of over fifteen million dollars to his soldiers and his slaves tramped for half a day to carry specie worth twenty millions more into the public treasury, while it was announced that the Roman people had been enriched by the addition of a similar amount to their yearly revenues.

The populace gazed with delight upon these unfamiliar splendors and there were those at hand to remind them (if they needed any stir of memory) that this triumph was the earnest not merely of Rome's sway over far lands and golden beaches, but of how the man who rode in the triumphal car had saved them, every one, from the quick death or the slow. When the anarch mob of gladiators, slaves and criminals had ranged through Italy, burning villas, torturing peasants, defeating consular armies and even threatening the city itself under the leadership of the inspired madman, Spartacus, who was it put down the revolt? Pompey!

That was the peril of the sudden death; the slow, following quick behind, had come from the pirates who had flourished like evil flowers in the rank soil of that servile war. The Romans, an un-seafaring people, had wakened to the danger only when they found the peninsula under effective blockade, the freebooters in control of whole provinces, making war and alliance like sovran princes. They crushed a Roman fleet in the mouth of Ostia harbor; they kidnapped the high magistrates of the Republic; they dammed the sources of the corn supply.

But great Pompey was called to the command against them and within forty days the western seas were clear, corn prices down, stocks up, and Pompey himself leading an irresistible onslaught against the raiders in a great sea-fight off Cape Coracesium. Their castles among the wild summits of Cilicia he carried by storm, and it was there that the messengers of the Senate had found him to say he had been called to redeem the Roman state and name from the disasters brought upon them by King Mithridates.

Down, down went Pontus before the sword of the hero. For every enemy Pompey faced yielded him a new triumph and every triumph tapped an inexhaustible reservoir of wealth. Pompey's soldiers never plundered because their rewards were sure; Pompey's ships rode through every storm. He was the darling of the gods, who added genius to fortune, and to genius, valor—something more than human as he rode through the shouting streets in the triumphal car, with his pale eyes fixed afar, cold, distrait, even aloof.

The attitude was neither a pose nor the accidental product of overindulgence in Cypriote wine on the previous evening. Gnaeus Pompey had, indeed, drunk deep, but it was in the diviner nectar of applause. The slight pouches beneath the eyes, so marring to the effect of the proud, heroic face, were pouches of fatigue, sign-manual of the merciless labors of detail fame exacts from her favorites. —"Great Pompey! Only your arbitrament can settle the question of which of us two peasants shall have this sheepfold."—The man in the car had already long ago received such a public ovation as he was now enjoying; twenty years ago, when he himself had hardly numbered more than a score of years. The present triumph, though the most splendid in Roman history, only applied the multiplication table to a sensation already experienced. His return from the East found Pompey the Great with a palate attuned to subtler and more powerful stimulants.

The achievements which lay nearest his heart now were not his military victories. They had become a matter of course. No, he preferred to be known as the founder of thirty-nine cities; he preferred the knowledge that one of the greatest of living philosophers had risen from his deathbed to pronounce a panegyric on a conqueror with a heart, who had placed irresistible power at the service of impartial justice, like the Zeus of the Golden Age. Even this triumph was a triumph of magnanimity—for the first time in Roman history the captives in the procession of honor were led not to execution but to release. And the tumult of sensations that had crowded in upon the conqueror during twenty years of victory left him with the capacity to enjoy yet one more—the pleasure of hearing Marcus Tullius Cicero refer to him as not merely the greatest living Roman but the greatest, the most humane Roman who had ever lived.

Gnaeus Pompey heard such praises with a pleasure almost voluptuous. They were the world's concession, the intelligent world's concession, that he belonged on a pinnacle above the passion and strife of parties, that he thought as the immortals thought. It was not vanity alone that made him agree with this flattering estimate. After all, while little more than a youth he had been first saluted as "Great" by old Sulla the Dictator, himself a man of gigantic mould. Modesty itself could hardly refuse to recognize something beyond ordinary human talent in two decades of unalloyed success with problems that ordinary human talent had failed to resolve. He desired a liberalizing reform of the economic structure and a centralizing reform of the constitution. Not in vanity, but in a reasonable conviction that the Senate would push both through at the mere desire of the man whose infinite wisdom they had recognized, he disbanded his army and entered Rome as a simple citizen, a modern Cincinnatus, with only his vast reputation as a support.

This spectacular experiment in moderation proved less potent than its promoter desired. The Senate had heard with qualms which it did not attempt to conceal that the terrible conqueror had landed at

Brundisium and was marching on Rome with 60,000 men. Several members, like Crassus the company promoter, who had good reason to believe that Pompey had for them no friendly feeling, found it convenient to retire to hunting lodges in the Apennines for a breath of fresh air. Then they heard with amazement that the 60,000 soldiers had been sent home and that Pompey was coming on alone. The vacationers returned to Rome. In the next session of the Senate they received the first orders from the Infinite Wisdom, brought on from the seacoast by courier—a demand that the consular elections be postponed for a few weeks to enable Pompey to make a personal canvass for a friend and lieutenant-general of his, M. Pupius Piso.

Pupius Piso arrived with the courier as a living example of what the Infinite Wisdom had in store for the Republic—a bronze-faced man, like a red dumpling, who had spent his life in army camps and interlarded his speech with the witticisms he had harvested there. He took well with the proletariat, who discovered refreshing candor in this public rendition of phrases usually confined to the guard-room, but the Senate heard his improprieties with cold distaste. Pompey's name, however, held so much of magic that they were on the edge of granting the request when up popped Marcus Porcius Cato with a long speech full of self-righteousness, the sacred constitution and scorn for the man who was trying to overthrow it. The senators, observing that no lightning fell on him from heaven, took heart of grace and denied the postponement.

Pupius Piso was much put out. It meant that he would have to spend his war bonus on the customary bribery of important vote-getters instead of floating into the consulate on Pompey's popularity. Pompey was more put out and did not know what it meant. He left the detail of mustering out his troops in the hands of a legate and hurried on to Rome. The people received him with paroxysms of delight; the Senate in a glacial mood intended to emphasize their feeling that Jupiter without his thunderbolts was a boresome old busybody. Pompey was deeply hurt. He had been away from the city long enough to forget how petty politicians can be.

Another and even sharper lesson followed immediately. With the tumult of his triumph over, Pompey entered the Senate to report that the territory subject to Rome had been doubled, her yearly revenue nearly doubled and her hegemony of the Mediterranean world placed beyond cavil as the result of his campaigns. For himself, he asked nothing in return; for the Greek cities and allied kings who had aided Rome, only the confirmation of the treaties by which he had secured them in peace and plenty; for his soldiers only moderate pensions in a form the state could well afford—allotments of small plots of land where they might spend their declining years. There was plenty of land in Campania, already public property.

It was this last suggestion that outraged the senators. Every man of them knew that every other man of them held large tracts of that Campanian land on leases of the most flagrant jobbery, playing tuppence a year in rentals and working the ground to death with slave labor. The oration was received in a pellucid silence that contrasted oddly with the ovation the conqueror had received only the day before. After a moment or two old Lucullus rose goutily to remark that the general's report contained many matters of such weight that it would be a mistake to extend a blanket approval to his arrangements. He moved that the house examine Pompey's treaties with eastern states in detail, regarding each as a separate transaction and postponing the other matters to a later date.

Pompey gasped but the Senate assented joyfully. The "other matters" were—was—the pension question, which they were especially anxious to avoid, as the customary method of pensioning returned veterans was a land grant and the Campanian land alone was available. With a little management Lucullus could be made to talk treaties till the exigent veterans died of old age, for he was a notoriously wordy old gentleman and his position as a former commander against Mithridates made him fancy himself as an expert on Levantine affairs. A few well placed interpolations would insure that he drag into the debate some of those thoughts on modern immorality which were so amusing to most of his hearers and keep the proceeding from being a bore. Immorality was a subject on which Lucullus felt strongly; he had recently divorced his wife, the lady Clodia, and she had opened a "salon" at which it was a literary distinction and a social disgrace to be introduced.

The program worked out beautifully; Lucullus rumbled on like a ruminating ox, condemning Pompey, Clodius and Clodia all at once and often in the same involved and endless sentence. But the senatorial tactic also had another and less pleasant result. Pompey, the soldiers' leader and revisionist, was forced into alliance with Clodius, the soldiers' friend. There does not seem to have been any formal striking of hands. It was unnecessary. Pompey merely began to remark that Clodius might after all, be innocent of sacrilege, while Clodius began an active campaign for the election of M. Pupius Piso. The young rascal was hand-in-glove with every scoundrel in the city; on election day all the *canaille* turned out to vote for Piso, and though the Senate succeeded in saddling him with a vacant-headed colleague of their own party, one Valerius Messalla, Piso was triumphantly swept into the consulate as a Radical, giving that party the high magistracy for the first time in many years.

He and Messalla took over just as Lucullus began to draw toward the close of his serial oration on the Eastern treaties, and a bill was brought into the Senate to set up a special commission for the trial of Publius Clodius Pulcher on a charge of sacrilege.

4

Justice—Soldiers never dare doubt; in their profession skepticism is a pawn to failure and a question may be treason. They demand the same cast-iron certainty from the spiritual world; when the star of faith has sunk they guide by the lighthouse of honor. Pompey the Great cared not two straws whether Clodius died on the felon's cross or lived to be as old as Tiresias, but he cared very greatly about his promises to the veterans and the eastern princes. In all honor he could not believe that Clodius had committed the unforgiveable sin by profaning the rites of the Bona Dea; during the Oriental wars he himself had violated the temples of divinities a hundred times more awesome. In honor's light the only person shamed had been the politician Julius Caesar; if he were too mean of spirit to revenge the stain why should the sword of state be unsheathed to help him?

But in his honorable effort to discharge his obligation to the veterans Pompey now found himself saddled with another debt—to the

Radicals who had put Pupius Piso into office. He must now get Clodius acquitted and he flung himself into the task as energetically as though he enjoyed it.

The method was characteristic of the man who for years had been matching wits with the statesmen of the treacherous Orient—trepan the opposition of its best brains. Marcus Tullius Cicero was the most brilliant orator in the Senate, the strongest man they had, who would surely prosecute the case. But he was a fellow of vulgar origin, who trembled with joy when a genuine aristocrat gave him a smile. "What do you think of this bill for indicting Clodius?" inquired the presiding officer of the House, turning to Pompey the day the motion was brought in.

"I think the authority of the Senate in such matters is paramount," replied the conqueror heavily, getting to his feet, "but I would like to say—" and he launched into an unbridled panegyric on Cicero and the services the attorney had done the Republic during his consulate a year before, when he had suppressed Catiline's plot—"You, Marcus Tullius, are a conqueror in a toga. To you alone we owe the safety of our lives and homes." It lasted for hours; Cicero drank it in with an expression of rapture that assured Pompey he was on the right track.

"There!" he remarked, sitting down beside the man he had been praising, "I think I have given a sufficiently clear answer to those questions." Questions? What questions? Questions of Pompey's own making, whose existence he had begun dimly to apprehend, and which he might have understood better had he not been too satisfied with his speech to observe the glance that Cicero, a little recovered from the buttering, was bending on him. It was a look at once speculative and quizzical, such as the king of the pismires might give a ferocious wasp that had unexpectedly offered to fly to the defence of his ant-heap.

For the orator's vanity was colossal; how could Pompey realize that he had given the man mortal offence by correspondence? It was merely a matter of letter and reply—Cicero had written to him with the tale of the Catiline conspiracy and how the Republic had been saved by his, Cicero's exertions. Pompey had retorted that it was very nice of him. How could the victor in a hundred pitched battles, who spent his life among naked blades and flashing arrows, know that Marcus Tullius really believed this bit of police work was a matter of world-saving import? How could he know that when Cicero got the "very nice" letter he would shut himself in his house for the day and when he emerged, tell everybody he met that Pompey was "neither courteous, candid, honorable, intelligent, resolute, nor generous?"

Yet the orator's vanity was colossal; he melted like wax under even halting appreciation from the man he had praised as the greatest of Romans. "I feel myself cooling down in this matter of Clodius," he confessed to a friend the next day, and the next day but one was damning the whole projected prosecution with inconvenient questions—the Bona Dea was an imported goddess, should not sound Romans rather reverence their own deities? might not Clodius appear in court with a gang of toughs to intimidate the jury, and so bring good law into disrepute? the proposed trial had no precedent: let Clodius rather be condemned by the common opinion of honest men . . . add it up and you discover that the friendship of the greatest man in the world was worth having.

But the more Cicero blenched the hotter blazed his rival Cato. He was a descendant of the famous censor of the same name, Marcus Porcius, thought himself a reincarnation of that celebrated prig, and was all hedged round with unpleasant virtues like a porcupine with quills. Pompey heard he had a couple of nubile nieces who were a drain on his finances and sent him an offer for a double marriage, himself to espouse one of the girls, his son the other. The women of Cato's family nearly swooned with delight; when the lord of their house refused the glittering bribe they gave him so rough a time that the normal acerbity of his speeches was intensified in the exact proportion of his sufferings.

He harried the trial bill over every obstruction and through the Senate. The Radicals were not beat yet; the measure provided for a new legal procedure, so the assembly of the people must pass it to confirm and the point of defence was changed to that body. Pompey fussed around importantly, begging old soldiers to vote against it.

Consul Piso introduced the bill in the Forum with a speech contrary and while he was talking the place filled up with a gang of half-drunken rowdies who proclaimed their intent of beating up everyone who voted for the bill. People began to shout; Cato heard the tumult from his nearby house, dashed to the Forum surrounded by his clients and began a harangue against Clodius, Piso and Pompey. Perceiving that the moderate men were rallying around him, if only for dislike of Clodius' roughs, the senatorial leaders plucked up heart, called out their own clients and hurried to join him, and the prospect of a regular riot battle blew up sudden as a thundercloud.

That did not suit Pompey's book; his help to Clodius was only a means to the end of getting the eastern treaties approved, and he would never make it if tempers gave way in unforgiveable blows. He had Piso hastily prorogue the assembly of the people and summon the Senate to reconsider its bill.

It was a noisy meeting with everybody jabbering at once and all indignant, but the Senate stood by the bill, four hundred to fifteen, when the vote was taken. Just as the result was announced, an old army sergeant named Fufius Calenus whom Pompey had managed to get elected tribune, stuck his snipe-like nose into the building and swore that he would veto the bill before the people could vote on it. He had that privilege; in fact it was his duty, as the office of the tribunes was to put a stop to any proceeding that might cause strife among the orders. But the idea that he meant to fulfill this legal duty against the bill for Clodius' trial unleashed the whole bag of Aeolus. Even Cicero, swept away in the torrent, forgot for a moment what side he was on, got up and pronounced a beautiful invective on Fufius and Piso as a pair of scoundrels with a single redeeming vice—laziness.

Fufius sat silent, the impact of the bitter words etching a military stubbornness deeper into his rusty countenance. When the tide of words ebbed, Senator Hortensius, a fine old parliamentarian who had taken no part in the proceedings except to note the unyielding visage of the tribune, made a suggestion of compromise. The original Senate bill provided a trial *in camera* before a special jury drawn from the senatorial list.——Why not split the difference with the Radicals?

(said Hortensius) let the trial go on, but in public, with a jury chosen by lot from the ordinary citizens' list. For his part he considered Clodius' guilt so obvious no jury could fail to convict.——"A sword of lead would do to cut *his* throat!" finished Hortensius with an oratorical flourish and sat down.

The Senate, which was recovering its bearings, began to murmur approval—but would Fufius accept the compromise measure?

The tribune had no orders on this point. He looked anxiously to Pompey for instructions, but everyone else was gazing in the same direction and the great soldier dared not, for the sake of the proprieties, signal his opinion. For that matter the proposal had caught him off balance; he needed time and a council of war to make up his mind and had neither, so he sat still, avoiding Fufius' eye. Forced to make his own decision, the tribune stammered a lukewarm acceptance, the amended bill was passed *viva voce,* the house adjourned and the trial began next day.

"The most disreputable crew I ever saw outside a gambling hell," Cicero described the jury, a trifle unfairly. It was true that the defence had challenged the solid citizens whom the lot brought into the panel, but the prosecution had similarly challenged the obvious rogues. The fifty-six who remained to hear the evidence were the middle cut of the joint—aristocrats on their way down hill, the precise extent of whose delinquencies was unknown, petty commercial men on the make, the exact quality of whose intelligence was uncertain.

The prosecution brought out old Lucullus as its first witness. Yes, he knew the defendant, believed him capable of any crime.

——Upon what ground? inquired the prosecutor blandly. The Proconsul's eye lighted; with evident relish he launched into the tale of his wrongs at the hands of the Clodian family. The defendant's sister Clodia had been his wife; during the Armenian campaign he had been surprised and hurt to receive stiff and chilly letters from so brilliant a lady. He had ascribed the coldness of these notes to her literary pretensions and had remonstrated with her for writing rhetoric to her husband. There had ensued a brief second summer of returning warmth, which he was now, alas! forced to conclude had been simulated by the shameless hussy for the sole purpose of inducing him to take Publius Clodius onto his staff. He had accepted the wretch, the world well knew with what result. But, gentlemen, this was not the worst—(at this point Lucullus emitted a few heart-rending groans, then paused to compose himself) . . . not the worst; for he had lately learned that Publius Clodius, not content with

Lucullus

loading his military reputation with disgrace, had dishonored his home as well. In other words, his wife had a lover, and the lover was none other than her own brother—Publius Clodius Pulcher. (Sensation.)

The defence tried to have this testimony thrown out on the ground that Clodius was being tried for sacrilege and this had nothing to do with the question. The jury, ears agape for more scandals in high life, ruled the point was competent as proving the defendant's depraved character. Cicero thought that day he detected a few honest faces among the "disreputable crew." The prosecution brought out the Vestal Virgins, who gave their evidence with calm detatchment, very impressive. Several other ladies confirmed the story; then the prosecutor called on Julius Caesar, probably more in the intention of

driving a wedge between him and Clodius than in that of strengthening an already overwhelming case.

Caius Julius came to court mantled in the icy dignity which Roman
politicians exuded so liberally for the benefit of inferior races, but
which they found uncommonly aggravating when turned against
themselves. Mentally, he appeared to brush the whole business from
his skirts with an elegantly manicured hand.

"What do you know of this affair?"

"Nothing whatever."

"But it took place in your house."

"It took place in the temple of the Bona Dea, from which it was
my pious duty to be absent on such an occasion."

"Why did you divorce your wife then?"

"Caesar's wife should be above reproach." (Inextinguishable
laughter.)

The prosecution withdrew the witness, and Caesar's house slaves
being unavailable (he had sent them out of the city to prevent the
examination under torture which was the legal procedure) closed its
case.

The defence was an alibi; a scalawag named Caius Canusius swore
that Clodius had been with him in Interamna, ninety miles from
Rome, on the day of the Bona Dea. The jury received this incredible
yarn with patent mistrust. The defence replaced Canusius with
Cicero, who had been reached by one of Pompey's agents and dra-
gooned into assurances of friendship which the conqueror interpreted as a willingness to perjure himself for the cause.

As he approached the tribunal, Clodius' bravoes, who did not know
of Pompey's private arrangement, began to shout and flash weapons,
but the jury rallied round the orator with a "strict and unanimous
uprightness" that caused him to revise his opinion of their integrity.
Thus sustained, he dared to tell the truth. In a loud voice he announced that P. Clodius had called at his house in Rome not three
hours before the sacrilege; he could not possibly have been in Interamna and Canusius was a liar. The alibi collapsed like a jester's
bladder, and Clodius' train of thugs set up such a howling that the
jury adjourned for the night, with a request to the Senate for a

military guard on the morrow when they were to pronounce their verdict.

The consuls held office in alternate months; it had become the turn of Valerius Messalla, the Conservative. He summoned the senators at twilight, hurried through the necessary sanctions and as dark closed in the streets resounded with the heavy tramp of a troop of regulars marching in from the Janiculum. It was a night of torches and agitation. The rooming-house districts were astir, and there was an unwonted activity down in the financial quarter, where the watch recognized two or three of the jurymen, slinking along with mantles drawn about their heads. Probably the only person who slept quietly was Julius Caesar, the wronged husband for whose benefit these alarms and excursions were theoretically being organized. After having given his evidence he had immediately changed to traveling dress and gone out to the Field of Mars, where he joined a small suite of officers. His term as a judge had expired with the old year. In the morning he would take horse for the long ride up through Italy, the Alps and Pyrenees to Lusitania, of which province he had been named governor, and he was not even waiting for the verdict.

The dawn brought shouting groups marching through the streets. Most of the jewellers failed to open up their shops and the members of the jury moved toward the Forum like criminals, each the center of a little knot of soldiers, with a long tail of rascality hooting behind. The guard formed square around the voting urns, shields and spears at the ready. Cato was there, his lean, pinched face showing as much satisfaction as it ever did over anything; Hortensius was there congratulating himself and everyone else on the success of his compromise plan for getting Clodius into the prisoner's dock. Clodius was there but no one spoke to him except the toughs he had brought as a bodyguard.

Consul Piso examined the ballots and stepped to the rostra, holding up his hand for silence:

"The jury," he announced, "has voted by thirty-one to twenty-five that the accused is *not guilty*—"

His voice was drowned in the universal shout; of delight from the followers of Clodius, of dismay from the Conservatives. The guard withdrew to side and side; the jury stepped out to join the now thoroughly amicable mob. As they passed the little group of lowering aristocrats, old Senator Catulus growled out at them:

"Why did you want the guard? To keep your pockets from being picked of the bribes you took?"

II

THE SHORES OF THE ATLANTIC

First in This Village—Ambition cannot afford to keep many personal feelings. They are tame bears, merry companions till grown to strength, when they will brook no other loyalty. Boundless ambition, indeed (and there is really no other kind, since "limited ambition" is a phrase signifying something its possessor is ready to sacrifice, like "limited honesty")—boundless ambition is predicated either upon an utter contempt for humanity or upon a peculiar universal affection for mankind, stirring the ambitious one to Promethean exertions to enable his fellow-creatures more freely to cultivate those flowers of individuality in which he delights. Both types of ambition exclude personal hatred and personal attachments, the former more than the latter; and this fact, without the reasons for it, is so generally apprehended that the discussions as to whether Julius Caesar was infinitely ambitious may well have begun as he clattered along the dusty summer roads through Italy with the Apennines rising and falling along the horizon like the waves of a rocky sea.

The topic afterward became one popular in schools of rhetoric, where it was used for disputations in the Greek manner. One of the arguments always advanced for Caius Julius' ambition was the lack of personal attachment he showed when he coldly divorced Pompeia. The premise was subject to the obvious retort that it would have been remarkable if he had shown feeling for her in any case. She was his third wife, and by a marriage of convenience. There was also the rhetorically less pleasing but more frequently adduced rebuttal that his sex life was abnormal. In his youth he had spent a couple of years at the Bithynian court of King Nicomedes; he had returned from that visit laden with presents of such royal magnificence that Roman wits, with a wink and nod, called him "Queen Nicomedes." As usual scandal confined itself to surface appearances, quite overlooking that Caesar was at the time a Roman noble in most excellent good odor with the government at home and therefore worth the cultivation of any small potentate. If there had been anything abnormal about him, indeed, he would not have found nearly as much favor in Bithynia, for the court worshipped Ashtaroth and there was quite good evidence that Nicomedes' daughter, the Princess Nysa, had induced the young Roman grandee to assist her in the rites of that goddess.

Which left the question of his ambition in doubt. A more cogent argument was the strange incident at Gades, which occurred when the new governor arrived in that town to survey the provincial records before beginning his tour of inspection. The temple of Hercules is situated on a high, bare hill; on the marble porch stands a heroic statue of Alexander the Great, one arm outflung toward the fathomless ocean as though to reproach it for setting a period to his glories. Caesar stood before that statue for a long time, as immobile as the sculptured figure. One of the members of his suite finally touched him on the arm, and taken aback at seeing that the eyes turned in his direction were bright with tears, made bold to ask the reason.

"Do you not think I have just cause to weep?" asked Caius Julius, "When I consider that Alexander, at an age less than mine had conquered the whole world, while I have done nothing worth remembering?"

Was it because Gades and its temples held sentimental memories for him? Thither he had come seven years before as a young quaestor, standing on the lowest rung of the ladder of honor, to look at the heights above with heart and hope. There he had dreamed one night of lying with his mother, and the priestly soothsayers to whom he took the dream for interpretation declared that it foretold he should be a better man than his father, coming one day to great power and stormy honors. That he should become a higher man than his father was no guarantee of distinction in Caesar's case, for the elder Julius had lived the blameless existence of a country squire whose fields insulate him from the combats of the world. But the rest of the prophecy affected the young quaestor deeply. He had a young man's longing for great affairs, and as a provincial quaestor found his duties limited to seeing that the bills presented to him for payment bore the proper endorsements. The appointment was thrown up; he hurried back to Rome, there to plunge into the stew of party politics which had led him, after seven years—back to Gades and the provincial administration, with a position only one step above the one he had abandoned.

No—those tears before the statue of Alexander did not prove ambition. They did not even prove that the weeper was telling the truth in the account he gave of them. They might well have been tears of angry disappointment, of nostalgia at revisiting scenes familiar from brighter days, of regret over his wasted years—a momentary sentimentality that Caius Julius Caesar, the man who sat as though cast in bronze while the Senate lashed at him over the Clodius business, would be the last in the world to confess.

Moreover, those who took the contrary side in the debates on Caesar's ambition had a point of much force in the financial status of the new governor of Ulterior Spain. It was not merely that he was extravagant and in debt—for these two states are as characteristic of a politician's life as obesity of a bullfrog's—but that he openly admitted his parched financial condition and did little or nothing to alleviate it. After all, a man in control of some thousands of votes in the Forum could hardly avoid opportunities for providing himself with funds— opportunities which in Caesar's case seem to have been uniformly rejected.

This was not the false puritanism of the usual rich radical, either; for no man more obviously enjoyed every sensual and aesthetic pleasure money could procure. He had books by the dozen; his collection of cameos was unrivaled; he spent huge sums on fine bits of sculpture when he was in funds, and when he was not, bought them on credit. Only a taste so impeccable that it made him the first connoisseur of Rome kept his home from becoming one of those museum-like barracks that are the result of so many collectors' efforts.

His public expenditures were distinguished by the same faultless artistic sense, the same failure to attach any value to money for itself. Upon returning from that first visit to Spain he had secured election as an aedile. The aediles were theoretically commissioners of markets and public works; actually the tribunes handled most of the market business and special commissioners all that of public building, leaving the aediles free to provide (at their private expense) the amusements for the three or four series of public holidays. Caesar brought so many gladiators to town for the shows that he was accused of raising a private army, and both his gladiatorial contests and his plays were arranged with such exquisite skill that there was not a boresome moment in the festivals. To lend a satisfying climax to the whole performance, he had temporary galleries built across the front of the Capitol and Comitium on which the performers were raised above the heads of the multitude, so that for the first time in the history of Rome everyone saw what was going on.

Such behavior is not characteristic of the cold and scheming politician Cato (for one) saw in Julius Caesar. It is rather that of a benevolent and hedonistic dilettante who finds the same aesthetic satisfaction in having a keen political intellect at his dinner table as in having a work by a keen artistic intellect on the wall behind it. Cato would have been still more nonplussed had he known that Caesar spent a good part of his leisure in composing poetry—which, with his usual good taste, he afterward suppressed.

Your true politician would not care whether the mob saw his aedile's spectacles or not; he would not care whether they were well arranged, or even whether the performers were artists or hacks. He would announce with a flourish of trumpets that it was the largest and most costly show ever assembled and trust that mass-suggestion would convince the size-conscious multitude that it was having a good time. Further, your ambitious politician is uninterested in the arts for their own sake. He buys his cameos by the gross and his statues by the ton, for the effect they will make on other people. His private life and public life are one. He has no time for objective experience.

Strongest of all the anti-ambition arguments was the fact that this incomprehensibly objective man made not the slightest effort to keep up his façade. On the social side, Caesar held a birthright so exalted that neither debt nor radical doctrine could altogether deprive him of it. On one side of the house he traced his descent to Ancus

Martius, most beloved of the old Roman kings, on the other to the goddess Venus herself. He was the last living representative of both families, the end product of seven centuries of aristocratic evolution. Yet he disposed of this valuable political capital at ninety per cent discount; sneered at Cato's hereditary virtues and damned Cicero for a tuft-hunter. His approach to politics was coldly realistic. One gathered that although he considered there was some value in those abstract principles of equity which are every demagogue's stock in trade, he thought them out of place in practical life; an attitude in which he differed from the average public man by being at no pains to conceal it. Nor did he hide the fact that he had given his aedile's shows by borrowing, nor did he disguise that the money-lenders had him deeply embarrassed.

"I need five million dollars to be worth exactly nothing", he remarked airily to a group of acquaintances about the time of Publius Clodius' trial, and a few hours before leaving for Spain he was actually under distrainder for debt, a governor unable to go to his province because his creditors had no surety that he would return to pay them. Ulterior Spain was a remote and ill-civilized country with a fringe of downright barbarism, and indigent Romans before Caesar's time had been known to step across the shadow-line that separates the acquisition of money by fraud through non-payment of debts, and its acquisition by force at the head of a gang of border ruffians.

In fact, he never would have made the trip but for the calculating generosity of M. Licinius Crassus, the financier, that same Crassus who had led the exodus from Rome when Pompey approached with his fearsome legions. Crassus was the wealthiest man in Rome, but five millions represented so considerable a drop in the bucket, even for him, that it is likely the amount gave him to pause. Still, he had made his fortune by backing long shots. In his earlier days he was famous for seeking out the owners of houses which were actually on fire and buying the rapidly disappearing property at prices dictated by the fact that the vendor might soon have nothing to sell. If the fire brigade extinguished the blaze Crassus was the gainer by a very fine, if slightly damaged mansion; he immediately put to work the large corps of Greek architect-slaves he maintained, and sometimes sold the former owner his own house at a considerable profit. Generally he preferred the tactic of retaining the deeds and renting, a procedure which had made him the landlord of a good deal of Rome by the time he reached fifty. He had also done very well for himself by backing Sulla the Dictator when that notable was only one of several promising candidates in a Kilkenny-cat civil struggle, and it was whispered that some of Sulla's proscriptions had been dictated less by the fact that the proscribed were in opposition to him than by that of their available landed property which Crassus might buy in at forced-down prices.

Of course, even such a financier as Crassus could not always turn up the winning cards. Thus when he undertook the suppression of Spartacus' servile revolt as a speculation in slaves the business had not only dragged to so unreasonable length that the profits were consumed before being earned, but the frightened Senate had summoned Pompey to finish it. The result was a lasting enmity between the two men. Crassus always claimed Pompey had arrived only in time to gather the credit after he had done the work and when people referred to "Pompey the Great" he was wont to inquire scoffingly—"How great is he? Over two hundred pounds, do you suppose?"

The soldier returned this contempt with so much of the feeling that men of action have for those who grow fat on other people's misfortunes that Crassus had reasonable ground both for fearing Pompey's return from the East and for holding a celebration dinner when it became evident that the conqueror intended to play at politics instead of some ruder game. Still Crassus did not feel altogether secure; summoned Caesar to a conference with the idea of offering to pay the latter's debts and thus provide himself with a sort of fire-insurance against the event of Pompey's setting the Roman world ablaze with some bit of legislation that would place a military man at the head of the state.

We have no data on that conference. It was no doubt very frank because both were candid men. We only know that it took place while the sacrilege case against Caesar's political lieutenant, Clodius, was being given to that jury "of strict and unanimous uprightness." Undoubtedly Caesar stipulated something beyond the settlement of his obligations, for that night Crassus' agents called on all the jurymen. Some of them returned the call forthwith. In the morning Clodius was acquitted, Crassus posted bonds for the payment of Caesar's due bills and the new governor of Ulterior Spain left the city a free man.

. . . The manoeuvre has little enough bearing on the question of ambition. But perhaps the final test of that quality came neither in Gades nor in Rome, but while Caesar's cavalcade of officers was riding through a wretched hamlet in Narbonnese Gaul. As the horses tramped down the dusty street with startled chickens dodging before their hooves, one of the suite was moved to wonder whether there also, as in Rome, parties contended over who should rule.

"For my part," Caesar flashed out. "I would rather be the first man among these fellows than the second in Rome."

Then he fell silent.

2

The Discovery—The suite, young men on their first turn of colonial service, like Caesar himself the septennaid before, regarded Gades with dismay, and Caius Julius was inclined to agree with them, though for more objective reasons. They saw only the mean streets and hectic gayeties, the indescribable air of premature senescence, of adolescent decay, which is somehow acquired by towns that exist for the purpose of exchanging the products of civilization against those of a barbaric hinterland.

Being young and Roman, therefore sensitive to the supernatural, they probably also felt the emotional impact of their surroundings rather keenly. It was a land of magic, where men seemed to exist only as the playthings of unseen and pitiless powers—*Spania,* the world of the lost, the Phoenician mariners had called it, not for its distance alone, and the delicate Greeks reechoed the judgment in their name of *Hesperia,* the twilight land. And a land of twilight it was, where the sun, no longer the clean rational Apollo of Italy or the islands, but a malevolent Baal, grimaced ferociously from a sky of brass, inhibiting movement, life even, till evening drove him beneath the turn of the western sea and the calm moon brought the Gaditaneans into the shadowy streets for their daily affairs.

They were half-Semites (for the Phoenicians had lingered long), moon-worshippers and moon-sorcerers by blood, and they had that much in common with the native Iberians, queer, squat figures, long-armed, broad-shouldered, dark and furtive, who themselves seemed the children of some incredible lunar miscegenation. Their mountain peaks and rivers bore the name of the moon in all its variations; they reckoned the year by the moon's passages and their day from her setting to her rise. Their very coins were stamped from the metal of the moon and bore the image of the moon, and when the moon attained her widest diameter, a madness came upon them so that even in Gades, one could hear the throb of tom-toms from the surrounding hills and know the Iberians were dancing in wild Maenad circles beneath the pale beams, drinking metheglin and howling like wolves.

Yet the next morning these same dancers would appear in the governor's office, dressed in all respects like Romans, very grave, very civilized, to complain that the business of the province moved halt-foot under a paralyzing load of debt to Italian money-lenders. The appeal held truth; the provincial records showed progressive declines in tax receipts and harbor-dues and were the subject of Caesar's objective dismay.

He had on his staff a man named Balbus, Cornelius Balbus, an engineer by profession, fat, tactful, worldly-wise and cultured, a native Gaditanean who had been found worthy of Roman citizenship, yet preserved enough contact with his own people to tap deep-lying cisterns of information. Him Caesar placed on a commission of inquiry and the delighted Spaniards, who had made their protest *pro forma* as part of the regular ceremony attendant upon a change of governors, opened their hearts.

Balbus reported that the roots of the trouble lay in the old wars, now ten years agone, when the native particularism of the Iberian race found armed expression and leadership of genius under Quintus Sertorius. He had raised a bitter guerilla warfare of ambush and midnight surprise that lasted for seven long years, or until the Senate had thrown invincible Pompey into the scale against him, but it had been alas! a warfare of devastation in which Sertorius could win only by depriving the country of everything it had to lose. Harried from the left by Sertorian raids, from the right by the taxes which furnished Pompey's legions, the miserable Spaniards slid down into the barbarism from which they had only just emerged and now the new governor was faced with the Sisyphus-task of pushing them up into the light once more.

Yet a war is not a stone to be rolled away with hand or lever and ten years had grooved deep the traces of Sertorius' struggle. The taxes were too heavy, of course; the taxes are always too heavy. It was probably more with the idea of gaining the good will of the governed than from any conviction of the inherent justice of this complaint that Caesar sent a sharply worded dispatch to the Senate pointing out that the income from the province would be greater if the income demanded from the individual tax-payer were less. Meanwhile he granted a temporary reduction by executive order and further to convince the provincials of his good faith, spent the sums then on deposit in the treasury on having the streets of Gades straightened and graded.

The universal load of debt was a problem incompetent of any such facile solution, for the leading creditors were those Roman bankers' syndicates in which M. Licinius Crassus was a heavy stockholder and Caesar would risk his own and the province's future merely by suggesting a diminution in either principal or interest. Yet even this difficulty was not proof against the governor's intelligent realism. He summoned debtors and creditors to a conference, at which he pointed out to the latter that though interest might be vaulting on the back of interest till their loans showed a book value in astronomical figures, the process could have but one end—namely, that the Spaniards would abandon field and shop, leaving the bankers under the necessity of managing the businesses themselves. The debtors were shown how much they might save from the wreck by reasonable composition.

Both pleas were doubtless reinforced by numerous and striking examples, for a man of Caesar's political experience was not above creating examples had none existed, and a man of practical realism would certainly not offer theory unsupported by fact. It is likely that he even used a threat of the police power to bring the opponents to terms. Something of the kind seems indicated by the upshot of the meeting, for no matter how great were Caesar's persuasive abilities, it seems unlikely that he could, by the word alone, have secured the agreement of either the grasping Roman business men who stood behind him, or of the selfish and violent Spaniards who stood before, to a compromise by which the debtors were to devote two-thirds of their incomes to the service of their obligations while the bankers forewent any further interest.

There was doubtless also the grumbling from both sides that usually accompanies a reasonable settlement of irreconcilables, but it speedily gave place to an almost passionate delight in the discovery of a Roman governor who was neither inimical nor stupid. The Spaniards had long since come to believe that their woes were those that flesh is heir to and all Romans were alike. Sertorius had understood them indeed, but he had used his understanding to hurt. Pompey was a soldier who neither knew nor affected to know that the province had any need but to be delivered from Sertorius; and on his heels had come a succession of governors, avaricious and correct, who dispensed an even-handed, uncompromising justice by the law and milked the colony dry, not caring so much whether it were ruined as whether it went to pieces in accordance with the principles of Roman jurisprudence.

Do new brooms alone sweep clean? There must have been other administrators in the ten years since Sertorius who had made promising beginnings in Ulterior Spain. It was unquestionably with a question in their minds that the Senate of Gades voted Caesar an extraordinary subvention for his personal use (to encourage him in good works) and prayed him to take up the serious problem of the bandit raids.

Banditry along the borders is the specific disease of frontier commercial settlements, in the case of Ulterior Spain aggravated by the Sertorian troubles, for the technique of his war had been that of quick, wounding stabs, and the collapse of the uprising had driven into outlawry leaders above the average both in training and talent. The harsh country, itself in perpetual rebellion against authority, stood peculiarly their aid, with parallel combs of mountain that re-

stricted trade caravans into movement by definitely marked valleys .
and themselves furnished natural fortress-bases for the robbers.
One such mountain barrier, the Herminium, formed the northern
boundary of the province—insofar as it could be said to have a
boundary—and flanked the valuable trade routes along the Tagus.
The country behind it, wild as Gaul, had never been civilized, hardly
ever visited by civilized men. It was inhabited by three tribes called
the Asturiae, Lusitani and Callaicae, whose custom of sacrificing
prisoners to the moon-goddess made them especially obnoxious
neighbors.

Governor after governor had attempted to come to terms with
them. It was a procedure unprofitable from their point of view since
it involved giving up the productive business of banditry. As governor
after governor had failed in diplomacy he had looked into the question of armed suppression, but had always reported against it, as
being outrageously expensive in both money and time. This was true
enough as far as it went and the governors could hardly be expected
to make it a matter of public record that the reason behind this
official pacifism was the fact that they held office only for a single
year, during which a man must apply himself rather keenly to the
business of acquiring a fortune if he were not to return to Rome as
poor as he left it. Guerilla campaigns are inevitably long and trying,
especially in the mountains, and the Lusitanians had no cities whose
loot might compensate the lost financial opportunities in civil administration.

Unfortunately, this *après nous la déluge* policy has an end at the
point where the working capital of the province will no longer support the double burden of enriching a Roman governor and barbaric
invaders, and this point had now been reached. Fortunately the point
was reached under a governor so deeply in debt that it made very
little difference what his financial opportunities were, and so careless
of all debts that he only paid them when they interfered with his
business.

The ground was thus clear in a financial sense, but Caius Julius
Caesar did not embark at once upon an expedition against the Lusitanian tribes when he entered into office. A man of exquisite artistic

sensibilities, he found nothing so distasteful as fumbling performance, whether in cookery, sculpture, administration or police work. He could not bear the thought of making a holy show of himself. It was only the reflection that he was carrying through a brilliant political intrigue to give him the last laugh on those who were amusing themselves at his expense that had enabled him to bear up through the ordeal of having his shortcomings as a husband dashed in his face at the time of the Clodius affair.

He could not bear the thought of blundering; and his military experience was small, his military training nil. It is true that he held a crown vallary, the highest decoration for military courage that the Roman Republic could bestow, but it is also true that it had been won by the kind of fortunate accident that might befall any man with a quick eye and good reflexes. It dated back fifteen years to the time when he had gone east as an aide-de-camp in the train of Admiral Minucius Thermus, who was conducting a naval campaign in Aegean waters as a side issue to the first war against King Mithridates. Minucius had little military use for a staff-officer who had reached the age of twenty-five (at which most Romans were veterans) without having seen any more formidable force under arms than the wooden-sword parades the city vagabonds organize for the Saturnalia. As the young man possessed birth, appearance and a persuasive wit, he had been employed as standing diplomatic commissioner at the court of King Nicomedes of Bithynia.

Caesar was a great success in this capacity. During one of his trips to headquarters it happened that he found the marines of the fleet preparing to storm the city of Mitylene, and having expressed the desire to take part, was allowed to do so. In the breach he saved a man's life. The action caught the admiral's eye and formed a convenient peg on which to hang a decoration that would considerably increase Caius Julius' prestige in his diplomatic work.

No—this was hardly the most desirable background for a man about to undertake a mountain campaign against irregulars, a business which every soldier knows as one of the most recondite of military operations. No one realized this more clearly than Caesar himself and when his messengers to the barbaric chieftains returned with the news that no accommodation was possible, he went to quite extraordinary lengths to avoid the melancholy failure his lack of knowledge seemed to promise.

The provincial establishment consisted of two legions of veteran professionals; he raised a third legion of volunteers and in addition to drilling with them while the latter body was being whipped into shape, made use of his phenomenal memory for names and faces to become personally acquainted with most of his men, a trick difficult but not impossible to a man who had already found it a passport to the loyalty of voters. The barbarian country and people were thoroughly scouted by means of cavalry points and information from pack-a-back traders. We may also take it that supply trains were organized with peculiar and unusual care, and an alternative supply base was provided in the shape of a good sized fleet which was fitted out to accompany the move up the coast.

Cornelius Balbus was invaluable. He had served a couple of campaigns under Pompey during the Sertorian troubles and was full of useful information about that great soldier's methods. When the campaign actually opened he went along as chief of staff, which, if there be any analogy with modern conditions, means that he undertook the detail work and tactical direction for which Caesar's ignorance of war disqualified him, leaving the commander to handle the broad strategic questions.

Unfortunately ancient history is tantalizingly uninformative on just those points which are essential in tracing the development of individual or idea. We only know that the army of 20,000 men strode across the Mount Herminium barrier on winged feet, cowing the Lusitani to peace and promises by mere accomplishment of a task to them incredible. Beyond the range lies Munda River. Caesar dropped small garrisons in a chain of blockhouses on the banks of this stream to secure a supply line with the coastal fleet and rushed on to the headwaters, where the northern tribes were assembling to give battle.

They drove their herds before them to the fight, half-wild cattle across a dusty plain, but the legionary ranks held fast and when the rushing animals had gone charged home on the savages and avenged many a moon-sacrifice in a great slaughter. Caesar followed the fugitives like a tiger, stamping out all resistance down the Durius valley, then the army turned back south, for the Lusitani had risen behind and closed off retreat and supply by breaking the blockhouse chain among the mountain spurs through which Munda cleaves its way to the sea.

. . . Just here the lack of information is provoking. We hear that Caesar flanked the barbarians from position after hill-position, driving their dispersed parties into one confused whole as a sheep-dog gathers his flock—but how? for among the stark tumuli of Lusitania it was an operation presenting such difficulties as to be almost without a parallel in war. Was the technique that of Caesar or Balbus? No clue—we only know that the Lusitani came to a stand on an island separated from the mainland by a tidal strait. Time clipped Caesar close, for away on the slopes behind Durius the Asturiae were rising and provision was too sparse in the Roman camp to attempt a blockade.

Fertile ever in expedient, he had trees cut down and formed into crude rafts which paddled to the island's edge while a cohort of legionaries tried to rush the strait. The effort failed; The Lusitani drove off the rafts under a storm of bowshot, the hurrying tidal waters engulfed the soldiers in the strait. It was only a check, not a defeat; messengers hurried down the coast to bring up the Gaditanean fleet, the warships closed in on the island, clearing a space for a landing with their catapults and stone-throwers, the transports ferried the Romans across and the trapped barbarians were shattered beyond recovery.

Northward the Asturiae held the passes of the western Pyrenees; no hope of surprising a passage as at Mount Herminium. Nor did Caesar try; he loaded his men onto the ships, flanked the mountains by sea and landing at Brigantium, fell on the Asturian rear and reduced them to submission without a battle by quick marching and the surprise of his big ships, which terrified them inordinately. "Hardly any commander had ever before completed so difficult a campaign in so short time with so few men; for not only had Caesar reduced to the Roman authority tribes not less valiant and skilled in

military affairs than the Romans themselves, whose very names
caused all the rest of the Spaniards to tremble, but he had accomplished this with very small losses on his own part, and gave the
barbarians so just and reasonable a peace that they abandoned their
old savage practices and willingly counted themselves among the
supporters of the Empire."

Yet if it be thought that the import of this campaign lies in the fact
that some thousands of Iberians ceased to bay the moon and drink
the mingled blood and metheglin poured by their priests around the
wizard-altars, the point has been missed. It had another and deeper
significance. For whether it came on some night of meditation in
camp beneath the Spanish moon, whether in some startled ejacula-
tion from Cornelius Balbus at an unexpected bit of strategy, or
whether on the beach of the island with Lusitanian arrows dancing
on helm and shield we do not know—but somewhere, sometime in
this campaign there came to Julius Caesar the realization that in the
crash of battle might lie the key to the greatness which had thus far
eluded him—that he had accomplished a feat beyond the capacities
of most commanders then living—that he might accomplish such
another and so leave behind him something worth remembering. "It
is well that war is terrible; otherwise we might grow to like it," said
one of the greatest of modern soldiers as his regiments swung past.
But they were marching to slay brothers of the same race and name
in one of those tragic misunderstandings of modern civilization; and
Julius Caesar lived in a world where the light of the world was surrounded by armed shadows with "Our blood or yours" on their lips.

So he became a man enchanted. The extraordinary subvention
from the Senate of Gades, his share of the proceeds from the sale of
slave-prisoners, which might have bought so many cameos and
incunabula, went to the payment of his debts and he returned to
Rome worth exactly nothing—unless the gratitude of the province
he had saved be counted a thing of value. There was no change in
his outward semblance.

Dancing Girl of Gades

III

THERE IS A SILENTIARY

Return of Ulysses—Caius Julius Caesar stood outside the city gates at the head of his victorious legions and sued for permission to enter in formal triumph, laurel-crowned. To all his contemporaries but one it seemed the pardonable vanity of an amateur captain who, by favor of the gods and a clever subordinate, had achieved unmerited success where professionals might easily have failed. Cato indeed, saw deeper. He knew Caesar was immune to flattery, even self-flattery, and proud of nothing but a single fact so dubious that it offered no reasonable ground for vainglory—his reputed descent from Venus Genetrix.

But Cato peered at the world through the blue spectacles of his own morbid bigotry—"The man is building up a military power to make himself king!" he cried in the Senate House, the old cry against any Roman whose activities lifted him a hand's breadth above the lazy aristocrats. So when the bill for Caesar's triumph was offered Cato talked it to death, not by argument but by lung-pressure and the clock, squalling his thin denunciation till the session ended before anyone else could speak or a vote be taken.

For though the ordinary triumph came as a matter almost axiomatic, taking place by acclamation when a general returned so thoroughly victorious that his soldiers could accompany him home leaving the new frontier unguarded, Caesar's triumph was a ceremony of a special order, requiring official authorization. Not that it was incomplete—ah, no, Spain lay under the peace of death, the legions come crowding home round their commander, swearing their bald-headed chief was another Alexander.

A victorious general was supposed to be satisfied with his applause; when the fireworks were over he was to send his soldiers home and retire to his estate like Camillus, the ideal Roman; and this custom had frozen into the force of law, in the following manner. The year's elections were held before triumphs for military operations of the preceding year. The triumphator could not enter the city before his triumph and could not stand for office unless he entered the city in time for the election. The arrangement had sense; it was designed to keep a victorious general from sweeping the polls with soldier votes to his own advantage. It was postulated partly on the fear that the victorious general would make himself into a permanent general, or king, partly on the theory that the Roman Republic was so richly supplied with talent that it could retire any general after one year's service.

If five centuries had not exorcised the fear, they had brilliantly justified the theory; for it was the special glory of the great Republic that it had almost never failed to find a new leader as competent as the one it laid on the shelf. And the system had only come to an end when it swallowed its own tail, like the worm Ouroboros. It was not difficult to find men who could bear themselves well in a single campaign at the head of the small armies of the early Republic, but endless victory had made the Republic ruler of the world and the number of men with intellect enough to rule the world, or any large section of it, is always limited.

Old Sulla the Dictator had realized this ever so clearly; when he revised the constitution twenty years before he made the collective intellect of the Senate emperor of the new world he had built, with the executives so many robots of that agglomerative Mind, octopus tentacles which could feel, strike or grip, but only at the will of the central intelligence. But the tentacle Julius Caesar was displaying a will of its own, very disturbing to the brain of the beast.

For it was no secret that the tentacle Caesar had returned from Spain a changed man, disinclined any longer to play his assigned role of dilettante radical. He was demanding not only a triumph for a war the Senate had not ordered, but also a consulate which the Senate had every intention of denying him. With the matchless impudence of the high-born he had asked openly for the privilege of appearing at the hustings by proxy and thus gaining both the office and the celebration.

Of course, there was precedent for such a request; Sulla himself
had asked and received as much, Pompey had received more, for he
was under the legal age for a magistracy of any sort when he got
that and triumph as well. The request itself was a fair offer of compromise, preserving the spirit of the old law; for Caesar undertook
to keep his soldier-voters outside the walls till the election was over.
Yet there was not a man of the Senate who did not breathe a sigh of
relief as the westering sun brought Cato's acrimonious speech and
the session of the house to a close without the proposition reaching a
vote. Too well for any compromise they understood the voting power
of the miserable rabble who idolized this returned governor of Ulterior Spain. Too well for any accommodation they realized that were
he once consul, the tentacle Caesar would introduce changes in the
molluscoid constitution, and those changes would not be in the interest of strengthening the central intelligence.

How fortunate! (they thought) that vanity had proved his weak
spot. The idol had feet of clay; let him feed to satiation on empty
honors. Give him a triumph with all the apparatus of decorated streets
and resolutions of gratitude from the Roman people. It would be a
display more hollow than Pompey's, for it would be in itself a dem-
onstration of how thoroughly the agglomerate mind of the aristocracy could control other elements of the state, whether they assaulted
the sacred citadel of power with votes in their hands like Caesar,
with arms, like Pompey, or with gold, like Crassus.

During Caesar's Spanish year the governing intelligence had taken
occasion to demonstrate how inefficacious was each of these rival
weapons against it. Pompey, wildly angry at the failure of the Senate
either to provide for his veterans or to ratify the eastern treaties, had
descended into the political arena only to discover that the gods are
respected in inverse proportion to their familiarity. Few listened to his
speeches and those who did listen laughed. In truth he was not a
good popular speaker; the small, high voice uttering elephantine
platitudes—for soldiers think in platitudes by training, it is part of
that obedience to authority which is the most priceless possession of
the military mind—voice mouthing platitudes was at such contrast
with the elaborate triumphal regalia habitually worn by the con-

queror that it produced an effect irresistibly comic. He managed to
get another general, Lucius Afranius, elected to the consulate, but
Afranius was one more Piso, simple and direct, whom the astute
senators led in bewildered prancings like a bear with a ring in his
nose. Afranius accomplished exactly nothing. He could neither prevent Lucullus "examining" the treatises for another twelvemonth
nor obtain a pension bill. When Caesar returned from Spain the
struggle was all over; Pompey, his soldier's honor irretrievably
smirched, had given up, locked himself in his home and was out to
callers.

As for Crassus, the Senate had long owed him an evil turn as the
stock bogey-man from the business world. The Clodius business sent
their temperatures so far above boiling point that they voted an investigation "into the conduct of business-man jurors", an undeserved
slur on the commercial classes, for the aristocrats among the famous
fifty-six had swallowed their bribes as greedily as the business men.
More so; during the night when Crassus received them before the
announcement of the result the business men of the jury had taken
their money and given their bought verdict calmly and sensibly, an
ordinary commercial transaction, but the few aristocrats, when
offered bribes, had wobbled this way and that till Crassus overcame
their scruples with promises to "recommend" them to certain hand-
some boys who were deeply indebted to him. An undeserved slur—
"The fools!" said Cicero angrily, perceiving that the Senate could
remain on its feet only by leaning on the crutch of organized capi-
talism; "The fools! They think the world wags soundly as long as the
carp in their fish-ponds will take bread from their hands."

Business men seldom suffer long from insults. A golden poultice
is their specific for every spiritual wound, and who knows how
quickly the breach might have healed but for Cato? The syndicate
that had bid in the right to collect the Syrian taxes was in bad shape,
the Mithridatic war and a starveling harvest having ruined the
provincials' capacity to pay. Most of the big banking firms were
caught; money went tight, the price of corn rose and the distressed
financiers begged to be let off their bargain, a step which the Treasury
could well afford, since it had been stuffed to the grunting point with

the gold of Pompey's victories, which after all had been taken by
military force from some of the men who should have been paying
it in taxes. Some vague proposals for a financial-senatorial alliance
were even made. But "No, by Hercules!" shrieked Cato when the
bill to rescind the tax-bid was offered, and he filibustered it to death
in the name of the sanctity of contracts.

Cato

The bankers were furious but helpless, Cicero upset. "Cato is a man
of virtue and I love him for it," he said, "but he acts as though he
were in Plato's Republic instead of the sewer of Romulus, and these
grandees of the fish-ponds support him blindly. So this one year has
overturned those two bulwarks of the state which I erected with so
much care. The prestige of the Senate expired when Clodius was
acquitted and now the concord between Senate and financiers has
flown out the window."

It was Cicero's own vanity that led him to the error of supposing
he had erected those bulwarks; actually he had only been the officiat-
ing priest at the *mariage de convenance* which always takes place
between aristocracies of birth and purse. But he had touched an essential point—the need of bulwarks—for his low origins gave him
preternatural insight into the strength of little things.

The world of fish-pond barons saw no need for such melancholy ardors. Why fret? On the night that closed the year Cicero so much deplored, the night when the Senate had talked Caesar's ambition to death as Pompey's honor and Crassus' purse had been talked to death before, one can picture them making their way home, comfortably self-satisfied with having proved their capacity to rule the world—by unlimited speech-making, the least wearing of all methods of government.

It is even possible that those who passed through the streets near the Flumentanean gate met a little group of sunbrowned men in a circle of torches and heard the clap of a sudden cheer. For that was the night when Julius Caesar, back from the wars, threw up his hoped-for triumph and rode into the city with a few friends to stand for election as chief magistrate of Rome.

2

Brought to Audit—There is a residuum of mystery. Was it vanity that led Caesar to apply for a triumph in the first place?

Yes and no. There were two Caesars, so different as hardly to be on speaking terms. There was Julius Caesar, the descendant of a line of kings, the connoisseur of art and life, who set the best table in Rome and garnished the meat with conversation so Olympian that if he had done nothing else his name might have ridden down the ages as prototype of Petronius, arbiter of elegance. This Caesar, Caesar the individual, took a barely dilettante interest in politics, an almost professional interest in women—an uneasy, cultured, speculative spirit, who wept at the feet of Alexander's statue and discovered that war may surpass all other arts in its opportunities for self-expression. To this Caesar, whose artistic sense implies a feeling for proportion, there could be nothing more ridiculous than the managed gayety, carefully metered as to quantity and degree, which was characteristic of a Roman triumph. Especially when he considered that the most recent of these authorized jubilees had been for the conquest of twelve million people, capping a victory that had rescued Rome from starvation, an achievement which made his own excessively petty.

But the dilettante Julius Caesar, in his search for new varieties of experience, had made a hobby of politics. It gave him magnificent opportunities for human contacts and subsequent psychological experiment but in return demanded that he raise up a double, Caius Caesar—Caius, the most common of Roman names. One could express the implication to a modern mind by calling him "Jack" Caesar. And Jack Caesar, though possessed of the intellectual powers of his prototype, was necessarily a person of less delicate perceptions. He was, he had to be, the quintessence of the great unwashed, a sort of living model of proletarianism at the nth degree. He rejected the golden artistic mean for that cult of superlatives, of the superiority of mass, which is the most characteristic of popular ideas, because the mob itself is a mass. It was this Jack Caesar who had given the public the most superlative circus in the history of the aedile's office. Julius Caesar had generously helped to make it a *succes d'estime* as well as one of volume, a favor which Jack was unable to reciprocate, for he could contribute little to the combination but those crude stimulants which the aesthetic Julius must despise in order to retain his objective viewpoint.

Yet if Caesar, either Caesar, did despise the clamor of popular approval it was an affectation, for no man can remain altogether indifferent to that uproar, since in the final analysis it is the artist's one sure clue to whether he has performed well or ill his self-appointed task. It may be objected that the commonalty as a whole has no taste. This is doubtless true with regard to the majority of the arts, with which the public comes in touch but rarely and of which it never thinks at all. But there is one art of which every man is a critic, because it has concerned him almost since the day of his birth—the art of human relationship.

The Romans were specialists in human relations. Their ability to produce a medium in which social contacts could be carried on with a minimum of strain had gained for them the hegemony of Latium, then of Italy and finally of the world. In this field they were critics of indefectible taste; and it was in this field that the aesthete Julius Caesar, after having adjudged himself a failure as a poet, had chosen to practice. His *alter ego,* Caius-Jack, was only the conventional actor's mask he assumed for the purpose, a concession to the inherent ritualism of the popular mind, which demands that its heroes and villains wear labels—to save it the labor of thinking.

The curse of the theatrical professions is that the best performers live their parts so thoroughly that their private existence becomes a gouache of all the roles they ever played. In Caesar's case the development of the Caius role can most easily be traced through his contacts with the women of his family. We have no sure information as to the amount of his affection for Pompeia. At the time of their divorce it was certainly no longer a consuming passion; yet the marriage, if a family alliance had not been a political one, and the icy formality with which he dismissed her, sans regret or farewell, is at such contrast with the earlier Caesar that it needs explanation.

For that earlier Caesar had loved his first wife with so clear a devotion that even in the days when his whole past was being combed for scandal, his enemies never failed to allow him one generous moment. The marriage flowered among the black embers of the Civil War, when old Sulla the Dictator was wiping out to the third generation the families of those who opposed him, and all day long dolorous processions of men, women and children passed toward the Wailing Stairs, never to return. She was a Cornelia, and of the proscribed party; the recent death of his father had made young Caesar head of a family interest so powerful that Sulla himself took the marriage under advisement.

The "bloody dictator" was an astute psychologist. His menaces were veiled beneath the flattering offer of a high administrative post under the new constitution he was building for Rome, accompanied by the hand of whatever lady Caesar preferred among the dictator's own family. Bird-lime? By no means; old Sulla knew how to play fair. Gnaeus Pompey, though still a youth, had similarly been asked to discard a daughter of the people's part, had done so, and had immediately been rewarded with the dictator's niece and command of an army, at the head of which he was already entered upon a glorious career.

The prospect thus opened before the eighteen-year-old Caesar was splendid beyond his wildest dreams, but in his eyes it had one insuperable objection; namely, he must divorce Cornelia and see her turned over to the executioner. He refused; Sulla immediately made good the implied threat by depriving the young aristocrat of the minor priesthood he held and confiscating his property. Young Julius fled to the Greek islands, there to live and love with Cornelia for a year and a day. She died, leaving him with a daughter on whom he lavished whatever was left of the passionate attachment he had given her mother.

The child was named Julia, after Caesar's favorite aunt, and at the interment of that aunt we find him mid-passage between the Julius Caesar who had sacrificed the world for Cornelia and the Caius Caesar who sacrificed Pompeia to the world. The elder Julia was certainly a very great lady and one whom the aesthetic Julius could honor without reproach; still it was a trifle unusual to give her a funeral with orators and a procession as though she had been a victorious general. The motive for these unconventional additions to the ordinary burial ceremonies became apparent as the procession moved down the Sacred Way. For high among the painted masks of bygone distinguished relatives was borne a representation of Caius Marius, in his great plumed helmet and dark frown, with the list of his victories placarded beneath.

Marius! The populace rent the sky with shouts of delight and no more work was done that day. Marius! The great hero of the proletariat, who had risen from an origin so obscure that neither he nor his laboring-class father had a third name. He had stepped out of the ranks to destroy the greatest barbarian danger Rome had ever faced, oh, saved the city and them all, never doubt it. Marius!— who, having crushed Rome's enemies from the outside with the proletarian soldiers of his new model army, brought them home to rid the city of her inner parasites, those lords of the fish-ponds. For one brief moment he had made Rome a worker's paradise with debt abolished and every man a king.

There had been, alas, only one Marius. He was mortal, he died, and bloody Sulla came tramping in from the East at the head of bourgeois legions to throw down the workers' paradise and build upon its ruins a constitution that closed government to all but the Optimates, the best people. His vengeance was frightful; Marius' bones he had dug up, ground to powder and flung into the Tiber. The very name was placed under interdict; the law said it was never again to be pronounced. The Marian family and connections had been exterminated—all but this same Julius Caesar, cousin by marriage to the great proletarian for all his aristocrat birth.

Sulla consented to spare the youth on the plea of the feminine members of his own household. They could not bear to think of so beautiful a head lying on the block, and beside young Julius was needed at dinner-parties, where his charming wit made the dullest occasion a delight. Yes, Sulla consented to spare him, though with misgivings— "There is many a Marius under that dandified head" he remarked presciently, even before he heard of the Caesar-Cornelia marriage. After it and after Caesar's refusal to rupture the alliance the grim dictator repented of his mercy. His messengers scoured Italy with orders to remove the dandified head from the shoulders that bore it, but they never came near him but once and then he gave so good a simulation of an epileptic fit the assassins would not touch him, epilepsy being a sacred disease.

At the time of Aunt Julia's funeral those days were sunk deep beyond the horizon of the past, the bloody dictator was long in his grave and the dandified head bald. Julius Caesar had become a political figure, a clever speaker who professed devotion to the cause of the masses, but damned by his own high lineage and wealth. He might complain that he had suffered for being a Radical; the hearers suspected that what he claimed as a passion for democracy had really been a passion for Cornelia.

It had become absolutely necessary to the career, to the continued existence of Caius-Jack that he produce some concrete evidence of the genuiness of the coin he was offering in exchange for Radical suffrages. What could be more appropriate than thus turning Aunt Julia's funeral into a Marius-festival? At a single stroke it informed the populace that Caius Caesar set party solidarity above family and decorum, that the greatest of Radical leaders was his kinsman and model, and that he was quite prepared to embark upon one of those campaigns—so difficult to suppress—of violations of social law which are the kernel of radical political tactic.

Admirable!—it leapfrogged Caesar forthwith into the party's leadership and the dismayed aristocrats dared not make a scandal before the shouting thousands by prosecuting the young man for his tribute to the great revolutionary. His request for a formal triumph on returning from Spain was made in much the same spirit, not out of personal vanity, an emotion which Julius Caesar considered anaesthetic, but out of official vanity, for the benefit of the part which Caius Caesar had made his own. It would be an acknowledgement wrung from the Senate itself that the Optimates held no monopoly of military talent, that a man might leap over the barrier of special privilege they had erected around themselves and still serve Rome well. An acknowledgement that another Marius was possible.

And now this leader of the rabble, this aristocrat gone wrong, was in the city and a candidate for the first place in the Republic. Another Marius!—the noble lords trembled at the brinks of their fish-ponds. They held a meeting in the Senate house at twilight; the situation was one of utmost emergency, at any cost and by any means Caesar must be kept from the consulate. Cicero, summoned as attorney for the defence, advised conciliating Pompey. With 50,000 veterans and the greatest soldier in the world on call, the Senate might bid defiance to embattled roguery—this had been Sulla's prescription, and 'twas sanctified by success. The oligarchs looked sour— No! What, conciliate a man who had approved himself their lackey? Conciliate at the price of the fat Campanian (every member doing mental acrobatics—minus so many gold-pieces a year how can I afford—?) lands?

Cost too great. We can do it cheaper, they agreed, by contributing, each according to his means, an electoral bribery fund. It was Cato's idea, pure Puritan Cato, who having found it immoral to be generous with the financiers (on the tax contract), now found it necessary to lie in the bed of shame with cheap politicians, a spectacle which stirred Caesar to his most mordant sallies when he heard of it. The slush fund shook him never a whit. Not only was he master of a more powerful spell, but his running mate on the Radical ticket was Lucius Lucceius, a friend of Crassus, whose own vast resources were a guarantee that no voter need sell his class principles for a mess of pottage since he could get as high a price by sticking to them.

It was a fierce election; wine ran rivers fiery as Phlegethon where the rival bribery-parties passed. In their wake gangs of clubbers moved through a morris dance of wrath; there were street fights, broken heads and shouting. The aristocrats brought in clients from their country villas to pack the polls; Caesar counter-packed them with the Spanish legionaries and the assorted skullduggeries cancelled out to leave a crazy approximation of honest balloting.

The vote—First, C. Julius Caesar, Radical; second, M. Calpurnius Bibulus, Conservative; third, Lucius Lucceius, Radical, but third does not count when you are electing two men and Caesar and Bibulus were named consuls. Once more the Senate had proved it could rule the world, for it had elected its man over all opposition. But this time the proof was brought to audit and the accountant was one to demand that the balance be perfect to the last fraction of a groat.

3

See How the Wicked Prosper!—Aristocrats, whether of birth like Lucullus, or by conviction, like Cicero, possess an astounding force of pragmatism. They accept the tailor-made concepts which are supplied to them as soldiers do a uniform, finding deviation from the official ideological costume a trifle more shocking than nakedness, which may be careless, while variance is downright intransigent.

Cicero was a humanist of exquisite sensibilities; yet he was so clothed in the ideas of his adopted class that he could express his delicacy of feeling only in the amelioration of details within his immediate orbit, such as generosity to his tenant-farmers and efforts to preserve the purity of public life. That public life under an oligarchy is essentially impure never entered his head. Integrity was his virtue; it clove for him a straight, narrow path through a world of clotted nonsense, with side-walls high enough to shut out any dismaying vistas of precipice or thunder-fit. It helped him to a delicious melancholy over the death of a favorite slave, of instance, without urging him to inquire whether the defunct was on the same plane of hu-

manity as himself. "I ought to be ashamed of myself for feeling so
badly over a mere slave."

Was it a rut? Cicero thought not; could even catch a glimpse of
rainbow at the end. "What will people say of me six hundred years
hence?" he wonders. "It worries me that they may find Pompey the
greater man of us two." (Ah, Cicero, not in six hundred years;

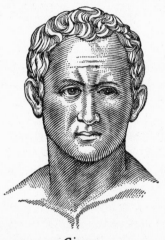

Cicero

people will not think of you or of Pompey or anything but the needs
of the immediate hour in a world gone barbaric then—give us two
thousand.) What will people say? They will say, friend With-the-
wen, that a great humanist refusing to be one of the architects of
a new and better world for fear of gossip may seem a very small
creature.

The offer had come unasked. "You know Cornelius Balbus,
Caesar's familiar friend? I had a call from him; he assured me
Caesar will consult me and Pompey in everything. What if I can
make this Caesar, now sailing full down the favoring breeze, a better patriot?"

Cicero toyed with the idea like a respectable old grandfather
mouse with the cheese in a trap. The interview was conducted with
calm Roman politeness and twice as much meant as either man

said, but the trap-wires were clearly visible. "Consult with . . . Pompey in everything"—and accept his ideas on the pension question, that is, on the alienation of the Campaign lands from their Senatorial lessees. Indeed, at the time of Balbus' call it was no secret that Caesar had already drafted a bill which would give these fields to the "Roman poor", civilians as well as veterans. Anarchic!—to take from the capitalists who were developing them along lines of scientific agronomy, those lands, and turn them over to a shiftless, parasitical proletariat. The orator caressed the butt of his nose in characteristic gesture, balancing the possibility of winning both Caesar and Pompey to his own peculiar brand of patriotism against what people would say of him if he ratted on his announced principle of opposing the Radicals in everything. Balbus' voice flowed smoothly on.

Nice cheese. "I must hold my peace, which is equivalent to retiring from politics, or else I must assist the measure, which is what Caesar expects. On this latter side of the sheet may be placed an intimate connection with Pompey and if I like, with Caesar, too; reconciliation with my enemies, peace with the populace and ease in my old age." But what will people say?—that is, the best people, for there are no others. The fount of Balban eloquence ran dry and the two men stood up for their farewells. As they embraced Cicero remarked that he found the city oppressive at this season of the year. He thought he would retire to his seaside villa at Antium to recruit his forces for a couple of months—could he execute any little commissions there for his friend Balbus? No sale; or I am afraid to oppose but will not support.

Caesar's offer was naïve, the only time we catch him ingenuous. He behaved as though he expected that the Conservatives, having been worsted in a game for which they themselves had made the rules, would stand aside and let him have his swing—overlooking the fact that the rules had been made to let them always win the game, a legalization of collective greed, the most irreconcilable of human forces. He was not a revolutionary in the ordinary sense. A revolution with the most favorable result could only leave Caius Caesar perched in a state of unstable equilibrium on the rim of a rapidly spinning wheel and take from Julius Caesar the thing he valued most—leisure to cultivate his intellectual garden. He was not a revolutionary; he was only trying to make the Senate share with the whole people some of the treasure (not financial alone) purchased with the united political acumen of the former and the blood and devotion of the latter. In a sense indeed, he was almost a conservative, wishing to preserve the existant balance of the state, to achieve an equitable division of profits before some second Catiline should rouse plebs to the idea it had been bilked and start it cutting throats.

No, no, he did not want revolution. When the Kalends of Janus brought in the new year and the twelve lictors thundered their crashing salute at his door, Julius Caesar, chief magistrate of Rome, stepped forth to begin the most humdrum of consulates. They expected him to introduce a confiscatory land bill into the assembly of the people and pass it over the Senate's head. He never mentioned land bill and reported to the Senate for orders like a minor functionary. They expected him to ramble about the town with a mob at his heels, making radical speeches on the street-corners; he hardly left his home and when he did speak it was with glacial moderation.

Indeed, for the first month he did nothing at all. His colleague Bibulus, a paunchy buck with the face of a spoiled infant, acquired an expression of permanent astonishment during this period; the Senate watched like a stoat at a rabbit's hole. They had broken the backs of popular consuls before this (Pupius Piso for one); they had their measures ready, from legal obstructionism down to armed bands for a riot. Seeing the new man made no move they even tried a bit of provocation. It was the privilege of the house to name the province a consul should command when he finished his year in the city magistracy. To Caesar, amid cheers and laughter, they voted the superintendency of rural roads and pastures, a post normally given to a consul's clerk. Caesar accepted it without a murmur, implication and all, calm as though he were at the meeting of the college of priests. Perhaps the fellow had lost his nerve? Or had an allopathic dose of power cured him, like so many others, of his radical megrims?

January climbed the crest of the hour into the second month; Caesar appeared before the Senate and begged permission to introduce a bill. The veterans of the East (he said) were starving. The Republic was at unreasonable expense in finding free corn for poor and idle citizens who would be better employed in raising it for themselves. (Now it was coming; lips tightened, foreheads leaped to frown.) The Republic owned much territory in Campania. A proposal had been made to cut it up, but he felt it would be wrong to touch land now under leasehold and cultivated, and he did not wish to offend the holders. On the contrary he proposed to set up a rotating fund from Pompey's eastern revenues. It should be used to buy land from those who wished to sell and leases from those who would be quit of them. The land so acquired and present wastelands would give ample space for colonizations. The project would be limited to fathers of three children. The needy who accepted the farms should not be permitted to alienate them for twenty years' space, and the whole settlement would be placed in the hands of a commission of twenty senators with Cicero as their president. . . . If any clause in this bill displeases you, Conscript Fathers, I will be glad to amend it.——

He sat down. The startled senators, charmed dumb by reason where they had expected force, glared emptily, all of them sure they did not want that bill nor any other, none of them able to find anything wrong with it. Then up sprang Cato, yammering like a beagle. He could see it all; this apparently rational proposal was the thin end of a wedge. This Caesar was bribing his way into the good graces of the populace with the Republic's money. And for what purpose. Yah! TO MAKE HIMSELF KING!

The Senate roused with a whoop; Lucullus, Bibulus, a thin dyspeptic named Favonius (they called him "Cato's ape") took up the cry, while Caesar sat silent as ever, watching four hundred old men rule the world by vituperation. It struck him that the spectacle was worthy of being shared; he had a secretary note down the leading remarks, wrote them out and affixed copies on the Forum proclamation-board under the heading "Daily News Bulletin."

Nothing is so deadly as exact quotation; next morning the whole town was laughing over the missed climaxes and feeble logic of the lords of the world, but the ridicule did no sort of practical good, for the previous day's session had ended with Lucullus mumbling liquidly through his toothless gums about monarchy—bribery—immorality, and according to parliamentary rules the bill was lost by not having come to a vote.

Caesar re-introduced it, again offering to meet objections with amendment. The Conservative leaders had been in consultation during the night; all heads turned toward Cato, who got deliberately to his feet and began dripping words with the weary patience of a water-clock. The purpose was obvious, he meant to talk the bill to death, the old tactic so successful in Pupius Piso's consulate and in that of Afranius, who followed him. But Caesar was a consul of keener ring than these; he stood up and raised his hand for silence. Cato jabbered on; Caesar slashed right across the cobweb of words with an iron-sharp order—"Take that man to prison!"

There was a universal gasp; then the discipline of the house collapsed in yells of fury as the lictors slammed through the press and jerked the screaming orator from his place. The whole Senate tumbled into the street behind him, moaning and wringing their hands as though at a funeral, Senator Petreius in the lead, shouting as he went along that he would rather be in jail with Cato than at liberty with Caesar.

Contest a draw. That night one of the tribunes appeared at the door of the prison, pronounced the intercession of his office and set Cato at liberty. It was one of the Radical tribunes, sent by Caesar himself, whose sensitive ear had caught echoes not altogether favorable on the imprisonment of Cato, who was regarded as the embodiment of the ancient virtues, even though nobody believed a word he said. The Consul needed all the strength he could gather for the struggle on the morrow when he meant to bring his land bill before the assembly of the people; hence the tribune.

The day came clear and brilliant. Everyone in Rome was jammed into the Forum, so there was hardly breathing-space. Caesar stepped forward to the pediment of the Temple of Castor, to be received with tumultuous cheers; the news of his flash at the Senate and following generosity had spread and been approved. He stilled the racket with a gesture, then read the proposed law, to which he had made a new and appalling amendment—that all senators should take oath to support the bill if passed, death the penalty if they foreswore their word. Just then Bibulus came pushing through the crowd at the head of his lictors, with Lucullus and Cato by his side. Caesar asked him if he had anything to say against the bill.

"I want no revolutions, and by Hercules, there shall be none while I am consul," gritted Bibulus, and sat down, his baby face in a pout, while the people hissed.

Caesar merely turned and motioned; Pompey the Great stepped forward, clad in a robe gleaming with the emblems of the victories of Rome. "What do you think of this law?" demanded Caius Julius.

"I approve it to the last letter."

"Would you support it if opposed by force?"

"By Heaven! If others draw the sword, I will at least bear a shield." The old soldier's eye lighted, and the audience burst into a paroxysm of cheering which rose to a crescendo of shrieks as Crassus stepped from behind a pillar and declared that the business-men of the city were one and all for the new land bill.

Caesar turned to put the question. He was interrupted by Bibulus, who rushed to the rostra, shouting that he had seen three crows flying from the right—there was blue lightning in the western sky— the sacred chickens would not eat—the omens showed forth the will of the gods that no further business be transacted that day, "and if you persist in this bill, by Hercules, I will find unfavorable omens on every other day. You shall not have your law this year though every man of you demand it."

At that moment—"Veto!" bellowed a leather-lunged Conservative tribune from another point of vantage. There was an angry growl within the crowd, a surge toward the temple steps, then someone from somewhere above emptied a basket of filth over Bibulus' head and at the same moment a lictor's rod rose and fell. The growl soared up to a shout, the mob surged around the temple, throwing stones and fruit at Bibulus, Cato and their tribune. Lucullus had vanished. His consular lictors tried to protect Bibulus, they were thrown down, their fasces broken by a concerted rush of men in the worn tunics of veterans of Pompey's army, and lictors, Conservative consul, tribune, Cato and all were kicked down the steps, rolled in the mud and hustled from the Forum.

Julius Caesar, who had been looking on with a gaze that contained more of speculation than excitement, raised his hand for silence again.

"The proposition placed before the people will now be put to a vote," he announced evenly.

4

Revolution in the Saddle—Bibulus appeared before the Senate the next morning and said he wanted to die. He had suffered fatal injuries to the dignity which, as he was not overly intelligent, was his most valuable possession. He was disposed to hold grievance that the Senate had not protected him to point and edge, and a snarling shuttlecock of "Your fault" began to grow up, which was interrupted by a message that plunged them all into the well of misery together. It was from Caesar; in accordance with the final amendment to the land bill just passed by the people, the senators were required to appear at once in the Forum and swear perpetual support to its provisions. Cato made a long, acrimonious speech, in which he swore that he would never swear; his ape, Favonius burst into tears, then both of them joined the procession to the altars and lugubriously swallowed the oath.

Their physic was unsweetened by any thought that they were the leaders of an effective opposition. The Senate itself had split; Bibulus presided over a sulky meeting of the august body in the tetrastyle of his town house and proposed a resolution that Caesar's law was illegal, but it lost by a narrow margin on the vote. It was not that the recusants were afraid of getting their skins punctured, either. Personal courage was a virtue that most Romans carried to the point of a vice. Rather the defeat had unchained a whole rout of hatreds and malices. A good few of the senators were giggling internally at seeing such proud magnificoes as Bibulus and Favonius stood in the corner, and were little disposed to interfere with anything that produced so salutary a result as long as it did not interfere with their personal pocket-books. Caesar himself controlled the votes of a few senators and Pompey and Crassus those of a great many more.

The appearance of the last two at the Consul's side in the Temple of Castor had, indeed, operated on the Conservative senators like some paralytic toxin, leaving them horrified but immobile. Their vertigo went through a still more violent stage when they learned that the triple alliance had been cemented by a public reconciliation between Crassus and Pompey and the marriage of the latter to Caesar's beloved daughter Julia. They had imagined they were dealing with the ordinary little Radical snap-dog; they discovered that the beast had three heads, one of them armed with the redoubtable iron teeth of the military power and another slobbering liquid gold. The thing had no right to exist; three-headed dogs were legendary, Pompey and Crassus were sworn enemies, Pompey and Caesar avatars of inimical spirits, who had had nothing in common within the memory of man.

Yet there the animal was, it lived, it moved, it barked with a bark not worse than its bite—as the Senate soon had good cause to learn, for when Lucullus undertook the perfectly normal opposition step of a court suit against Caesar, the Consul counter-attacked with a prosecution for maladversion of funds during the famous Armenian campaign on evidence supplied by Pompey. Lucullus was no more guilty than any other provincial governor, which was very guilty indeed. Caesar pressed on the prosecution with a vindictive energy that showed he meant to carry through a public trial and a confiscatory fine, and the old man was horribly frightened, for his being revolved around the magnificent gardens he had laid out with the proceeds of his peculations and the superb entertainments he gave in those gardens. He wrote a note asking composition; there was no answer; and the morning visitors in Caesar's atrium were presently treated to the sight of the Proconsul and Senator Lucullus, ex-general of the armies of Rome, scrubbing the marble with his knees while he begged for mercy with perfectly genuine tears coursing down his hard old face.

Still the Senate would not give up. Not in vain had the four hundred old men claimed to rule the world by words; they were experts in propaganda. Bibulus had retired to the monasticism of his four walls whence he issued daily proclamations that the acts of the new government were void since (1) he had that morning observed the omens of the skies, they were bad, therefore the day was sabbatical, and (2) one of the consuls, to wit, himself, was taking no part in the proceedings. Nobody minded. But in April, just as the land commission got to work, a change crept in; Bibulus' proclamatory style tightened, his pronunciamentoes changed from legal documents to bawdy and diverting comment on the members of the "three-headed hydra:"

——Caesar was a lecher ——Why had Pompey divorced his wife Mucia? Or had Caesar arranged the whole matter with malice prepense to provide a husband for his overripe daughter? ——Caesar was more than a lecher ——Queen Nicomedes, ha, ha, ha. ——How had Crassus got his fortune? By betraying his friends, bah! ——Pompey was a tin soldier, decorated for victories won without fighting, gained after some other commander had done the hard work——

Etcetera, etcetera, ad infinitum, ad nauseam, and backed by a dinner-table whispering campaign, ninety per cent untrue, one hundred per cent unprovable, pro or con, and only fifty per cent believed, but that fraction did a lot of harm, especially the parts about Crassus, for the proletariat felt acutely uncomfortable at cooperating with the financiers who, by a proletarian article of faith in all ages, cooperate with the poor only when they can deceive them. ——Are we betrayed? asked the slums when Caesar, faithful to the obligations of his political alliance, brought in a bill to relieve the bankers of the onerous Asian tax-contracts by refunding them a third of the price they had bid. The bill went through, but amid murmurs; Caesar gave the great companies warning that they need never again expect such a concession, a proceeding which the insiders treated as a kind of Olympian joke, but which was really a necessity of the Consul's position as a leader of his party.

Are we betrayed? Caesar was proposing new laws at a furious rate. So was his henchman the Tribune Vatinius. One of them very stringent against bribery in elections, obviously intended to keep poor citizens (who might live half a year on their vote-payments in a tight canvass) from selling something of no value to them but greatly desired by other people. There was a rumor that Caesar and Pompey had guaranteed the exiled King of Egypt his throne again for the princely bribe of six thousand talents—what had this to do with honest Radical rule? Varro the agronomist, one of Caesar's own land commissioners, lashed out with a bitter pamphlet against "the three-headed monster" and a hundred copies were made of it. Scribonius Curio, the young Conservative orator, declared the three were preparing a tyranny like that in the old Greek cities and the reaction was setting in.

Pompey was little help to the alliance; wandered about the city like the ghost of himself, apologizing for everything, for the first time in years experiencing a new sensation—the sensation of unpopularity in society—and liking it so little that he was moved to ask Cicero what specific he should use against this malady that was destroying his peace of mind.

"Break with Caesar," snapped Cicero. Pompey gave him a strange look and left the house—break an honorable compact with a man who had loyally fulfilled his part? But that evening he left the city and was next heard from in Capua.

Are we betrayed? The flood of new legislation went rushing through the popular assembly, passed by acclamation because Caesar asked for it and he was a good fellow who gave consular games of unusual splendor. The laws themselves were frankly incomprehensible. Why should there be new enactments against robbery or adultery or counterfeiting or in protection of magistrates? Such things were punishable already; if done by a slave or a minor, the head of their house might inflict what pain he would on the culprit; if done by a peregrine foreigner, some unpleasant form of death would be the penalty; if by a citizen, fine or banishment; if by an ambassador —no matter, they were all there, categories and categories of punishments, one for every status to which a man might belong, but certainly none omitted. Only a jurist like Servius Sulpicius Rufus, a great jurist and a philosopher, could trace in the new laws the appearance of a startling new principle, now so common that it is difficult for us to conceive a world in which it was not yet existant—the principle of the *ius gentium,* the law of peoples, applying to Greek or Roman, bond or free, prohibiting the same acts to each and levying against each the same penalties.

——There is a universal law that rules the world—a divine law emanating from the universal Reason. Human law comes into true existence only when man becomes aware of this divine law and recognizes its claim on him. Morality is thus identical with law, for both are called into being by the Right Reason, which is the universal primary force—— Or, to make it simple, this business of being born into some special privilege before the law—let it end. . . But this was in the mind of Servius Sulpicius Rufus the justiciar, meditating on universal law in the light of Zeno's philosophy. Caesar himself gave no clue, nor even had time to tie the knots, for people were asking Are we betrayed? and there was not enough land to supply all the fathers of three who requested plots in accordance with the farm allotment plan.

There was a gala performance in the theatre, with the actor Diphilus on the boards. As Caesar entered he was received in silence. Vatinius drew a few hisses and Scribonius Curio a round of cheers. The play started; Diphilus declaimed the line

" 'Tis through our misery that thou art great"

and the audience burst into a shout of applause. Cicero, sitting near the Consul, though he detected a stir behind the ineluctable mask. The play went on:

"The time will come when you shall rue that power!" cried Diphilus from the stage and the audience stood up to cheer him so long he was forced to repeat the speech. In the turmoil Caesar slipped out; before dawn an express was pounding the roads to Capua, and Pompey set out for Rome an hour after its arrival. There was a hasty conference behind closed doors; the next morning Caesar appeared before the popular assembly, and announced that he would submit a new measure to the vote.

Some mysterious chemistry of excitement had run through the city, stirring in everyone the feeling that a great moment had come. It had; the new law provided that all the Campanian leases he cancelled and the land was to be distributed to the poor.

It went through with shouting acclamations. Are we betrayed? withered like a leaf in the flame and the startled Senate held a meeting to take counsel of despair. The blow had come deadly swift; there was no time to organize resistance or counter-attack. Propaganda, a weapon of mass, moves lumbering as an elephant, obstruction was a broken shaft, resistance in arms hopeless with Pompey's fifty thousand on the other side.

"This is really tyranny and insupportable," moaned Cicero, "Yet support it we must." True; no counsel of despair could draw them from the pinch, they had to send a delegation to Caesar to eat humble pie and offer any reasonable compromise . . . ——Too late now, , gentlemen. I tried to be your friend, you would not have it. Shall we say that the loss of the Campanian lands is the not-extravagant price you pay for your amusement over the Nicomedes story?——

The senators glowered and mumbled; their revenues, their lands, their right to legislate for the Republic were all going lost together, and revolution was frankly in the saddle. More new laws now, leaning ever more toward the left—law against corrupt state contracts, law making poor citizens jurors of the high courts, and finally law for the abolition of special privileges to the business classes.

For the business men had taken the lead against the three-headed monster under the spur of senatorial propaganda. They had what they wanted, the remission of the Asian tax-bid, and had reverted to their normal position of friendship with the aristocracy and opposition to reform. Not that there were no honest men among them; capable Crassus stood like a rock to his word, and they produced a few disinterested patriots, like Cicero. But the curse of a commercial bourgeoisie caught between an aristocracy of birth and a depressed laboring class is that it gets carried away by the glamor of the former, or wishes special purse-privilege to balance special birth-privilege . . . From which defects not even Cicero was immune;

and if Cicero, a great humanist, made himself devil's advocate in this cause—?

Yet, by the strangest of paradoxes, it was the law among all the rest most unpalatable to aristocrats of birth and purse that sent the first thrill of doubt shivering down Cicero's spine that he might be on the wrong side. The famous *Lex de Repetundis,* law for the suppression of rapacious provincial governors. It provided stiff penalties against extortion in office, which had been done before, but it also permitted provincials to bring the cases before the Roman courts, which was new, and meant that the prosecutions would be pushed not languidly like the trial of Catiline by Clodius, nor for ancillary effect like that of Lucullus by Caesar, but tooth and nail by men who had the liveliest personal interest in driving through to conviction.

"A most enlightened law," said Cicero, rather surprised at himself for praising something of Caesar's, "which has destroyed corruption, made life possible for the provincials and saved the honor of Rome." But Cicero was a humanist who could weep over a slave's death. His friends, the fish-pond barons, found the new law good only in the abstract sense, like the Stoic doctrine that pain is a toy without terrors for the mind fixed on the infinite. "Unnecessary!" glumped Cato, when he heard of it; the rest said less but did more, and the year tilted toward its close with tempers rising toward the flashpoint and gangs of bravoes shouting through the streets at night or clashing in hot affrays whose echo rose over the city like smoke-puffs over Etna. It was fall; the consular elections were at hand, when out of the welter loomed the sinister figure of Vettius the spy, and P. Clodius Pulcher was delivered of his fourth practical joke.

5

*A Metabolic Process—*L. Vettius was a creature out of a picaresque tale, overfed, with larval-white skin—a noisy breather. It would take two thousand years and scientific psychology fully to explain him, but in the meanwhile he was one of those incredible characters who bob up in moments of stress with stories of gigantic plots which have been confided to them for no apparent reason. Back in the days of

Catiline's conspiracy he had appeared before Cicero (then consul) with a circumstantial report implicating Caesar in that mess. He even offered to produce documentary proof. Cicero sent him packing; so far from being a member of Catiline's plot, Caius Julius had been the leader of an adroit undercover investigation which had yielded much of the evidence on which the conspiracy was destroyed, though L. Vettius could not know it.

Vettius, dissatisfied with his reception, went before the minor magistrate Novius and laid a formal complaint against Caesar, which was an error both of information and of judgment. Of information because as soon as the complaint was filed Cicero made public the fact that Caesar had been helping him trace down the plot; of judgment because Caesar was then a justice of the superior court. He sent down a mandamus bringing the case into his own jurisdiction and demanded Vettius' documentary proof. When it was not forthcoming he sent Vettius to prison as a perjurer and the minor magistrate Novius to keep him company as a fool who had entertained an illegal prosecution against a higher ranking judge.

Vettius escaped the toils by promising to keep the authorities informed of happenings within his circle, which was large and tangent to the straight line of the law at every point. Pickings were good for a while; then people began to find him out, he had trouble in maintaining his paunch and began to long for the good old glorious conspiracy days when everybody in Rome had listened to him.

Did he, just at this point, stumble onto the track of a genuine assassination plot? Coincidence must stretch from Beersheba to Dan to explain it, but coincidence sometimes has arms longer than those of the Colossus of Rhodes, and there is nothing inherently improbable in an assassination plot among the young nobles of Rome, where murder was a recognized method of eliminating politically insoluble elements.

The whole truth we shall never know. Only this is certain: Bibulus sent Pompey a warning that there was a plot to kill him. Pompey laughed; he had survived the lethal intentions of more people than Rome contained. A month or so later Vettius approached Scribonius Curio, the young Conservative orator.

——I am (said he) one of a band who have found Pompey a menace. We are resolved to assassinate the "ex-Great" next time he comes into the Forum. Would you like to be one of us?——

Curio played with Vettius and informed Pompey. Pompey, perceiving that if the thing did have backing among the great families, he could both scotch it and cause the instigators acute embarrassment by publicity, make the charge public in the Senate and asked an inquiry. The Senate's bailiffs laid Vettius by the heels before he had time to hide; or perhaps he did not wish to, for once before the senators, the self-accused plotter launched into a rambling narrative in which he accused Curio as the leader of the conspiracy and named L. Aemillius Paulus, Senator Lentulus and M. Junius Brutus as well as Bibulus as members. Bibulus had sent him a dagger and bidden him be in the Forum on a certain day, when a gang of armed slaves would join him. The Senate burst into laughter over this farrago, for they knew what Vettius evidently did not—that Curio himself had opened the inquiry, Aemillius Paulus had been visiting in Macedonia since the beginning of the year and Junius Brutus was a special intimate of both Pompey and Caesar.

Senator Lentulus, however, was one of the Conservative candidates for Consul. It occurred to other members of his party that political capital might be extracted from the incident by declaring that the whole business was a put-up job, arranged by Caesar to discredit the opposition candidates. The whisper-propaganda department began to spread this idea, but the senators were slow, for as soon as Caesar heard of Vettius "revelations" it occurred to him that the Senate might try to use them in just that way. He visited the spy in jail that night, told him he would have to repeat his story before the assembly of the people the following morning and warned him that he had better make it more convincing than he had before the Senate.

Vettius, however, was constitutionally incapable of telling a straight story about anything. When Caesar led him to the rostra he informed an incredulous assembly that the plot had originated with Lucullus and that Cicero was in it as well. The fellow was obviously placing the blame on men so thoroughly out of active politics

that no one would believe him. Behind this there could lie but one
thing—such deadly fear of vengeances or of his real backers that
making himself out an arrant liar was better than naming them. But
who were they? The Senate said Caesar and Vatinius; Caesar said
some shadowy band of young aristocrats who were really plotting.
We shall never know—for the morning after playing his last star
role before the Roman people L. Vettius was found in the Tiber
with the red welt of a bowstring around his oversize neck, dead as
a roasted sprat.

Cicero laughed at the accusation. He was laughing at everything
that autumn, laughter being the only thing strong enough to bear
the weight of what he felt, justly or no, an insupportable tyranny. He
found an astringent humor in the thought that "Caesar's plot" would
recoil on its maker and the Conservatives thus carry the election. He
was wrong; Aulus Gabinius and Calpurnius Piso, the Radical candidates, were swept into the consulate by huge majorities, and what
was far more ominous from his point of view, P. Clodius Pulcher
was elected to a tribunate.

"Pulchellus", the pretty little girl-boy, Cicero called him, punning
on his name, but the pretty little girl-boy was as venomous as a
coral snake, which is also dainty, and it is only a little after the election that we find the orator writing, the smile quite wiped from
his countenance—"Clodius is uttering threats against me. The peril
is real, and I am afraid I shall have to call on all the friends I possess
for support."

It was not till he caught the note of envenomed hatred in those
threats that Cicero realized how deep an enmity he had aroused. He
had destroyed Clodius' alibi in the famous sacrilege trial, not the
sort of thing one would do to a friend, but still not enough to make
a man your enemy. The pretty little girl-boy could have laughed
that off; it put him in danger of penalties, not of ridicule. But harder
to bear was the scene after the trial in the Senate, when the orator
vented his disappointment in a series of blistering Ciceronian sar-
casms:— "You think, Publius Clodius, that this acquittal has let you
loose to do as you please. You are mistaken; the jury saved you for

the gallows, not for public life. Their object was not to keep you in the country but to prevent you leaving it."

Up leaped Clodius with an interruption: "The jury did not credit you on oath."

"On the contrary, twenty-five jurymen did credit me. The thirty-one acquitters gave no credit at all, but took their money in advance."

The house laughed, Clodius sat down and the *bon-mot* was repeated in fashionable circles where it made him the butt of a jest, which hurt more than the gallows. Still Clodius had tried to smooth the matter over. Meeting Cicero one day at the entrance to the Circus in a crowd of friends, he saluted the orator gaily, asking if he might sit with him—"for my sister has brought such a crowd of friends to our seats I can't get any more than standing room near her."

"Oh, don't grumble about standing with your sister," snapped Cicero. "You can always lie with her, you know."

The pretty little girl-boy's face went white to the lips; Cicero turned away, feeling very satisfied with himself, and repeated the remark to friends as an example of good Latin epigrammatic style. It never occurred to him that a great humanist with claims on six centuries of future renown might one day stand in need of even such friendships as Publius Clodius could give. It did not occur to him, either, that he was digging more trouble from the bottom of the sea with that super-sharpened tongue of his when he defended one Caius Antonius before a huge crowd in the Forum a week or so later. The charge was misspending public funds while Antonius was in Macedonia—"What has he done?" thundered Cicero, sweeping along on the tide of his own eloquence, "that the present rulers of Rome have not? Impeach him if you will, ungrateful people—but he spent the money for the good of the Republic and the preservation of its alliances, while these, our triple kings, filch from the public treasury to buy their way into a tyranny of their own!"—and went on, with sword-like logic and burning arrows of wit, while the Forum rang with applause.

At the time Cicero thought of nothing but the fact that he had made a fine impression:— "I was the man who revived the faining courage of the patriots. I did not leave the victorious party a word to say for themselves. The Senate I aroused from its despondency; the triumvirate I cast into despair." It never occurred to him that Caesar would take this triumphant exercise in rhetoric seriously. He, Cicero, was out of politics. He had refused a post on the land commission. It was not till years later, mulling over the mistakes of his career in a far country that he thought of connecting the speech for Antonius with another event which occurred just after it and which, at the time, puzzled him greatly—the translation of Clodius to the plebeian order. It was accomplished secretly but with careful regard to the legal religious ceremony. Caesar himself presided as High Priest of Rome, Pompey took the auspices, and Clodius was declared adoptive son of a man younger than himself. A kind of joke, but a joke with grim undertones, like all Clodius' witticisms, for it made him eligible to the tribunate, and the next news was that of his election.

Without quite understanding how the man had reached such a position Cicero was fully awake to the peril of having his enemy in so powerful an office. He called on Pompey, who received him in the most friendly manner and bade him have no fear, so the orator went home to read a book of inferior poems by Alexander of Epiros which had come in by the latest post, feeling quite comfortable. He was sure that Caesar was merely the executive head of the "triple monster" and Pompey its brain—an error in proportion.

Pompey, for instance, had nothing to do with the bill that Tribune Vatinius put through the assembly just at election time, overriding the Senate's allocation of country roads as the field for Caesar's activity when he had finished his consulate. Pompey, a fair-minded man, did not indeed, approve of Caesar being turned into a road-mender, but he thought Vatinius' substitute measure extreme. It made Caesar governor of Cisalpine Gaul and Illyricum for the next five years and gave him command of three legions—15,000 men—an arrangement for which the only and obvious reason was that without violating the law against armies in Italy it would place Proconsul Caesar within striking distance of Rome at the head of an armed force sufficient to make certain that his new social legislation would not be upset by violent means the moment he turned his back. Pompey thought he and Crassus and the new consuls could attend to that detail, esteeming all these soldiers a trifle extravagant, but he made no protest as he was, after all, enjoying his ease and the arrangement promised him the delightful sensation of power without responsibility.

At this moment the Senate suffered another access of cleverness. Metellus Celer, the gentleman who had caught the fascinating Clodia on the rebound from old Lucullus' arms, found the pace she set him too swift and died of it. He had been governor of Transalpine Gaul, the great wild province stretching northwestward from the mountains into the mists of barbarism. His death coincided roughly with the passage of Vatinius' law, and about the same time the rumble of a coming tribal uprising drifted down from the frontier. It seems to have been with the idea of giving this clever Caesar enough rope to hang himself with that the Senate voted him Transalpine Gaul and another legion in addition to the provinces he had been assigned by the Vatinian law. It would be months before he could get there. There was no one to deal with the tribes in the meanwhile but the deceased Celer's clerk, and things might easily get into such a state that Caesar would be too occupied with them to have any attention for affairs at home.

Caesar accepted the new charge silently. He had not yet studied the Gallic problem but he foresaw that the assignment would give his busy brain something to do during the coming year. Cisalpine Gaul and Illyricum were, after all, garrison provinces, and if a tribal rising were imminent in the Transalpine province it would be important to reach it at the source rather than letting the wave swell up to tidal size.

The Kalends of January came; he laid down his consular office and went outside the city to organize his staff, recruit a few new men and make preparations for leaving. On one indispensable he was determined; there should be no overthrow of the laws he had given so much to bring about, and he was waiting near Rome to see how the new administration would handle things. The result of the first few weeks was disappointing, as it rapidly became evident that Gabinius

and Calpurnius Piso were weaklings, Pompey without political talent
and Crassus to be trusted only so far as his clear interest lay. In a
practical sense the whole tree of reform, judicial, social, economic,
was braced only by the inertia of its existence and might be blown
down by any aristocrat with ability enough to raise a storm.

There was a brief period of quiet with Caesar watching the Senate narrowly from his headquarters outside the walls. Fortunately
the aristocracy was not rich with cloud-compellers. Scribonius
Curio, though able and energetic, was too small and young a man to
puff up a whirlwind; Lucullus was already knocked out. There remained just two who united the malice and the mentality necessary
—Cato and Cicero, and of these two Cato was presently eliminated
by an appointment as financial commissioner to the city of Cyzicus
in the East, a job that would take him at least a year.

Caesar did his best to draw Cicero's teeth gently. The first offer
was a glamorous appointment as ambassador-at-large among the
Oriental powers, where the orator's persuasiveness might do the
Republic a real service in view of the threatening condition of affairs on the Parthian border. Cicero refused; he liked his seaside
villa and his Apennine farms; he liked the clash of intellects he
found in the city; he would not be at home to meet his brother, who
was absent in Greece. Caesar, boundlessly patient, boundlessly conciliatory, tried again.—There was trouble brewing in Gaul (he
said in a note) he had room on his staff for an able man. Would
Cicero do him the honor of accepting an appointment as chief of
staff and second in command?

No. "I don't want to run away; I long to fight. After all, I am
high in the esteem of all men here; my reputation will protect me."
—"My reputation" and Pompey, he might have added, for he clung
like death to the picture of Pompey as leader of the three and
thought no shame to attack the triumvirate as governors while
appealing for their protection as friends, an attitude which lacked
contact with reality.

The year changed to its second month. One of the new praetors,
a Conservative, brought in a motion to rescind Caesar's laws *en bloc*,
and saw it fail. The tribes were astir beyond the mountains; an

express came down from the Cisalpine province to say that colonists there were quitting their homes. The recruits drilled to trumpet and drum without the city walls, and Publius Clodius suddenly proposed a bill "that anyone who has executed a Roman citizen without trial shall be interdict from fire and water."

There was only one man in Rome to whom that bill applied; the man who had snipped the heads off Catiline's conspirators and no questions asked, three years before—Marcus Tullius Cicero. With a start he awoke from his dream of six hundred years. Something must be done, and quickly. But what?

He appealed to the middle classes in a public oration, very classical and refined. The bankers put on mourning and marched to the Senate in a body where they presented a petition that the house do something to prevent the threatened banishment of its most distinguished member. The Senate also put on mourning and did nothing at all—"There were few among them who had not been stung by his irony or irritated by his presumption." Cicero hurried to Consul Gabinius' house; Gabinius was not at home. He rushed off to see Consul Calpurnius Piso; found him at eleven in the morning in a boozing-dive and in his slippers. On being notified that Cicero was at the door the chief magistrate of Rome staggered unsteadily to the lintel, leaned against it, hoicked, spat, and remarked:

"The state of my health is such that the doctors have recommended a draught of wine in the morning."

Cicero, his high-bred nostrils crinkling with the odors that assailed them, asked about Clodius' bill and whether the Consul approved it. One of Calpurnius' eyebrows ascended to make contact with his hair-line.

"I disapprove of cruelty," he said and spat again.

The orator turned disconsolately away. That afternoon he had another note from Caesar, still friendly, still conciliatory—the offer of a staff post on the army for Gaul was still open. Cicero refused; he was not reduced to charity yet, he said. Pompey the Great was his friend, to Pompey the Great he would go, and distasteful though it was, remind the conqueror that he had pronounced him the most illustrious of Romans.

But Pompey was not in the city; the porter said he was taking the airs at his villa in the Alban hills. As Cicero hurried through the streets on his way to the gate he was followed by a hooting rabble who threw clods after him. That day Clodius announced that he would push his bill to a vote, and that the three triumvirs approved of what he was doing.

Alba is fortunately not so far but it can be made in half a day. Cicero arrived in the late afternoon, but as he stood at the porter's gate of Pompey's villa one of his slaves gave an exclamation. Cicero turned round to follow the pointing hand; a little group of horsemen had just emerged from the back gate and were hurrying away into the woodlands as though on a hunt. In the middle of the group he could recognize the stately figure of Gnaeus Pompey.

Roman Altar

The orator, numbed and bewildered, his intelligence in a state of collapse, journeyed back to the city, where he heard Clodius had drawn another bill, banishing him specifically by name and declaring his properties forfeit. No help for it; he had to go, to leave the clash of intellects, the seaside villa and the Apennine farms. For a day or two he wandered among the houses of his friends, talking morosely of suicide; then took a little Greek statue of the goddess of wisdom which he had long treasured, and inscribing it "To Minerva, the Guardian of Rome" took it to the temple and passed on out the city gate along the long road to exile.

That same night a Narnian horseman arrived at the city gate. The tribes were up; the whole horizon of Gaul red with the flame of their burnings. Julius Caesar left with the dawn and the first day he rode seven hundred and eighty stades.

IV

FOOTNOTE ON POLITICS

(which may be omitted without interrupting the narrative)

The modern reader is constantly coming up against the term "equites" or "knights" (here generally rendered "business men" or "bankers") in ancient historical writing and wondering what it means, for it seems to refer to a sharply defined class of birth, with a strong feeling of unity. We have business men and bankers today; they are not knights, except sometimes in England, they are seldom united upon any subject and they form so little a separate class that a man may be a business man on Monday and a laborer on Tuesday.

The fact is that there is no good translation for the idea expressed by the Latin word *equites,* and the Rome of Julius Caesar's day, in which they formed an important element, has no close parallel in any modern society. Leaving aside the slave population, which did not count politically, Rome was a three-class state, with the mass of the proletariat at the bottom, the equites in the middle and the great senatorial families, the Optimates, at the top. The arrangement is not, superficially, unlike that of pre-revolutionary France, with its peasants, bourgeois and aristocracy, but there are differences so fundamental as to vitiate the analogy, and most of them center around the business class, the equites, the equestrian order.

Like the French bourgeoisie, it was a class concerned with commerce; unlike it the equites were concerned only with the upper ranks of commerce, a class of bankers and business-managers. The mobile wealth of the Roman world was almost entirely in its hands, as well as all financial operations and the directorships of the big companies. The Roman proletariat thus comprehended approximately the same elements as the French proletariat and bourgeoisie together, with the equites forming a special class, a kind of commercial department of the aristocracy.

It had one characteristic of a full-fledged aristocracy; admission to it could not be achieved, for it was a class of birth. Being a "knight" carried with it social and political privileges—the right to serve on juries, the right to sit in a reserved seat at the theatre, the right to wear a special type of gold ring and to go to war on horseback— whence the name. Unlike any modern commercial class, the equites had the class feeling that goes with birth, and the complex Roman voting arrangement gave their suffrages a weight out of all proportion to their actual numbers.

That they did not make more use of their privileged political status was due to two factors; concentration on money, and the existence of the upper class, the Optimates, who specialized in government as did the equites in finance. The Senatorial order constituted a genuine aristocracy with all the usual features of great holdings in land, social superiority and monopoly of military and civil office.

In earlier days, after the suppression of the old "Patrician" and "Plebeian" labels, which had lost all but a ritualistic validity two centuries before Caesar's time, the arrangement of the Roman state had been the normal one of a single aristocracy of property, the equestrian order, from which individuals were elected as magistrate-generals. After their year of service these former executives passed into the Senate, which thus became a kind of governing committee of equites who had been chosen by their fellows as the best fitted to govern. In this earlier period the line between proletariat and equites was not strictly drawn, either; it was merely a matter of attaining sufficient property to be able to keep a horse.

The extension of the Roman suffrage and the manumission of numerous slaves had gradually made the proletariat an undesirable recruiting-ground for the equestrian order. At the same time there was a persistent tendency to elect as consuls the brothers and sons of successful generals, and an equally persistent tendency on the part of wealthy equites to avoid military service. Both equites and Senate thus became closed corporations in a practical sense, though there remained a certain amount of seepage from the equites into the Senate—as of such characters as Cicero.

It is important to remember that Rome, like every other ancient civilized state, was surrounded by greedy and active barbarisms who kept the republic in a constant state of war. This made the Senatorial oligarchy for a long time an aristocracy of service as well as of birth and prevented its decay into elegant idleness. The young Roman of Senatorial rank had received a thorough practical education in both war and government on the staffs of several commanders and administrators before he reached the age of twenty-five. It was not only the sole career open to him, it was also the only means by which he could maintain his position—estates never pay, a landed aristocracy inevitably coasts into poverty unless it receives a constant influx of funds from some outside source. The commercial sources were closed to the Senatorial families by the equestrian monopoly of banking training, technique and ability. Victorious war, in other words, loot, was the alternative.

At the time Caesar appeared on the scene there were then, three Roman classes—a warrior-governing class, a banking class, and a third class, which comprised everything else. The first of these classes, by the processes of both natural and artificial selection, had acquired a considerable skill in the tasks of government. The arrangement had only fallen out of balance by reason of its enormous success. The training received by Roman generals and governors combined with the racial ability for cooperation and combination, had produced for her Optimates such an influx of wealth that they became debauched. They wanted to sit back and enjoy their gains forgetting the conditions by which they held them.

At the same time there were fewer of the Optimates to share both the riches and the responsibilities. Like all closed aristocracies the Roman was afflicted with a declining birth-rate. The supply of trained leaders began to run out just at the moment when the Republic, by virtue of its imperial position, was most in need of administrators with minds large enough to embrace the problems of millions and long enough to envisage the problems of decades. When the terrible crisis of the invasion of the Cimbri and Teutones came, the best leaders the governing class could supply proved incompetent to the issue. More than unwillingly, they had been forced to import a man from the proletariat, Caius Marius, and he made them pay heavily for it.

For he hastened the process of decay in the Optimate class by the merciless proscriptions in which he sent so many aristocrats to the block. He decapitated them less for their aristocracy than for their ability, that is, the likelihood that they would furnish an effective opposition. Finally Pompey's success in the East had produced another whole chain of provinces that needed governors, and as Caesar began his rise to power the situation was one of obvious seriousness to anyone who took, as he did, the long view.

His remedy was radicalism; that is, the admission to a full share in the rights and profits of office of the meanest citizens, the elevation to Senatorial rank of the whole Roman population, so that they might form a kind of equestrian order for the world, as the early equites themselves had governed the smaller Rome. He hoped to force or to persuade the Optimates to share their privileges with the whole people in order to produce an enlarged set of privileges for all. Reform of some sort was necessary, for the machine was creaking at the joints. The Cimbri-Teutones invasion showed it, the Spartacid revolt repeated the lesson, the pirate troubles Pompey had suppressed reenforced it, the increased tendency of provincial governors to enrich themselves at the expense of the governed was the final touch. The reform Caesar proposed seemed to his basically orderly and reasonable mind the most simple and reasonable method of restoring the old Roman spirit of cooperation.

But he was dealing with unreasonable men whose intelligences had been softened by overwhelming wealth. The Senate had been forced to yield, but it would not cooperate, and without its cooperation Caesar's homeopathic radicalism was doomed to failure, for without cooperation there was no way of training up a new class of executives. Only the proletariat were numerous enough to supply the demand for administrators and for them to gain education and find talent by trial and error would be an experiment disastrous to the whole structure. The Senate had so obstructed him at every step that he was not even given time to complete the legal reforms that should have been the basis of the new Rome, and in the sense that he was forced to leave the structure half finished, his consulship had been a failure.

He might, indeed, have crushed the Senate and thrown the whole mass into solution. It would have been a tight fit, since the equites would in all probability have joined the struggle against him as they had against the Gracchi, but he could no doubt have managed it. But Julius Caesar was too much of an aesthete to relish destruction in any form. He was an artist, a creator, a producer, to whom waste was horrible. And there was another element in the situation, an element all too frequently forgotten by modern theoretical critics, who argue from analogy as though Rome were a state in a civilized world. Rome was the civilized world; it existed like a bowl of water on which half a dozen needles are floating, upheld by surface tension. Agitate the water, the surface tension breaks and the needles go stabbing through. If Caesar altogether destroyed the privileged class he would also destroy the only class with military talent. His new classless state would never have an opportunity to prove itself; it would take a generation to find new leaders and in a generation the whole business would have been trampled under the hooves of yelling savages. The thing had been tried in the Greek world at Megalopolis, at Callatis on the Euxine and at Syracuse, and always with the same result—extinction. Caesar could not afford to sacrifice immediate strength to ultimate strength.

The difficulty with which Caesar was faced then, was this; nowhere among the three classes of the Roman state could he find the requisite combination of governing ability and patriotism. The Optimates had the ability but they were stubbornly determined to use it for their personal benefit. They persisted in looking upon the state lands as their private appanage and the state treasury as their private bank account. The equites were helpless at anything but the financial tasks in which they had been specializing for nearly three centuries. The lower orders, still sound, still valiant, still able to think in terms of duty, lacked both intelligence and experience.

Caesar was thus driven to the creation of a fourth order, a new aristocracy of service which should at once protect his civilization against the exterior dangers which threatened it and furnish a reservoir of experienced talent for the task of ruling the world. The Senate's war of pasquinades, the conspiracy of Vettius, minor events in themselves, have this profound significance—they showed Caesar that conciliation was impossible, orderly and logical evolution within the existing structure of the Roman Republic hopeless. They forced him to go outside, to make a new class, powerful enough to eat up the other three, in which performance replaced family as the basis for rewards and in which the path of promotion should be open to all. The army was such a class and it was the only such class.

Caius Marius had already professionalized the Roman army and both Marius and Sulla had used professional armies to override existing authority at Rome and introduce constitutional changes. But both men had used military power as a special implement of force to wrench the course of Roman political development violently round into a new direction. Both had removed the pressure as soon as the change was accomplished, expecting that the Republic would thenceforth continue along the new path in a normal manner.

What Caesar contributed was the realization that any change brought about in this manner was impermanent. As soon as the pressure was removed, everything snapped back into its old position. Sulla's great and valuable administrative reforms could not re-endow the Optimates with their lost sense of responsibility; Marius' blows and grimaces could not force them to share their monopoly of administrative ability nor produce a substitute for it in the lower ranks of society. When the problem descended to Caesar, he realized this and rejecting entirely partial and impermanent solutions, attacked the thing at the root and with the sword.

But for the development of a military governing class one element is indispensable; outstanding military success of obvious value, since only through such success could the new military order attract to itself the talented and ambitious young men of all classes who were devoting their energies to other pursuits. Caesar, in short, meant to undercut the Senatorial oligarchy by draining off the best of its young blood into his new order of soldier-administrators, and there

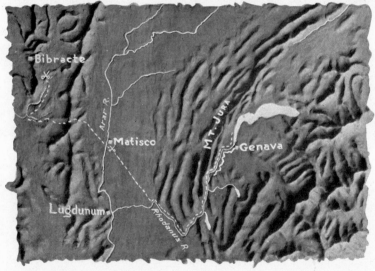

THE CAMPAIGNS AGAINST THE
HELVETIANS AND KING ARIOVISTUS

Below—The Helvetian campaign. The dotted line shows the march of
the Helvetians; the crossed swords indicate the point of battle.
Above—The campaign against King Ariovistus. Dotted line shows
Caesar's march.

combining it with the best of the blood of the other two classes. He was synthesizing his new state outside the limits of the old because the old had rotted too deep for saving. But to accomplish this, he must again obtain cooperation; this time the cooperation of the young bloods. And to obtain that he must offer them more splendid rewards than they could obtain by sticking to the old castes and the old dispensation.

And "ambition never chose a more dangerous or less promising route for itself"; for Gaul was to be the place of this synthesis and Gaul was inhabited by the fiercest, the most militant barbarism of the ancient world, a race that had already once burned Rome, had shattered the Macedonian Empire, a race whose word for "soldier" was the same as that for "men", who despised civilization because they felt it reduced the martial spirit, who were a thousand times more numerous than the four legions that faced them and who were in every respect as well armed and as well equipped as they.

In every respect but one. The Romans had Julius Caesar.

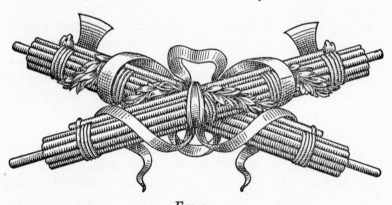

Fasces

V

GAUL DIVIDED, CAESAR UNITED

The Men of the Mountain—All Gaul is divided into three parts, of which one is inhabited by the Belgae, one by the Aquitani and the third by the Celts. These peoples differ in race, language and institutions, the Aquitani, who lie beyond Garumna river, being akin to the Spaniards; the Belgians, north of the Sequana and Matrona rivers, to the Germans, while the broad central belt from Alps to Ocean includes the people called Celtae or Galli.

Celts: that is a race of spoiled children, amiable, unstable, mystical, brave and treacherous, the best of acquaintances and the worst of friends. They were men who could adorn anything but build nothing, whose classes lived in poetry and dirt while the masses were so miserable they found it a privilege to become Roman slaves.

Their un-neighborly qualities furnish no justification for attacking them. Neither does the dogma invented by modern imperialists that Gallic barbarism had reached its cultural limits, for this remains at best not proven, although it is difficult to show that Celtic culture contained any progressive element, and Celtic intellect has ever and everywhere been concentrated upon regret for a mythological past.

Yet even if they had reached their limits, why not let them work out their own destinies? Surely, barbarous or no, they have a right to the complaisance of civilization. If civilization means anything it means that those who have it possess also the largeness of mind not to crush others' intellectual development by means of purely technical advantages they have gained. The argument is specious, based on the conditions of a modern mechanical civilization, whose barbarians are inoffensive folk located on sundown islands, and by moderns projected into a past to which it does not apply. It fails at three points to meet the case of Rome and Gaul. The advantages civilization had given Rome were not purely technical but purely intellectual, the Gauls were not distant and they were not inoffensive. They were by no means satisfied with civilization's complaisance. They were international gangsters, muscle-men, lazy and avaricious, who wanted the incidental products of progress (wine, for instance, jewels, soft women, everything that goes with easy life) without being willing to submit to the mental discipline by which the Mediterranean races had so hardly won these things.

For many years Rome had been complaisant to the extent of a policy of peaceful infiltration, maintaining commercial treaties (called "alliances" but without military character) with the frontier tribes. Significant that the Druids, the only educated and professionally intelligent men in Gaul, were Romanizers. But desires clashed; the news that sent Caesar whirling up the peninsula at ninety miles a day was that to continue any longer the Gallic right of self-development was to extinguish the Roman right to self-defence. The great Helvetian nation had burned their homes, destroyed their crops and granaries and taken to the war-path, three hundred and sixty-eight thousand strong, ninety-two thousand of them full-grown warriors.

Neither their purpose nor their destination were secret. They were moving because the territory they held (roughly a triangle between the Jura range, the Rhenus river and the lacustrine sources of the Rhodanus) was so bound in by natural obstacles as to give them few opportunities for raiding, "and on this account they were greatly distressed, for they were men that longed for war." They were going to the lands of the Santoni, where Garumna mouth meets Ocean. Another tribe, the Sequani, had agreed to join them on the way and found an anarch empire which would have unrestrained freedom of murder and pillage across the plains of central Gaul down to the Alps.

No Roman could view with indifference the establishment of such an empire. Rome had been indifferent to such an enterprise once and within the twelvemonth the savages were in Italy. But there was a peculiarly compelling reason against this movement even if the remoter possibility of invasion had not existed. The easy exit from

Helvetia lay across the Rhodanus and through the Roman province of Ulterior Gaul. Could 368,000 wild men with arms in their hands be trusted in that fat land? Never—the villages already flamed along the horizon and Caesar rushed north at ninety miles a day, sleeping in his traveling carriage, waking to dictate crisp orders as he rode.

Ulterior Gaul had only one legion, the 10th. The new commander gathered this up and rushed to the key-point, Genava, utmost outpost of Roman power, where Rhodanus leaves Lake Lemannus to curve round Jura's feet. The Helvetians heard he was there and sent an embassy asking free passage for their host through the province. They longed for war, but not war against the Eagles, which they had seen borne into action too frequently before. Caesar's need was

See map
facing page 96

time; he made some trumpery excuse about it being against the Roman religion to make such a decision before the change in the moon. The barbarians, being of a race that called themselves "Children of the Night" (Dis was their high god) accepted that. They would return for a decision on April 13.

Caesar burned the bridge at Genava and set his men feverishly to work—the 10th and the provincial militia to throwing up a palisadoed wall with redoubts at all the fords from Genava nineteen miles along to where the Jura pinched the river, the industrial population of the province to making catapults and stone bullets, for he was outnumbered more than ten to one.

At dawn on the 13th April the envoys came back and got their refusal. Before sunset the attacks began all along the line, sometimes at fords, sometimes on huge rafts made of linked bateaux. But the catapult-balls drove in among them as they struggled at the water's edge and the legionary cohorts, gathering rapidly, showed so stout a front that the Helvetians could not make it.

There is a pass, however, round the flank of Jura, on Rhodanus' right bank, a narrow route and difficult, where the wagons must go in single file. The Helvetii began to stream through it, turning sharp north into the plain beyond, with the design of ascending the Arar river a way, then swinging west.

They moved slowly with their families and herds. Caesar left a legate, Titus Labienus, in command of the 10th and rushed back across the Alps in a passion of speed to the great stronghold of Aquileia, where his three other legions, the 7th, 8th, and 9th, had spent the winter. He got them onto the march at once, but it would be death to face the 92,000 Helvetian warriors with only four legions. Without authority, but also without hesitation, he called for volunteers from the Cisalpine province, enrolled two whole legions— partly young men, partly time-expired veterans—numbered them 11 and 12, and hurried to the frontier at a pace that automatically weeded out all but the strongest in the rank.

The Alpine tribes, stirred by the rising of the Helvetii, were up; they tried to bar his passage. Caesar went crashing through, fighting them off front, flank and rear, and arrived on the Rhodanus front hardly more than a month after he had left it. At Lugdunum he checked; the political situation was set with spikes. An inch across the river would carry him out of Roman territory into independent Gaul, and the land just north belonged to the Aedui, of all Gallic nations the largest and the best affected to Rome, but proud as sin and sensitive of their rights.

The Helvetians solved the difficulty. Up ahead, their lumbering column, fifteen miles in extent, had gathered in some Sequanan recruits, then swung northwest into the heart of Aeduana and was now crossing the Arar near Matisco, pointed on Bibracte, the Aeduan capital. They ate out the land like locusts, they burned and smashed what they did not take, the Aeduans were powerless before their numbers. An embassy came down to Caesar's headquarters, headed by Liscus, high chief of the nation, and Diviciacus, the head Druid, an old man of singular charm and mental breadth, who had visited Rome the year before and delighted Cicero with his philosophical conversation. They prayed Caesar, in the name of the ancient alliance between Aeduans and Romans, to help them ere they perished. The resources of their nation would be at his disposal.

As he had no cavalry of his own he asked for four thousand light horse. They came under the leadership of Dumnorix, the greatest war-chief of the country and Diviciacus' brother, tall, moustachioed men who rode like Centaurs, swinging great two-handed swords.

Caesar crossed Rhodanus at once, spreading the Aeduans ahead of him as scouts and screen. They reported that three of the four Helvetian cantons had crossed the Arar; the fourth, Canton Tigurinus, was still on the east bank, gathering boats and rafts. Caesar marched like wildfire by forest ways onto their rear; came among them in the thick of the night and slashed into the unsuspecting multitude with trumpets howling fiercely from the dark. Canton Tigurinus could not withstand the shock; it was cut to pieces and the survivors dispersed to the forests with the Aeduan horsemen riding after them.

Caesar's engineers threw a pontoon bridge over the Arar and he crossed in the morning. The Helvetians had spent three weeks getting over; it occurred to them that a man who marched so swift and struck so sharp might be better conciliated than fought, and they sent an embassy to see about it. A bent patriarch named Divico was the leader, in his younger days a famous battle-chief, who had surprised and massacred the garrison at Genava and was therefore supposed to understand Romans. The conference was what might have been foreseen. Divico offered peace in the name of the Helvetii; they would continue their march to whatever part of Gaul Caesar appointed, but advised him to be careful lest such a disaster as that of Genava befall him. Caesar replied in a tone as lofty that the only part of Gaul he wished them in was Helvetia; if they would give hostages to return thither he would be glad to forgive the treacherous exploit to which Divico referred. Divico answered that it was the Helvetian custom to receive hostages rather than to give them and the conference broke up in mutual disrespect and anger.

The next morning the Helvetii took the road again with Caesar following slowly, his legions in order of battle, the Aeduan cavalry out in front to hold contact. The problem was beyond his experience, two of his legions green levies and the enemy double his numbers with no sensitive flanks or lines of supply—how to grip such a hedge-hog? As he pondered there was a cavalry clash up ahead; the four thousand Aeduans were routed and came streaming in on the legions with tidings that they had been beaten by only five hundred Helvetian riders, bad news for Caesar, to whose outnumbered army the moral factor was doubly important.

At the same time food ran short. The Aedui, who had promised to supply the army, kept feeding them on promises, and Caesar perceived there was mischief afoot somewhere. He summoned a council of chieftains. As soon as he began to address them he felt that atmosphere of hostility every orator knows and dreads; already annoyed with the turn of events, he unreined his temper and lashed at the Aedun conduct toward an army that was fighting their battle in terms so incisive his audience was left pale and muttering.

Liscus the high chief made a long, almost tearful reply. ——The Aeduan people (he said) were friends of the Romans, but there were some ill spirits among the chiefs, too powerful to be restrained by his magisterial authority. They had ordered the people not to furnish supplies——and he broke off as some of the others began to glower and finger sword-hilts. Caesar was on familiar ground now; he made a few remarks in a milder tone, then dismissed the meeting, but signed Liscus to remain and when they were alone bade him speak his full mind.

The root of the trouble, as Caesar had begun to suspect, was Chief Dumnorix. He had a secret understanding with the Helvetians. The whole invasion project was, in a sense, his; he was using the horde to crush personal opposition to himself among the Aedui with the idea of becoming king. The cavalry defeat was his work; he had set the example of flight from the center of the skirmish.

Caesar was thunderstruck to find how deep the canker had eaten; even half-true this malicious complaint accounted for everything and showed in what position he stood, surrounded by open and secret foes, with a starving army in a hostile land. Retreat would suit the traitor's book exactly—how many days before Dumnorix would be guiding the children of the night through the passes into Italy? No weakness; he summoned Diviciacus, who as High Druid, was head of whatever barbaric courts the Aedui possessed, announced that Dumnorix must be tried and executed out of hand and inquired simply whether Diviciacus would prefer to have his brother condemned by the national judges or by a Roman court-martial.

The old man fell on his knees, bursting into tears. He had known of the treachery, of course, but himself engrossed in the contemplation of infinite verities, had not dreamed men could be so grim in this game of empires. Caesar raised him from the ground and pressed his hand; then sent for Dumnorix, told him that everything was known, but that he owed his life to his brother's pleas, and sent him to his quarters under guard. Liscus took over the cavalry command; the army moved on.

The change worked wonders for the service. Caesar speedily learned that the barbarians were camping without proper outposts or watch, and planned a dawn surprise to make the most of his smaller numbers and better discipline. Titus Labienus the legate took two of the veteran legions in a night-march circuit around the hill where the Helvetii were encamped. Caesar with the other four and the cavalry advanced against its front. Labienus hid in the woods, with orders to attack the Helvetian rear when he heard the crash of Caesar's onset.

A good plan, but it miscarried; the scouts Caesar sent to report whether his legate were in position came back with the improbable but alarming tidings that Labienus must have been ambushed as there were thousands of barbarians where he ought to be. Caesar held up the attack while he went to see for himself; the Helvetians, calmly unaware of these bafflings and excursions, meanwhile packed up their baggage and moved out of the danger-zone.

They had crossed the watershed. Next morning they turned down the westward streams but Caesar, still lacking provisions, struck diagonally northwest toward Bibracte, where he could be sure of getting them before continuing the pursuit. Gallic deserters carried the news of this eccentric to the Helvetians; they interpreted it to mean that the Romans feared them, and martial enthusiasm blazing up hot as a straw-fire, turned back to wipe Caesar out.

The Proconsul threw forward the Aeduan horse to gain time to form and ranked on a little elevation that crossed the T of a valley, with the 11th and 12th back as a baggage-guard, the four veteran legions in triple line of battle on the slope. The Helvetians stopped to build a wagon-laager, where they left two small tribes, Boii and Tulingi, to guard their women and children. It was noon by time they ranked and came surging up the hill, shouting and brandishing weapons above the line of shields locked in front to hold off the Roman javelin-fire.

The last device failed its purpose; many a Gaul went down with a spear through throat or head, many another dropped his shield as the soft iron points of the Roman weapons bit in, then bent, rendering the shield unmanageable. The Helvetii did not hesitate for that; they drove right in and closed. There was a hard fight for a space but the braves could not break the legionary line, and began to give back down into the valley with the deadly Roman broadswords slashing and stabbing into their rear as they flowed up one of the side hills to make a stand. The Romans pressed on after them, pivoting on their left wing. At this moment the Boii and Tulingi abandoned the wagon-burg and came swarming onto Caesar's right flank and rear, the worst possible place, for a legionary's right is his shieldless arm.

Caesar had a moment of warning as he saw the rush begin. In that moment he faced the rear rank of legionaries around and met the Boii and Tulingi shock for shock as the revived Helvetians on the hill came storming forward again. The advantage was with them now, position and momentum; their onset was both fierce and long-sustained. The Roman first line was relieved and fell back through the files, and returned to relieve the relievers. Still the fight went on. The sun swooped down; still the Gauls hurled their big bodies against the close-knit line of smaller men behind the big cylinder shields, but it was all useless, the Romans would not break; slowly, slowly the Helvetians were driven back in both directions and dark came on to find them at the edge of the wagon-burg with women and children hurling things at the Romans from the tops of the carts and jabbing at their legs with spears through the wheels. The place was hard, but the Roman spirit was up now, too, with a fighting tradition seven centuries old behind it; wounds and weariness forgotten, they stormed the barricade and made an appalling slaughter of everything within.

In the morning there was not a living Helvetian to be seen. Those remaining had fled north into the land of the Lingones, but their fighting men were mostly dead, they could get no food, the whole nation was sunk in a misery beyond despair. When they heard that the terrible legions, rested from the battle, were on their track, they sent in an unconditional surrender. Caesar had a census taken of them (there were about 110,000 left) and sent them back to Helvetia, where they would serve as a barrier state against the savages from beyond Rhenus, all but the Boii, who were allowed to remain as clients under the protection of the Aeduans. As they had destroyed their seed-corn and houses to prevent a return to that land the Proconsul ordered that these things be furnished to them from the Roman province.

There was some complaint about this in the camp, where such magnanimity was considered a quite unpardonable oddity on the commander's part. The army felt Caesar might at least have followed the procedure usual with contumacious enemies and sold the prisoners for the benefit of the soldiers' purses.

2

The Men of the Forest—Caesar moved slowly south from the land of the Lingones. At Bibracte the Gallic chieftains had assembled for a grand pow-wow and he thought it advisable to be present. There turned out to be no cause for worry; genuine relief at delivery from the Helvetian trouble mingled with that lively appreciation of favors still to come which is sometimes described as gratitude and the combined emotions found expression in several days of speeches on Caesar's generosity, courage and intelligence. The subject of this adulation waited patiently for the inevitable request to do something, while his soldiers salved wounds.

It came in the form of a delegation headed by Diviciacus, who delivered a homily on Gallic history:

——Since old time (he said) there have been two principal nations among the Gauls—Aedui and Arverni. The latter formed an alliance with the Sequanans of the Rhenus frontier, yet the Aedui still had the mastery in their perpetual wars till the Sequani, mad with defeat, waged fifteen thousand Germans to their service, not Gauls at all, but savages out of midnight beyond the great river, huge, hairy, formidable. Then the allies were victors indeed; the Aeduan nobility was almost wiped out and their state reduced to vassalage. But the issue was as dear to the victors as to the vanquished. The Germans liked so well the fertile plain of Alsatia that they demanded a third of the Sequanan territory as their price, and stayed. This bore hard on the Sequanans; they made common cause with Aedui and Arverni to drive the invaders out, but too late, for the Germans had invited in their friends, there were 120,000 in all, and they ruined the armies of united Gaul on the fatal field of Magetobriga. Now 24,000 more Germans had arrived in Sequana; their king, Ariovistus, had demanded a second third of the Sequanan lands and the keys of their fortified towns. Aeduan and Sequanan children were held hostage, the Gauls were powerless to resist. I alone, Diviciacus, dare do so much as speak. All the hope and refuge of the Gauls lies now in Caesar and the Roman people, for unless these come to the aid of the three nations we must needs do as did the Helvetii—quit our homes and risk what fortune may bring us.——

It was a powerful speech, somewhat marred in effect by the fact that both speaker and listener knew it was solely for the record. Caesar, from a point outside and above the situation already understood it better than the Druid; he had on his staff an observant philologist of Narbo, Caius Valerius Troucillus, who had travelled extensively among tribes on both sides the border in search of new dialects, and was able to give an impartial account of the mess. For that matter Diviciacus had made the same speech in Rome the year before, just after the overthrow at Magetobriga. Consul Caesar, having heard him at that time, made sixty per cent deduction for rhetorical hyperbole and carried through the assembly a set of resolutions on the matter—one confirming the "alliance" with the Aedui, one giving King Ariovistus the imposing but useless honorific of "friend of the Roman people" and a third advising both parties to keep the peace. The only difference in the situation then and now was that Proconsul Caesar was looking at it from the heights of Bibracte instead of the Capitoline Hill.

Yet that difference was curiously great, not alone because it brought the old wives' tales of German strength and ferocity from third to second hand, not alone because it included the defeat of the

Helvetians. The latter event had, indeed, made Caesar a kind of Great White Father to the Gauls, a position he would forfeit by refusing to act against the Germans, for indifference is the only emotion gods are not permitted to display.

The loss of Gallic admiration would matter nothing in itself to Julius Caesar, who only sought to introduce into his work a completeness and proportion that would satisfy his aesthetic sense without regard to what effect his actions had on less cultivated or more materialistic intellects. But seen from Bibracte summit and in the clear light furnished by Valerius Troucillus' scientific mind, the German problem was quite other than it had appeared at Rome. From that distance it had seemed a Horatius-Curatius duello between two practically indistinguishable lots of barbarians. The more they killed each other off the better it would be for the security of Roman frontiers. Here it had become evident that while the governor of Ulterior Gaul might indeed keep the frontiers clear during his own tenure of office by the traditional Roman policy of pairing off the tribes against one another, the feat would only be accomplished by running up a bill of hatreds that would be presented to some future governor for payment. Such a course would have run sharp counter to Caesar's artistic conscience, like producing a statue beautiful only when viewed from a particular angle.

The invaders from beyond the Rhenus were quite savage by nearly every criterion. The true danger in their irruption, however, lay neither in this fact nor in their extraordinary physical powers. It was rather in their inherent capacity for combination as illustrated in their acceptance of a tight monarchial rule and the curious institution by which half the men of the German tribes willingly submitted to till the fields for a year while the other half made war, and then changed places during the following twelvemonth. The Greeks and Latin races had passed through centuries of blood and agony to achieve such a spirit of cooperation. The anarchic Gauls had it not at all; their whole tribes would rush off, red-hot to fight a battle, then dribble home by twos and threes before the campaign was half over. It was obvious that in a contest between them and the Germans the latter must ultimately win. Diviciacus' melancholy prophecy of the fate of his nation was truer than perhaps even he could realize.

For the Gauls had no place to go once the Germans began to drive them. Ocean shut them in on the west, Rome on the south and the Germans on the east; under the two active forces they had already been reduced to a state of high compression. Apply one more ounce and there would be an explosion that might well blow up the Alps. Nor would the Germans themselves be any better satisfied with conquest in Gaul than had their ancestors, the Cimbri and Teutones of Marius' day. Sooner or later they would take the long journey toward the cities of the south; and if Caesar now turned his back on the Aedui they might well take up that adventure with Gallic allies to help them. No—a river can be defended against barbarians through all eternity, a mountain chain hardly ever. No—the only possible safety for Rome, the only possible course, was to halt the Germans where they stood, turn them back across the Rhenus, make it the frontier, if not of Rome, then of Roman influence.

. . . Caesar sent an embassy to King Ariovistus with a request to name some median point for a conference upon affairs of state. The King replied with a Teutonic courtesy that has not altered through the centuries that if he had anything to say to Caesar he would come and say it; if Caesar wanted anything of him, the Roman might wait upon him with the petition. Moreover, what business had any Roman in Gaul, of which he was overlord by right of conquest?

——Very well (was Caesar's reply) then here is your ultimatum; stop importing Germans into Gaul, restore the Aeduan hostages or take the consequences.——

There were more embassies, arrogant on both sides, like dogs growling themselves up to the fighting point, suddenly interrupted by action. German bands raided across the Aeduan border and spies said the whole host of the Suebi (*Schweifer, Rovers*) two hundred thousand fighting men strong, was pouring through the defiles of the Hercynian Forest on its way to join Ariovistus. The German King called his hird about him and moved forward; Caesar ordered forced marches and went striding across the mountains like an Orion to be first at the key-point of the campaign—Vesontio of the Sequani, the great river-hold where the Dubis throws a curve like a moat round the base of a granite pentagon studded with towers. Cavalry scouts felt north; the armies rushed toward each other like inimical stars, burning hot with the speed of their mutual approach.

Or not quite burning hot on one side. Into Vesontio were pouring fur-hunters from Hercynia pale with fear, bearing tales of giants in the forest, huge men of more than human mould, whose eyes darted fire so their glance could not be borne. The legionary soldiers were brave, but they came of a peasantry that believed in the physical existence of dryads and gorgons. The young dandies of the staff, indifferent alike to gorgons and fire-darting eyes, learned that their late opponents in the desperate battle of Bibracte were despised by these new invaders as weaklings. Their hearts froze; Caesar, walking through the camp by night, heard sounds of lament as the emotional Italiotes bemoaned that they were being sacrificed to his ambition; his clerks and notaries were kept busy all day sealing wills; there was an outburst of applications for sick-leave; and finally the legate of the 9th came to his tent and said straight from the shoulder that the army would refuse to obey an order for farther advance.

That was the last straw. Caesar, already worried by the march of the Suebi and the ambiguous conduct of the Gallic allies, called a council of war and read the riot act to his officers. ——What the devil business of theirs was it where he intended to march? (he demanded). He was the commander and believed he had given proof that he was neither an incompetent nor a dishonest officer. There was, then, no real reason why the soldiers should mutiny. The rumor that the rank and file of the 9th would not march was absurd, and for his part he refused to believe it. As for the Germans, what did they amount to? a bunch of undisciplined savages who had been slain by the thousands and tens of thousands in the days of Caius Marius. Were these present legions less men than their fathers, who had performed that slaughter? Even the Helvetians, whom they had just overthrown, were accustomed to beating Germans; they had, as all men knew, planted colonies beyond the Rhenus and carried fire and sword through Ariovistus' own land. For that matter, how had these

awful bugbears won their famous victory at Magetobriga? By hiding
in the swamps till the Gauls got ready to go home, then falling on
their rear. A pox on such paltry stratagems (O clever Caesar, who
knew so well that any suggestion of stratagem in war carried to
Roman ears an undertow of cowardice!); for himself, he felt that
the move against the enemy had been too long delayed, he was
issuing marching orders to the 10th Legion in the fourth watch of
the night. That regiment would not fail him, he felt sure. He could
conquer with them alone. The rest might follow and see the fun if
they liked.——

The centurions of the 10th burst into cheers and crowded round
their commander to thank him and clasp his hand. The rest retired
driven clear from fear to anger by one speech. All
afternoon and evening there was a buzz of chatter
among the huts. In the first watch of the night a delegation came
to beg Caesar's pardon and when the bugles rang a few hours later,
the whole army shouldered pack and shield and took the road, the
12th in the lead and marching quickstep the sooner to get at the
enemy.

See map
facing page 96

Diviciacus guided; he knew the routes. Caesar rode with him, cold
and impassive, on the strange two-toed horse that had been given
him in Aquileia, showing the eager soldiers no favor since they
would not be forgiven till they had proved their courage. Behind,
the army took a high circle north and east to void the ragged tangle
of forests and defile among Jura's foothills, then tramped through a
pass and down into the broad plain stretching to the Rhenus. They
had marched for seven days at hot speed; out ahead the scouts
reported Ariovistus twenty-four hours away and said the Suebi had
not yet joined him.

The King equally had scouts out and was evidently surprised at the
speed of Caesar's approach march, for he sent in a flag of truce to
ask a conference. Caesar took it as the expression of an honest
purpose; it would not be the first time the spectacle of Rome in
arms had moved some savage prince to reason. After a few pour-
parlers they agreed to meet at the summit of a bald knoll in the
plain with only cavalry for an escort. The last requirement, made a

sine qua non by Ariovistus, was so queer that Caesar dismounted some of his Gallic allied horse and replaced them with legionaries from the 10th. He was glad he thought of that; in the midst of the argle-bargle between the two commanders German riders suddenly rose from ambush and set upon his escort, but drew back dismayed when they launched against the big shields and bronze helmets of the regulars instead of the Gauls they had evidently expected.

Aside from this effort to kidnap the Roman leader the conference produced only one note of importance. The King, prodded to a kind of peat-fire rage by Caesar's sharp tongue, let fly the information that he had received messengers from the Roman Senate telling him that he could obtain solid proofs of favor from them in exchange for Caesar's head. Caesar passed the news along to Rome to be published in the Daily News Bulletin he had established and made ready for battle.

Next day came another flag of truce. Ariovistus had a proposition to make; he wanted Caesar to send a couple of legates to talk things over. Caesar had no legates to spare. He sent Valerius Troucillus instead. Ariovistus had been celebrating something or other with unusually copious draughts from his drinking horn that day; when the philologist appeared instead of the officers (whom he had evidently intended to keep as hostages) he blew up, stormed at the messenger for a spy and threw him into chains. That same day the tribal levy was complete up to 36,000 fighting men, fully equipped. In the evening he came swinging down toward the Romans and encamped on a mountain-spur six miles away.

The next move was his also, swift and able. At earliest dawn he took the march, across the chord of a wooded hill, right past the Roman flank, and sat down on Caesar's only line of supply. It was clean surprise; Caesar durst not hinder the movement by the only possible military means, which was an attack, for it would be a hopeless attack uphill and through trees against superior numbers, no chance for the close shock action which is discipline's reliance against strength.

Fortunately there was no loss in morale. The Roman soldiers, like other privates in the ranks, never comprehended the importance of

NORTHEAST GAUL

For the campaigns against the Atuactuci, Ambiorix and the Usipetes and Tencteri.

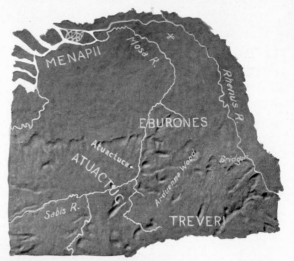

THE BELGIC CAMPAIGN

The dotted line shows Caesar's march through Belgic territory.

AMBIORIX' REBELLION

Distribution of the legions before Ambiorix' rising and Caesar's march to relieve Q. Cicero.

supply till their bellies were empty. When Caesar ordered them out in line of battle to face the new German camp next morning they responded with right good will. The Teuton cavalry boiled forth, fell on the Gauls who were covering Caesar's manoeuvre and routed them, but there was no battle, for Ariovistus kept his main-guard stolidly in camp, certain he could afford to sit still. The next day it was the same and the next and the next and the next; on the sixth, with rations running low, Caesar formed for battle in the usual three lines, but when the German foot did not come out, faced half-left, marched rapidly round the Germans to a hillock he had previously marked and while the two front lines faced the enemy, set the third to digging like mad on the foundations of a new camp. Ariovistus threw forward sixteen hundred archers with his horse in support. Caesar's first line rolled them back while his third line went on digging. By evening the new camp was ditched, palisaded and provided with a liberal supply of javelin-catapults; the supply-line was regained.

The new camp was only big enough for two legions, designedly, since Caesar hoped to provoke an attack on it. Ariovistus fell into the trap. At twilight on the next day he tried it with his full strength, and took a stinging repulse with his front line badly crumpled by the fire of the catapults, but got away before the other four legions, brought from the big camp on the run, could cramp down on his rear. The same night a Gallic spy who had been among the Germans came in with news that threw light on the capital mystery of the campaign—Ariovistus' unwillingness to engage. There was a spae-wife among the Germans; she had sought the future in the eddies of a mountain tarn and bidden the King not to fight before the coming moon as he prized his kingship.

Caesar counted heavily on the importance of morale. This news made him desire battle before the Germans could have their moon and their surety. He spent the night shifting archers and light-armed to the small camp to make a show of force while the six legions were gathered under his own hand in the larger. The morning was fresh and cloudless; the legions got afoot with the day, formed line and went sweeping across the plain straight at the German camp, Caesar himself leading the 10th on the right wing, Legate Labienus with the 9th on the left.

The German cavalry was brushed aside, the Romans came right on, with the evident intention of storming the camp. A strategist Ariovistus might be, but no engineer; his men lay in a mere tent-laager without defences. To fight in those close quarters was suicide. Woe for the spae-wife's warning; he let the warriors be ranked according to their several tribes and went forth to do battle. As they marched past the wagons the King had set across their rear to cut off hope of any security but in driving straight through, the women on them burst into a discordant dirge, imploring their men not to let them be sold into slavery.

The Germans locked shields front and overhead and rushed at the Romans so fiercely the legionaries never had time for a javelin-cast. The lines met with a terrific clash of metal under the shrilling trumpets; for a few moments there was desperate-hot close work, with German longswords and Roman broadswords licking like tongues of flame among the shields. Then the legionaries of the 10th, where Caesar led, got their ranks loosened and flung themselves upon their enemies like tigers. They wrenched the shields from the arms of the burly Germans in front of them and sifted into the gaps in raging little knots, hewing and cutting; they leaped up on the tight-locked bucklers overhead and stabbed down at wild bearded faces; they rolled under the shield fence, driving deadly short-arm jabs upward at hairy legs and groins. The Harudan tribe, who held the German flank here, could not stand such ardor; their front ranks went down, the tight phalanx broke, they lost heart and cohesion, they began to run, and the 10th, with a shout, went wheeling in to sweep down the German line.

On the other wing, though, superior German numbers lapped round the flank of the 9th. It was caught from two sides at once and the barbarians clipped the legionaries in so close there was no room to swing a sword. Labienus and his legion reeled back; the legion next in line wavered.

Legate Crassus (beardless Publius Crassus, brave young son of the financier) was the hero of the day. He stood behind the Roman left flank in command of the allied light horse, which had no place in such a battle. As the 9th gave way he saw the emergency, rode to the rear of the legions, gathered the reserve, ployed them into a deep column and flung the column into the rear of the tribesmen who were besetting Labienus. They sheared right into the German mass like a warship's ram into an enemy's side. For a tense moment the battle hung, then panic ran wild through the Teuton thousands, they broke, they went tumbling back, the 9th closed in to the wagon-burg on one wing as the 10th reached it on the other. The Germans were trapped, penned.

Even now the battle was not done; the barbarians fought back in hopeless fury from their circle. Caesar, now mounted and riding calmly above the storm, saw an easier way. He withdrew a legion to open one end of the net, the beaten Germans streamed through the gap and away, and as they fled young Crassus and the Aeduan light lancers flung into the rout. The pursuit went on through the day till the fragments of the invading host were driven into the Rhenus, sink or swim. At the river's brim Caesar, riding with the first of his advance, saw a man in chains and leaped from his horse. It was Valerius Troucillus, his friend and aid. The King had bidden the gaolers slay him, but the battle had come while they were throwing dice to see which should do the deed.

Ariovistus got across the river in a boat and escaped into the forest out of history, a king without a people. The Suebi, who had just reached the far bank, turned back in dismay. They would trouble Rome little more; for the German Ubii had a blood-feud against them and slew many of the Suebians as they made their way back into the forests of night.

All Gaul united in a shout of joy. Caesar put his legions into winter quarters at Vesontio and left Labienus in command while he went back to the citerior province to hold the November assizes.

3

Interlude on Conquest—There is a veil between us and a clear understanding of the Roman character. They seem forever actuated by feelings we cannot share and only with difficulty comprehend.

This is distressing to the seeker after causes, for somewhere near the heart of this emotional mystery must lie the secret of Rome's greatness—the reason for the devotion of those wonderful centurions and soldiers of the line, for the strange and exalted fire within them that made them pounce recklessly onto the Germans, tearing the shields from their hands.

Every soldier, every reader of military history, knows that such enthusiasms are as rare as anything in war. It is true that these Romans disliked Germans and that many of them no doubt feared Germans, but neither reason is quite adequate to explain so vivid an ardor. An energetic, even a simple performance of military duty, push and thrust and keep the lines closed up, would have furnished sufficient catharsis for these feelings; and the six legions were too new to Caesar's service to have for him that fanatic personal devotion which every man who served under him eventually acquired. There was something more, something bred into the Roman character almost from birth, an altogether selfless attachment to that most difficult of ideals, the state, an almost ant-like willingness to be an instrument of the collective will, something without any modern parallel unless among the Japanese.

In the modern world we are accustomed to thinking in terms of duty or of honor when we escape from the egocentric circle. The legionaries subordinated both to an abstract virtue of Romanism. They did not wish promotion, money or any other reward so much as to be looked up to by their fellows for brave deeds or noble deeds done for the benefit of the Republic. The thing had with them something the character of religious observance. They worshipped an entity which they would have described as the Genius of their city, and felt all sacrifices worth making to that cloudy ideal—an ideal so vague, so ill-expressed, as to be sub-intellectual, pre-barbaric, insect-like. It lay so deep beneath Roman thought as to constitute rather an instrument for the criticism of ideas than an idea in itself. It was a basic axiom, an absolute truth, the only absolute truth in a world from which anthropomorphic deities were being expelled by reason. Even Cicero, a delicate instrument, capable of searching self-analysis, is full of it. It would no more occur to him to question

Gallic Warrior

Rome's right to rule the world than it would occur to him to fly to the moon. Even Caesar, almost a disembodied intelligence, abdicated control of emotions when it became a question of his native city.

During the winter at Aquileia a door had suddenly sprung open upon a vista of dazzling splendor for any Roman. Labienus wrote down from Vesontio that the Belgic tribes were forming a network of alliances with the idea of making a great national movement against the Roman army and its stronghold. Various travellers (among whom we may undoubtedly number the observant Valerius Troucillus) told the same story.

Now there was one sure way to evade any trouble with the Belgae; viz., to retire the army within the borders of the Roman province. A Belgic invasion which reached them there must inevitably cross the lands of the Lingones, Sequani and Aedui, who would be sure to offer the most strenuous objections to any such incursion. Nor was there any such philosophical case against the Belgae as against the Helvetii and Germans. They exerted no pressure upon the frontiers, immediate or remote. If they roved one day, it would be to the misty shore of Britain or to the melancholy flats of Frisia right away from Rome.

The philosophical case for a Belgic war was bad. But the juridical case was so good it would be difficult to find a better. Caesar had never expressed or implied an intention of invading Belgia. He was interested only in Celtic Gaul; the Belgae were clean out of his orbit, his army at Vesontio was a hundred and seventy-five miles from their nearest frontier, with a great foreign nation between. Yet they were preparing to cross that intervening territory and attack him, partly because they felt he might some day represent a danger to their independence, partly because they were like the Helvetians "men who longed for war." Pure unrest on their part; or pure ambition—to be known as the conquerors of the conquerors of the Germans.

Caesar's own ambition rose in answer when he heard of their movement. Personal ambition undoubtedly spoke first, but personal ambition in the direction of conquest was something Julius Caesar would repress without a qualm after having crushed the two most formidable barbarian enemies the Roman state had known in a single summer of whirlwind campaigning. In the city they talked of nothing but his victories. Even Pompey's achievements were moonstruck and pallid by comparison; after all, he had conquered Orientals, far away across the seas, while Caesar had destroyed the most formidable fighters in the world at Rome's very door. For a moment the old irreconcilable Senate forgot that he was anything but a Roman and decreed a solemn thanksgiving in honor of the man who had revived the great days of Marius.

Personal ambition could well rest on such laurels, indeed might not wish to risk them in the further chance of war. Caesar had gained everything, in this first year, for which he came to Gaul— proof of his capacity to meet all emergencies, the prestige of a great name, that position within striking distance of the capital at the head of a powerful, victorious and devoted army which would enable him to prevent any interference with the political reforms that lay so near his heart. To reach for more for himself would be to discard that Platonian mean in all things which he made the order of his life. A campaign in Belgia would remove him far from any point where he could control events in Rome and by this token would imperil the existence of his reforms and even of his party.

Yet still ambition cried within him, not the ambition of C. Julius Caesar, but the ambition of Rome, that ambition which was so essential a part of the mental equipment of Conservative and Radical, consular, Optimate and proletarian. What an achievement!—to bring all Gaul, a land greater than Italy and Greece together, under the eagles.

As a thinker on military topics the Proconsul could see that such an opportunity would never come again—a perfect juridical *casus belli* against the tribes who held the military key of the Gallic situation in their possession of the left bank of Rhenus to its junction with Ocean. Once they were broken, like the Helvetians, or Romanized, like the Allobroges of the province of Transalpine Gaul, the great river would be Roman from mouth to source. Gaul would be seized in a net, cut off by a wall; struggle though it might it must eventually yield,

As a political analyst it was not difficult for Caesar to perceive that beneath the apparent weakness of the philosophical case for a Belgic war there lay a line of justification so profound as to be almost fundamental. That an earlier and greedy Rome had engulfed and assimilated all existing civilizations was not Caesar's fault nor that of his generation. Philosophically their highest task was to see that nothing went wrong with the combined culture, and that meant nothing must happen to Rome, for if she went down there was no other to take her place. The law of parallel development is inoperative when there are no parallels to develop. By retiring from Vesontio the war with the Belgae would be avoided, but it would be avoided at the price of abandoning all the Roman gains in Gaul. By a similar retirement from envy-exciting cultural gains Rome could have preserved herself from future clashes, mental or physical, with any Children of the Night whatsoever—at the price of sinking to their level. The experiment had been tried in the notable case of Sparta. Civilizations are pendula in constant motion; Rome refluent must ebb forever as Sparta had.

Did Julius Caesar follow out this particular line of argument? Possibly not, though it would be unintelligent to deny it. All we know for certain is that the glory of the Roman name would furnish, to him, a sufficiently compelling motive, as it would to his legionaries. In the early days of spring the Proconsul enlisted two new legions, 13th and 14th, and sent them over the passes under command of Legate Quintus Fabius. Himself he delayed to set the legal business of the Cisalpine province in order, then rushed north, riding day and night, horseback or in a litter, dictating orders and judicial decisions during all his waking hours.

4

The Men of the Marshes—The army that broke camp at Vesontio in the spring was twice as strong as the hurriedly assembled force that opposed the march of the Helvetians. Recruits from Hither Gaul filled up the ranks. The legions stood at 5,000 apiece, 40,000 infantry of the line, all told. The war would be fought in a country of forest and stream with underbrush tangles. To cover the flanks of his heavy columns Caesar's agents had spent the winter combing every shore of the inland sea. Now he had 13,000 light-armed Cretan archers, black faced javelin-men from Numidia, slingers out of the Balaeric Isles who could drive a leaden ball right through a cuirass at fifty paces. Old Diviciacus led a corps of Aeduan cavalry, a warrior-priest. For such a host in a wild country the trains alone were a problem; they were organized as carefully as the fighting corps so that no man might lack for bread.

Spies brought word the Belgians were assembling beyond Axona River under Galba, High King of the Suessionian tribe. Caesar put his men at their best pace to hurry in on the enemy ere they should have time fully to muster. In later May the Romans appeared _See map / facing page 113_ before Durocortorum of the Belgic Remi like a stone from the skies, outrunning even the news of their march. The town opened its gates; Caesar marched through and rushed on to seize a crossing of the Axona right in King Galba's teeth before the Belgae knew what he was doing. Their horde was monstrous big—300,000 said the scouts, which meant at least 200,000 in sober fact. Too many to meet in level battle; the Romans must make spades do the work of swords and hope difficulty of provender would sow discontent in Galba's ranks to make him fight at disadvantage or go home. Therefore Caesar had dug a camp on a long tongue of high ground with the river at his back, a strongly held bridgehead on the south side, and waited.

It was a supply campaign, but he had taken care of food for his own army. At Durocortorum the Romans had been received, somewhat to their own surprise with flowers, cheers, and a delegation of elder chiefs who offered the alliance of the nation. It seemed they hated the Suessiones and had a blood-feud with High King Galba. Caesar assured them he would knock out Galba, signed an alliance between the Remi and Rome, and sent their fighting men westward under Diviciacus to harry the lands of the Bellovaci, which tribe was the largest and most violent in the great Belgic alliance.

Galba was too close for the plan to affect his army; his men smelled near blood and plunder. The night after Caesar's arrival at

Axona a runner came in with a note in his breech-clout; the Belgae had turned aside on their march to assault Bibrax, capital of the Remi, eight miles north-northeast of the camp, and it might not hold out long. Caesar questioned his experts sharply about Belgian skill in siege-craft and was relieved to learn they had no great knowledge of the art, the only method they knew being to smother the wall-defenders under a shower of missiles and then rush. He shut off a few thousand of his missile-weapon men at once under charge of a good legate; in the moonless dark they got into Bibrax along a breakneck escarpment of rock at one side of the town where High King Galba had failed to complete his leaguer. When morning came the Belgae began again their usual rush, but ran into a terrible hail of bowshot that nailed the shield to the arm and the helmet to the head. Their own feeble archery was no match for the fell shooting of the Cretans; the attack broke down, they howled and fled away.

That same evening, from the praetorian gate of his camp, Caesar beheld a great crescent of watch-fires spring up, closing the whole horizon, eight miles for east to west, and knew King Galba and his thousands had come.

The tongue of land where the Romans lay reached diagonally west from the camp to the Axona, with a marsh and brook between them and the enemy. The Proconsul made his right wing secure with a double line of trench and rampart, reaching back from camp to river, forward from camp to marsh, then drew out his legions to await the Belgic onset across the swamp. Galba also brought his men out, and a stumbling, reeling combat of cavalry began among the reeds and tussocks in front. Caesar put in his slingers; the Belgic horse were driven in, but the Romans would not follow into such ground and Galba's men would not dare the issue either, so there was no battle.

As the legions marched back to the tents to sup there came a messenger in hot haste. The Belgae had obliqued right from their position and were even now winning a ford near the mouth of the brook with the threat that if they made it they would be in Caesar's rear. The Proconsul sent the light-armed and all the cavalry at the run; Legate Sabinus followed with six cohorts of the 14th.

Only one small party had already crossed. The cavalry caught them disordered, charged home and rode them down. As the rest of the Belgic mass struggled with the current in waist-deep water, sling-balls and arrows came driving in among them so hot they were fain to give over and go growling back to their lines while the dead floated down the reddening current into the twilight.

Corn grew short in Galba's camp. Belgic patriotism had been equal to the task of mustering 200,000 heroes but not to that of feeding them, and they could not make the Romans fight on even terms. They held a great council of war the night of the fight at the ford and voted King Galba a failure as a leader. It would be a better plan to go home; should the Romans enter the territory of any tribe the others would fly to its aid and they could be briefly heroic on full stomachs.

In the second watch the Belgians took up their march. There were no general officers, each tribe wanted to be first on the road and the whole vast army dissolved into a hurrah's nest of shouts, wrangling and tossing brands that woke the Romans in their camp beyond the swamp. Caesar went to the wall. He could see the streaming torches, hear the medley of cries, but suspected an ambush and held his men under arms till daybreak, and Legates Q. Fabius and Aurunculeius Cotta were pushed gingerly forward with the cavalry, Labienus being in close support at the head of three legions. They found retreat, slashed in heavily and turned it to panic, cutting down fugitives while daylight lasted.

It was only a one-day pursuit. Caesar's position on the Axona was supported on a long, delicate shaft of communications running back through Reman and Lingonan territory to Aeduana. He wanted an alternate line, and recalling his pursuers, he turned west to cut a thoroughfare through the Suessiones while they were still broken by the retreat. The men were given a good night's rest at the Axonia camp, then turned out for a blazing forced march that brought them to Noviodunum of the Suessiones as dark shut down. Caesar tried to storm the place out of hand, but though there were few defenders the ditch was deep and he had no fascines. When he saw that persistence would be a bloody business, he called in the stormers and built camp, preparing for siege.

In the morning all eight legions turned to with hammer, spade and axe, forty thousand skilled laborers under skilled engineers. Tall wheeled towers reared up out of the ground and began to rumble toward the walls, with archers in their upper stories to rake the ramparts, an undergrowth of mantlets among their feet as they moved. A ramp began to rise, a battering ram was set up and beat at the stones. A day or two of it was enough; the simple Belgians, terrified at the mere mass of the constructions, waved green branches and threw open their gates. High King Galba prayed peace on any terms. Caesar gave it to him on condition that he and his people be the tributaries of the Reman state, which was hard on the Suessiones, but made the Remi pro-Roman forever.

The army pushed straight ahead into the territory of the Bellovaci. They bore the name of the most formidable tribe in Gaul, but had been badly cut up in the fight at Axona ford and worse by the raids of Diviciacus and the Reman warriors, who had driven most of the Bellovacians into the walled town of Bratuspantium. As Caesar drew near the place he was met by a procession of old men in long white robes, with oak-leaves in their hair—the Druids. They begged for mercy; Diviciacus, for the sake of his office and the name of his race, seconded their request. Caesar granted it with the condition that the Aedui be overlords of and guarantors for the Bellovaci, a shrewd condition since it made Gauls do police work against Gauls, then right-angled north and east against the third of the great fighting tribes, the Nervii.

These Nervii formed an enclave of carefully cherished barbarism in the heart of Belgia. Their habit was to turn all traders back at the frontier, as they considered luxuries nationally enervating and all trade goods luxuries. They drank only water—wine was for sybarites, milk for children—and they had sent heralds through Belgia to proclaim their contempt of the nations who had Romanized. Three tribes of the northwest Belgae agreed to stand with them—Atrebates, Viromandui, Atuactuci. Caesar's scouts said the first two had joined, and the Atuactuci were on the march with the common rallying point beyond the Sabis River. It was July; the effect of last month's defeat on the Axona wearing off, and he hurried toward the Nervii by fast marches to catch them before the Atuactuci came in if that were possible. The Nervii and their allies, being 75,000 strong of the best infantry fighters in Gaul, were quite enough to deal with, and the Atuactucan reinforcement would hardly be less than 20,000.

The Roman march was a circuit, with the idea of getting to the tribal rallying point first. As the Proconsul came down toward the Sabis from the northern side he found all round traces of the near presence of the barbarians—trees cut across the road, saplings pulled into loops and interwoven with brambles and strong vines to make line after line of abbatis that must be cut through for the legions' passage. The cavalry could not make it, being crowded partly into, partly behind the infantry column.

Toward evening of a warm summer day the head of the march emerged onto the brow of a little eminence from which a cleared space slanted down to the Sabis, here neither broad nor deep. On the far side trees came down nearly to the water's edge. A few barbarians were visible, fiddling around among the trunks or washing themselves in the river. The cavalry gave a whoop of relief at finding open ground and trotted down the hill to engage them. Caesar, deeming the spot good for camp, had the bugle blown, and the six legions at the head of the column fell out to gather palisades and fuel as they came into the clearing.

Behind them the baggage train lumbered slowly into view. It was an unusual march formation, adopted instead of the ordinary 10th Legion-baggage-9th-11th-8th-12th-7th-light armed-13th-14th order of route because the Nervian tangles had slowed the train coming through the forest, leaving the leading legion too far ahead of the main body. It saved Caesar's life and his men's that day.

For the thorny tangles, the open space where they were not and the men by the river were keys and falls of an elaborate wolf-trap. Gallic spies, escaped prisoners, had told the Nervii of Caesar's usual march order; clever as Mercury, they had arranged the snares to attenuate and slow the column. The 10th (they thought) would gain; the baggage would hold back the other legions. Pinched in the brushwood mazes it could not deploy, while they swept away the 10th by one furious blow and smothered the rest. Among the trees beyond the Sabis the barbarian strength lay concealed. The appearance of the first baggage wagons on the hill was the signal; as they mounted the crest there was a titanic shout and the whole forest seemed to explode as 75,000 warriors dashed out of it, through the river and up the hill.

The legionaries' helmets were on their backs and their shields encased; their javelins were stacked, they were dispersed all over the landscape in search of camp supplies, as this tornado came rolling up against them. There was no time to form proper battle-lines. The soldiers ran together anyhow under whatever officers and standards they saw; the trumpets shrilled a discordant note, not together, but pipingly, as each musician caught up his instrument. It was the worst possible surprise; no head, no purpose, a hundred little groups all disorderly, unable to help each other. Caesar ran down from the praetorium of the camp to the nearest line, with just time to cry "Bear yourselves like men!" before the hurricane of fighting closed all down the front.

On the extreme Roman left the slope was steepest. The Atrebates arrived here, blown with their climb; the 9th and 10th, with Caesar himself at their head and Labienus, met them with a countercharge so lusty that the barbarians could by no means abide the shock. They were rushed back down the pent, torn to tatters. At the river they made a stand; there was a sharp, brief struggle in knee-deep water, then the Romans won and drove their enemies right up the opposite hill into the trees.

In the center the 11th and 8th clashed with the Viromandui. The Romans had the best of it, they went forward. But this very move laid bare the flanks of the other two legions, 12th and 7th, on the Roman right, where the Nervii themselves came on. The barbarians flowed round these two legions on every side, dispersed the broken cavalry which had been flung back by their waves, fell on the laborers and troops of the train and sent them flying in all directions to carry abroad the news that the Proconsul was killed and his army cut to pieces.

Caesar, from his position near the river, caught a glimpse of the rout, borrowed a horse from some officer and galloped to the spot. Things were as bad as they could be; the 12th was retreating and beginning to break up. Most of its officers were down, the fourth cohort of the legion had lost its standard, the flanks were surrounded. Caesar flung himself from the horse, snatched a shield from a private in the rear rank and leaped to the front of the fray, calling the men by name to follow him, loosen the lines and drive home. The retreat checked; in the high, strong voice that had dominated Forum mobs, Caesar called out that the rear rank should face round. Another officer got the rear rank of the 7th round also, and at that moment the 13th and 14th, who had been behind the baggage, came roaring into the battle. Labienus across the stream sent the 10th to help; the remnants of the cavalry turned and rode into the press with loose rein to redeem their reputation; in the 12th and 7th even the wounded began to prop themselves on their shields to give one more thrust before they fell senseless.

Yet the Nervii would not yield. With hundreds of their fellows going down around them, surrounded, overwhelmed, they fought back in fatal, dogged obstinacy, piling up their corpses to make mounds from which the survivors struck and cast till they were all dead.

Caesar camped on the field to rest his shaken legions. A day or two later came a chorus of old men and Druids to make the submission of the Nervian state, of what was left of the Nervian state, for they complained that of the great council of the nation only three had escaped out of six hundred chiefs, and that of 60,000 warriors barely five hundred remained. It was true; almost alone among Gallic nations the Nervii were so extirpated that they have left no memory of their race in the name of any modern town, district or river.

When the Atuactuci heard of the ruinous battle, they retreated to their own country and gathered their whole strength in the capital town at the confluence of Sabis and Mosa. Caesar marched thither and circled the place. The Atuactuci were unimpressed at the sight of his army, being particularly moved to amusement by the observation that Romans came in small sizes. They tried little probing sallies day and night; when Caesar had a wooden tower set up they burst into roars of laughter and shouted down that he had built it in the wrong place, which was true, but only until the tower began to amble forward on the wheels within. The Atucactuci had never imagined such a possibility. Their laughter changed to desperate fear, they perceived that the Romans were necromancers who had the help of the gods and sent in to surrender lest they be torn by demons.

Even with the gods one makes terms. The Atuactuci asked to keep their arms for self-defence against quarrelsome neighbors. ——No compromise (said Caesar) I will guarantee that your neighbors let you alone.—— The chiefs gave in; all afternoon they paraded their men to the ramparts with shields and swords, throwing the weapons over into the moat till the heap nearly topped the wall. Midway they got to talking and repented their bargain, deciding Romans were human after all, and an inferior brand of human at that. Word went round to hold out the rest of the swords and spears, giving up only shields, which had impressive bulk and made a loud bang when added to the pile. At twilight the gates were shut; men and women in Atuactuca fell to plaiting new shields of osier work, covering them with rawhides.

In the third watch of night the gates were suddenly flung open; the Atuactuci gave a shout and leaped for the nearest point in the siege-lines. No surprise; at the first stir of feet Caesar's trumpets blared forth and great bonfires, prepared in advance, leaped into flame. Through the red light the legions rushed; from tower and rampart catapults hurled hail-storms of missiles into the massed attackers. The Atuactucan shields were wicker against iron, their courage only brought them the heavier loss, they were driven back, back, back into the town with four thousand dead. In the morning Caesar brought up a battering ram, beat in the gates and carried the city. As a punishment for their treachery he sold into slavery everyone he found within.

That finished the Belgae. There were some coastal tribes who had sent in adhesion to King Galba's alliance in the spring, but while he was sieging Atuactuca Caesar had sent young Legate Crassus, the hero of the German battle, to round them up with the 7th Legion, and they made little difficulty. Indeed the ease of Crassus' conquest itself deliminated a new problem. He found most of the villages populated by old men and boys, the fighters having gone aboard their ships and sailed off to the Tin Islands, which lie close by the Gallic coast. Caesar began to wonder whether the strategic line of the Rhenus could be considered secure while those islands remained unsubdued on its flank. His scouts reported them fairly useless for their own sake—pestilential, full of fog, swamp and midnight—but at least a reconnaissance in force seemed indicated to clear the question up, and it seemed certain that the islands were the source of the fine pearls that occasionally turned up in Gallic markets.

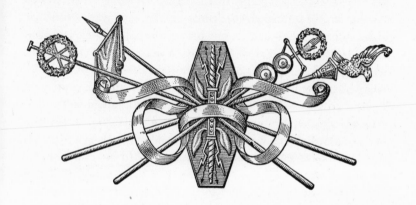

VI

THE LEAVEN OF PROMETHEUS

All Hands Round—Observers in Rome felt Caesar's star was due to set. Almost fanatic devotees of the cult of luck, the Romans generally attributed his victories over the Gauls to it, to the superiority of his Genius over the national Genius of the Celts, or to some other movement among the supernatural powers, for him of happy issue. From their distance it was apparent that he had won against huge numerical odds and it seemed apparent that he had won against the logic of the situation also—had he not been surprised by the Nervii? It was altogether too good to last, three great victories and a huge sweeping conquest in a summer and a half. Pompey had the experience of a lifetime of soldiering behind him and an army that matched his enemies' numbers during the eastern campaign, yet had taken years to accomplish less. There was no explanation of Caesar's success reasonable to a Roman but luck; and it would be as impossible for him to remain Fortune's favorite as it had been for Croesus, Midas or Timon.

The Romans felt they could rationalize the matter quite easily; their whole system of philosophy and religion was permeated with the idea of good and evil distributed to helpless mortals in exactly balanced proportions by some Force, Genius or Fate who was, in the long run, impartial. Fate had dealt this Caesar a nasty cuff in the matter of Pompeia's infidelity and the public humiliation that followed. He bore the trial with stoic fortitude; therefore Fate equalized things with a shower of blessings, but she had gone too far now, the string was done, the time for retribution had come.

Nor were signs wanting that the time approached. The proconsular army had been drawn out of Rome's nearness to remotest Gaul, where it was having a rough time, as witness the dispatches that spoke of surprise and desperate battle for existence. In the city the last elections had gone wrong for the Radicals; Cornelius Lentulus was returned Consul, a friend of Pompey indeed, but a far better friend of exiled Cicero, and none at all of Caesar's. With him Q. Metellus Nepos went into office, friend to nobody but the old Conservatives and the Senatorial camorra. Lentulus' first day in office was devoted to a long speech in favor of recalling Cicero. It was received with tumultuous applause, a bill to effect the recall was passed through the Senate and referred to the assembly of the people who would likewise have passed it had not Caesar's ban-dog Clodius seized the polls by night and held them through the dawn with bravoes and the naked sword in a riot so savage that the sewers of Rome were choked with corpses after.

Pompey flashed at Clodius; the recall had been his idea, to salve his wounded honor for the hurt it suffered when he fled out one door of his Tusculan villa as the orator and friend came in the other to ask a favor. Clodius struck back at Pompey; his followers hooted the great general through the streets, he got an armed slave into the senate house with instructions to murder Pompey and so frightened the conqueror that he spent the rest of the year behind locked doors in daily fear of assassination. Crassus laughed; a hot quarrel grew up between him and Pompey as to which should have a pending rich embassy to settle the broiled affairs of Egypt, where there was a revolution which could not be allowed to stand as Egypt was the source of much of the corn-supply.

That broke the triumvirate as far as anyone could see, and Caesar's star dipped toward its setting, for no one doubted that he was a mere mirror-sun, shining in the reflected light of Pompey's glory; a pensioner of Crassus' picked up by accident to serve the Great for a particular emergency, who would now be dismissed back to his mistresses and his cameos.

It occurred to none of them that their rationalization might be irrational—not even to Cicero, though perhaps for all his insight, he was the last man to whom anything of the sort would have occurred, for he regarded the world as an armillary of indefinite extent revolving about the central pinion, Cicero. Empires might fall; unless the event touched him directly, he were incurious. "I cannot endure life," he wailed from Thessalonica, which was as close to Rome as the exile-law would let him live, "Hortensius has treated me with the basest treachery, my friend Pompey is my betrayer. Only your appeals have kept me from ending my existence, and now see what a pass you have brought me to." Misery, misery, only because he could not live at Rome and mix in the political pudding. There was a rumor he had gone mad, not far from inaccuracy; his letters through this sad period are almost incoherent.

Not even to Cicero, with his insight. For the Romans were the worst of psychologers, as fatalists must needs be. Their picture of Caesar had been forty years in the building—would four reverse it? They had no apparatus for evaluating the prodigious adaptability of a mind which specialized in everything. The whole idea of such a mind was foreign to the Roman intellect, sharp, clear and essentially narrow as it was. The range of Caesar's interests itself escaped their notice. We are aware of it today only through side-hints, half-allusions and comparisons. Nor is it surprising that it escaped their notice, for the man's capacity for taking in ideas, his index of intellectual absorption, was in a sense masked—partly by aestheticism, partly by the intensity of his existence.

For Julius Caesar lived at such a pace that he had already run through half a dozen ordinary existences. Those who touch the arts only with the cuticle of the mind little realize the years of concentrated study one single art demands for genuine aesthetic appreciation—not merely from the practitioner, but from the critic, the connoisseur, the appreciator. The latter may indeed, be called an artist without the talent.

Yet when Caesar plunged into the Gallic adventure he had exhausted all the arts of his time. He was not an authority, but the final court on cameos and sculpture; we know he kept one of the greatest libraries of his time and criticized the drama with an incisiveness that surprised his literary contemporaries. Cicero had given his life to the study of oratory; yet he alone was ranked superior to Caesar in the pyrotechnical type of public speaking and the Proconsul exceeded him as a debater, and we have evidence of this fact in writings published before it was useful or important to flatter Caesar. The perfect connoisseur, the perfect litterateur, Caesar was yet enough of an athlete to be noted as a swimmer and to gallop a horse over rough ground with his arms behind his back. The elaborate dinners he contrived, his affairs with women (with all deductions made, there seems an irreducible sediment here) were little-noted outlets for an energy that could never set itself tasks enough because the mind that directed it was so efficient it instantly analyzed every problem.

Every man found his counterpart in Caesar—even Clodius. Indeed, it may have been some recollection of his own turbulent adolescence that made the Proconsul choose the latter as his political lieutenant at Rome. He himself had once played monstrous jests in the Clodian manner, as in the days when he was held to ransom by pirates at Pharmacusa while on his way to an island school of oratory:

——How much are you going to ask for me?——he inquired.

——Twenty talents.——

——Better make it fifty. The sum is large enough to give you a sensation of wealth which will brighten your last hours when I come back and crucify you.——

They laughed and made it fifty; during the fortnight before the money arrived he joined in their games and discussion, hobnobbing with the band in a way that made them honestly sorry to see him begone. The cream of the jest was that he did return with a formation of Milesian war-galleys at his back, carried the pirate hold by escalade and took the friendly raiders off to be crucified, strictly according to promise, though as they had been so gentle with him, he allowed them the favor of being strangled before they were nailed to the crosses.

It was an incident to which the Proconsul could look back as an amusing bit of juvenilia. Yet he can hardly long have expected Clodius' character to harden into one like his own, can hardly have missed the fact that the younger mind was all juvenilia, with no more central purpose or direction than an ape's, the sort of mind that would think it a joke to burn down a house to roast a pig. No—he was made Caesar's vicar more because of that crazy fantastical ingenuity, dealing strokes unwardable because no rational mind could follow the antic involutions of one acting purely on whim. Yet such a tool can effect use only in the hand of another mind clear enough to confect a large plan and strong enough to whip the ape to heel.

There lay the pinch. During the campaigns in Gaul the dizzard Clodius slipped control. It was by order of his principal that the young man, tongue in cheek, carried through a bill that Cato had served the nation well in Cyzicus and for reward named him commissioner in the annexation of the island of Cyprus, but 'twas his own mad humor egged him on to raddle Pompey and shout through a measure giving free state's corn to members of political clubs, that is, in essence, to his hired desperadoes.

Should he rule Rome by violence? Pompey swore not, and carried the matter to Caesar by letter. The summer of the Belgic war, whether of his own motion or by the Proconsul's advice, the conqueror appeared once more in the Forum, backed by a gang of toughs of his private superintendence, old eastern soldiers come up from Campania with the tribune Annius Milo to head them. More—he sought out Quintus Cicero, the orator's brother, and persuaded him to go surety that Marcus Tullius would do nothing to upset the triumvirs if allowed to return to Rome. Caesar accepted the brother's pledge; that fall a new bill was brought in for Cicero's recall and Milo's men overbore Clodius in a bloody ruffle, while it was declared passed, with people shouting from the housetops.

Cicero came home through streets thundering applause enough to gladden even his vain heart. The general, not knowing the underhand manoeuvres that had preceded the event, took it for one more proof that Caesar's star sloped to its nadir. The little Conservative lap-dogs who had not dared bay the Proconsul's trail while he stood yet before them lifted up their voices.

One Domitius Ahenobarbus, a kind of Roman hereditary evil genius (there was always a Domitius Ahenobarbus in politics, always in trouble, and always making trouble for others) announced his candidature for the consulate on a flat program of recalling Caesar from Gaul and bringing him to trial for illegal recruiting. Support swelled up behind him swift as a wave; it seemed he must win through. To cap the emergency Pompey began to itch for more

Meanwhile, here's something to be considered.

Message from: Rome
January 18, 1 B.C.

Dear Cassius,

Are you still working on the Y zero K problem? This change from B.C. to A.D. is giving us a lot of headaches and we haven't much time left. I don't know how people will cope with working the wrong way around.

Having been working happily downwards forever, now we have to start thinking upwards. You would think that someone would have thought of it earlier and not left it to us to sort out at the last minute.

I spoke to Caesar the other evening. He was livid that Julius hadn't done something about it when he was sorting out the calendar. He said he could see why Brutus turned nasty.

We called in the consulting astrologers, but they simply said that continuing downwards using minus BC won't work. As usual the consultants charged a fortune for doing nothing useful. As for myself, I just can't see the sand in an hourglass flowing upwards.

We have heard that there are 3 wise guys in the east working on this problem, but unfortunately they won't arrive till it's all over. Some say the world will cease to exist at the moment of transition.

Anyway, we are continuing to work on this bigoted Y zero K problem and I will send you a parchment if anything further develops.

Plutonius

Meanwhile, here's something to be considered....

Message from: Rome
January 18, 1 B.C.

Dear Cassius,

Are you still working on the Y zero K problem? This change from BC to AD is giving us a lot of headaches and we haven'tmuch time left. I don't know how people will cope with working the wrong way around.

Having been working happily downwards forever, now we have to start thinking upwards. You would think that someone would have thought of it earlier and not left it to us to sort out at the last minute.

(JULIAN CALENDAR)

I spoke to Caesar the other evening. He was livid that Julius hadn't done something about it when he was sorting out the calendar. He said he could see why Brutus turned nasty.

We called in the consulting astrologers, but they simply said that continuing downwards using minus BC won't work. As usual the consultants charged a fortune for doing nothing useful. As for myself, I just can't see the sand in an hourglass flowing upwards.

We have heard that there are 3 wise guys in the east working on the problem, but unfortunately they won't arrive till it's all over. Some say the world will cease to exist at the moment of transition.

Anyway we are continuing to work on this blasted Y zero K problem and I will send you a parchment if anything further develops.

Plutonius.

showy powers than that of shadow behind the throne and when the question of the Egyptian embassy came into the open there was another Forum brawl with him, Milo and Cicero on one side, Crassus and Clodius on the other:

"Pompey spoke, or rather such was his intention; for when he got up Clodius' hired gangs raised a yell, with insults and abuse. When he had finished, up got Clodius. He was met with such a deafening shout from our side, with doggerel of the filthiest description on himself and Clodia, so that he lost control over his faculties and his voice. Mad with rage, he screamed above the shouting, 'Who is starving the people to death?' His rowdies answered 'Pompey.' 'Who wants to go to Egypt?' 'Pompey.' 'Who do you want to go?' 'Crassus,' they shouted. As if at a given signal they began to spit on our men; we resented it, both sides charged and after a tussle the ruffians were driven out of the Forum."

That spoiled Pompey's patience. He went into the Senate next day and baldly accused Crassus of supporting a plot to murder him. Next morning Cicero followed it up by the announcement that he would make a speech against Caesar's new laws on the Ides of May. The triumvirate was broke, Caesar's luck gone and pledges to the three no longer mattered.

But they knew not Caesar who supposed him the easy dupe of maleficent fortune. He was of spirit too high to acknowledge any chance his master—or rather, held himself under the special protection of a guardian angel or Genius, superior to any shock. He was crossing a strait once (in the Tyrrhenian Sea?) with a small boat; a storm came whooping out of the north and as the seas raged past the boatman fell to weeping. "We shall be drowned!" and was for committing his soul to Mercury and his body to Neptune. "Fool!" said Caius Julius calmly, "Take your oar. You carry Caesar and his Fortune; there is no danger." The boat swam through where others foundered, and the storm died.

His dilettante seeming was a mask. It hid an energy we can but guess by side-hints. When he left Rome for Gaul the concealment of his private life, the fact that he had so full a private life, was stripped away. His entire existence entered the public domain and the boundless ardor that had been exercised, as it were, in secret, swelled to embrace a world. Even now we only catch sight of him moving cloudily behind results. An allusion tells us that he employed the interval between two bouts of barbarian skull-cracking, with the tramp of marching men all around him, in composing a treatise on Latin philology that remained a standard work. A reference says he

Coin of Caesar

drew a plan, complete with architectural details, specifications and costs, for tearing down "those old rat-warrens around the Forum", widening it out and housing its businesses under a stately marble colonnade—the plan having been drawn in his tent at night among the forests of Gaul. (Easy to draw plans, yes, but this one was carried out to the letter at a later day and found without defects.) A hint that he invented a method of secret writing or cipher, the first of its kind. The sure knowledge that he kept spies and correspondents in every important city of the Empire and handled all their reports in person. . . . Ha! This was the man Domitius Ahenobarbus promised to drive from public life with a Senate resolution that he had raised legions contrary to law.

Caesar lay at Ravenna in early spring, overseeing the affairs of Cisalpine Gaul, when word came of the emergency at Rome. Young Crassus the legate wrote from north at the same time that the coast tribes were aflame, holding Roman officers in gyve and raising a war. Old Crassus the triumvir came up from the city with the tale of

Cicero's defiance, Domitius' attack and Pompey about to quit the coalition.

The Proconsul wrote to Gaul that a fleet should be built and sent on another legate to take sailors up from Massilia; himself he hurried to Luca, where Cisalpine Gaul throws a horn across the Apennines, praying Pompey to meet him there.

The triumvirs sat behind closed doors. Caesar must have had his design of agreement cut and dried. He barely touched hands, then swept off like a meteor for northwest Gaul, but whispers had it that the three had settled all differences. They told no less than the truth; the new plan comprehended everything, Caesar's surety for his laws, Pompey's itch to have men march at his order, Crassus' desire for still more money. The two last were to stand for the consulate, the strength of their candidacy shunting aside naughty Ahenobarbus; at the end of their joint term, Pompey would become governor of Inner and Outer Spain with six legions, Crassus governor of Syria with leave to make war in the golden East. For exchange Caesar asked only the doubling of his term of command in Gaul and the silence of Cicero's sharp tongue. Mad Clodius, mad Milo, were out of the agreement; they were left to beat each other's brains out an they would, as they would.

Pompey took ship for Sardinia where Quintus Cicero was, and straightway chipped him roundly on his brother's pledge, but that interview was private and when the Ides of May came there was a packed Senate and breathless gallery waiting to hear the great orator talk down Caesar. Only a few days before had come the official dispatches from Gaul, with their tale of victories won and new lands conquered from Rome's hereditary enemies, the worst she ever had. They were the subject of the debate; Cicero sat silent. Domitius Ahenobarbus, thinking to give him courage, rose and made a motion to recall Caesar from Gaul; senator after sour-faced senator spoke for it. Cicero had pledged himself to abstain from the attack on Caesar, and pledged his senatorial associates he would never defend the man, but as the motion to recall gained strength, he stirred restively, he could no longer stay, he leaped impetuously to his feet, and half-unwilling, with lips he could not himself control, launched forth in the most fervid, the most Roman of his orations:

"Let the Alps sink!" he cried. "Nature placed them there to protect Italy, not without some special kindness of the gods in providing
us with such a bulwark. For had that road been open to the savage
disposition and vast numbers of the Gauls this city would never
have become the home and chosen seat of the empire of the world.
Now let them sink; we have a Caesar. They say the men they mean
to send to Gaul in his stead are valiant and lucky commanders, but
were they the most excellent of men, still I say it would never be
advisable to supersede Caesar in Gaul. Let it be left in the guardian-
ship of that man to whose valor, good faith and good fortune it has
been entrusted. A great war has been fought there; mighty nations
have been subdued by Caesar, but they are not yet established by
any sure guaranty of peace. We shall only see this war terminated,
this long danger laid to rest, if the man who began the task remains
to stamp out the last embers. Therefore I, a senator, an enemy of
the man himself, feel it my duty to be a friend to the Republic and
to him as its sword-bearer. It is true that that storm to which I
yielded so little time ago was raised by the instigation and with the
countenance of Caesar; but I hope that I can have more regard to
the common advantage than to my own past sufferings. I admit that
I was of a different opinion than Caesar in politics; in that opinion
I agreed with all of you here, but now I am doing no more than
agree with you once more. For you yourselves have decreed such
honors to Caesar as were never decreed to any man. Why, then, do
I need to wait for mediation between us? This honorable Senate
and his own achievements have mediated between me and Caesar; I
am a Roman and he has performed deeds that make him the friend of
every Roman. If, in any truth, he who has been distinguished by such
marked kindnesses of Fortune were unwilling longer to risk the
favor of that fickle goddess—if he were impatient to be borne in
triumph through the gates of the city—to take his rest upon the
laurels he has won—it would still be your duty to insist upon this
war being brought to an end not less glorious than its beginning.
But since the man who has done so much for the Republic now asks
only that he may do more, let us, I say, place all power in his hands

and thank the immortal gods that we have such a sword to defend Rome."

Like rain from a piled cloud the applause rushed forth; word ran through the streets that Cicero was defending Caesar and tearing his enemies to bits. The startled Senate stared dumb for a few moments; a tribune whipped in a motion that Caesar's command be prolonged for five years more, his new enlistments confirmed and a special grant be made for his soldiers' pay. Passed *viva voce*.

That fall there was a little jiggery-pokery at the elections and some mewling opposition from the Conservatives, but Pompey and Crassus carried their consulate nevertheless. Caesar wrote a warm note of appreciation to Marcus Cicero and dedicated the new philological treatise to him, thus beginning a friendship that wavered often but never quite went out; and up into Gaul to take a place on the Proconsul's staff rode Quintus Tullius Cicero, a big, bald man, red-faced and irascible, with chin and nose so hooked they nearly met.

2

The Blue Wine and the Red—A darker thread runs through; Caesar came north in the knowledge that the Gauls were like a sea fluid, avid of change, racing all together along whatever new tide stirred their neighbors. The rising on the seacoast bore a threat of universal war; it needed his strongest attention. But there were rumors of trouble also along the lower Rhenus, where a new German thrust seemed preparing, and clear down along the Iberian border in Aquitania, where the bandit tribes who raid the convoys for Tolosa were reported preparing a full-scale invasion.

Labienus the legate, already marked as the ablest general of those under Caesar, went to the Rhenus with a cavalry command and a levy of Remi. They could and did hold the Germans for one season. Aquitania went to young Legate Crassus. He had only a legion and two cohorts, but a store of youthful fire; he swept through the south like a whirlwind, breaking through an ambush the marauders set him to win a ringing victory, then stormed their encampment in another battle and wiped them out.

Among the seacoast tribes the main centers of disturbance were two—the Unelli of the north, whose chief, Viridovix, had gathered a bodyguard of wild spirits and homeless men out of Belgia, and the Veneti who live round the mouth of the Liger and are considered lords of the sea by the other Gauls. Legate Sabinus, who had done so boldly in the fight at the Axona ford, took three legions into the north to deal with the Unelli; Caesar himself turned west.

Since earliest spring he had had a legate in that country building ships—young Decimus Brutus, a kinsman of Cato, but a brilliant intellect in the making who could take color from whatever his surroundings were. When Caesar's arrived the young man took three legions for a march down the north bank of the Liger while the Proconsul himself kept the remaining eighteen cohorts under his personal command for a parallel sweep along the south bank, west toward the sea, with the ships carrying provisions between the two forces.

At the sea-rim both turned north into a land of flats and jutting spires of stone, with scant vegetation. It looked like an easy campaign, for the country was so open the legions could disperse across a broad front to hunt the Veneti into their strong places where they might be captured in groups. But appearances deceived; the Venetan towns were situate on peninsular heads whose necks lay under water at high tide. When Caesar's men, with toil and danger, had built a dike that gave them access to the walls the Venetan ships came round to the sea face of the fortress, took out the people and ferried them to another. The trick was repeated three or four times, or often enough to show it could go on forever. Half the summer had slipped past with nothing captured but empty cormorants' nests, and now supplies began to grow short in the Roman camp. There was no corn in the land. Wagon-trains could not well cross the wastes and when the Romans tried to ship supplies by water the well-handled Venetan ships captured them.

These ships were peculiar; strong and tall to resist the shock of the great Atlantic seas, but flat in the bottom so they navigated easily among the shoals. They were of oak, so high in the bulwarks Roman archery was without effect and so heavily built the ram was useless against them. In a sea-way they rode down the galleys; among the tides they tacked nimbly away.

The campaign was a failure unless the wolf could drink blue water. Caesar sent Decimus Brutus back up the Liger to build a battle-fleet and gave him a legion to man it. The construction took only a few weeks with the artisans available, as the ships were intended for only one battle and green timber could be used, but contrary winds held back Brutus till it was late in summer. The Gauls had news of his coming meanwhile and gathered all their strength in one great fleet to face him, filled with hope and confidence by the success of their defence throughout the summer.

It must have been October when the Roman ships came sweeping round a headland into a wide bay to find the army on a headland looking down at them and the Gallic armada before, two hundred and twenty ships, crowding out of a marshy estuary on the right, their square leathern sails gleaming in the sun as they slanted down the wind.

The Roman ships hesitated a minute—how to deal with these giants?—then the first division rushed in with a clash of cymbals, Brutus' galley conspicuous in the lead, with the red commander's standard snapping from her prow. At the instant of impact she voided, swept down the side of the leading Venetan, flinging out a fistful of long poles with knife-edged grapnels at their tips. They caught the rigging of the Venetan; there was a rush of arrows and Brutus' galley checked sharp round with flashing oars; a brief tug, and as the ropes of the Venetan gave way, yard, sail and mast came crashing to her deck and she rolled masterless on the swell.

The Roman ship turned again in a long serpentine curve that ended at the Venetan's side; up sprang the legionary soldiers and leaped aboard. Swords tossed briefly, then came the peal of a trumpet and a thin shout drifted across the water. The Roman army on the headland began to cheer; the other galleys flung themselves into the Venetan pack with their grappling hooks swung out. Another sail went down and another; the legionaries charged home across the reeling decks, the Venetans had no time to master this surprise tactic, and their big yards swinging round as though in response to a signal, they turned to run.

Caesar's Fortune and Rome's; at that moment the wind died. The big Venetan ships were locked fast as islands; Brutus' galleys wove in and out among the helpless hulks, storming one after another while daylight lasted. The onshore breeze came with dusk; some half-dozen vessels alone, out of all that navy, crawled away into the dark, and the Veneti were ruined, for the fleet was their future, it had held nearly the whole of their fighting men. Caesar's army easily mopped up the remains. Next morning he sent off a runner to Sabinus that he was on the way with aid against Chief Viridovix and his army of scoundrels.

The march was never made; on the way the messenger crossed one from the legate to say the emergency among the Unelli was over. Outnumbered, Sabinus had played a waiting game. Viridovix came up against the Roman campment and taunted him for a coward. It seemed to Sabinus that capital might be made out of that idea; that night he sent a Gallic auxiliary out to represent himself as a deserter, telling a tale of panic in the Roman camp and preparation for flight. Viridovix believed it since it accorded with his own opinion. At daybreak his Gauls came hurrying up a long slope to storm the camp, arriving at the crest blown and weary with haste and the weight of the faggot bundles they carried to fill up the ditch. Sabinus raised the standard just as they got there and blew for battle. The legions rushed out and met the disorderly mass before them with so fierce a shock that the barbarians could make no stand, and as they fled the cavalry cut heavily into their stragglers.

That ended the war in the west; Caesar drowned the revolt in blood, mercilessly executing the men of the Venetan council who had stirred up the trouble, and selling the last of their warriors into slavery. It was a hard punishment, justified only by the inherent danger that the rising might spread farther and the whispers running through Gaul that though the Romans might slay in hot blood they would never kill in cold—which meant to Gauls that a man was free to plot whatever treacheries he chose if he only gave these southerners fair words till ready to strike with all his force. The tribes, too, had laid ambassadors in suasion, which was a witless, barbaric thing to do, yet for that same reason an act unforgiveable, since it struck not at the persons of the ambassadors, nor at Rome even, but at civilization itself, that begs of all that hasty passion stand still till things can be reasoned out. Seen in this light the Venetans' council were common criminals since they had ordered it as a deliberate policy; and in announcing his judgment on the Venetans Caesar placed it on that basis alone.

Yet seen in their own light these Veneti were men who wished to live free and took the shortest road thither . . . but that's the rub, Caesar could not see them in their own light. He saw things in an intellectual light which was not necessarily unsympathetic, but with a sympathy dominated by that intellect so that he looked upon humanity from long range as a race to be saved from its own impulses. "If the eye offend, pluck it out"—there was no room in this sympathy for poor witless Veneti.

So he executed the Venetan council and put the legions under marching orders for their winter camp near the Rhenus to meet another hurricane which had been gathering beyond the rim of the forests in dim, wild Germany.

3

Terror—Labienus and his cavalry held the Rhenus frontier good only for the summer. In late fall the new German horde went down the right bank of that river to its junction with the Mosa and the Batavian island. A Belgic tribe called the Menapii lived there. The Germans burst in upon them suddenly, slew most, drove the rest out and settled down to eat up the Menapian corn during the winter. When the ice went down the river they began to stir once more; their horsemen were seen far south in the neighborhood of Atuactuca. There appeared to be about 400,000 of them, a quarter of the number full-grown warriors, in two tribes, Usipetes and Tencteri, moving westward like lemmings under pressure from those same Suebi who had marched to join King Ariovistus. Gaul offered them a life of easy plunder. They were there to stay, and some of the minor Gallic chieftains had already formed alliance with them to save their own necks. No alternate—they must be struck and hard, a lesson that would keep the Germans out of Gaul forever.

In earliest April, with the weather still chill and rainy, Caesar broke camp and set out at his best marching pace for the frontier. His cavalry were Gallic, many of them being chosen from among those clans who had promised aid to the Germans, Caesar affecting ignorance of their waverings and taking them with him to keep them steady. A few days' march from the Teuton laager ambassadors appeared. They minced no words—the Romans must go away or be driven away. They, Usipetes and Tencteri, had taken Batavia by right of the sword and would hold it. They acknowledged the right of none to give them orders but the Suebi, against whom the immortal gods might struggle in vain.

Caesar gave them a temperate answer. ——He had lately made a treaty with the Ubii, a Germanic tribe east of Rhenus. They asked help to stand off the Suebi; let the Usipetes and Tencteri take land there since it was land they wanted. Against the Suebi they would also find a war worthy of their talents and disposition.——

The ambassadors, not being men good at dialectic, could think of no answer but to suggest a three-day delay while they reported the matter to the tribes. Would Caesar consent to stay where he was for that length of time, making no hostile move?

By their hang-dog look and hesitation as they made this request Caesar could see what the trick was, the common old German trick Ariovistus had served him two years before—first defiance, then long-spun negotiations while they called in their scattered band and made ready for battle, then a quick, driving blow while he trusted to the truce and peaceful intentions. He gave them not a day nor an hour; they might go home and consider the matter if they wished, but his march toward them would continue meanwhile.

It did continue; at twelve miles' distance from the barbarian camp the ambassadors returned to say they would arrange matters with the Ubii and go live there—would Caesar wait three days more? His scouting service, always adroitly conducted, had brought in word that the tribes were lacking a large force of their cavalry, now be-

yond the Mosa river on a raid, but that these horsemen had been summoned and would take exactly three days to return to the main body. ——No (he said) no delay, not for a day. Accept the terms now, go back across the Rhenus, leave Gaul to the Gauls.——
——Would he, then, (they asked) only have the forbearance to instruct his cavalry vanguard not to engage any scattered parties of Germans they encountered by accident?—— Yes, he would do that. The orders to the cavalry went out, the embassy left.

There were five thousand Gauls in the Roman cavalry force. They moved along gaily through the aisles of forest next morning, keeping no very good watch because of the truce, when there was a whoop and a tempest of fighting Germans rose from the ground all around and among them. Some few of the Gauls tried to make a stand; they were cut down, the rest swept away and flung in upon the marching column of foot in utter rout.

The check ruined Caesar's temper and fixed his resolve. The only argument these savages understood was the sword—well, they should have it. The legions pressed on, grim-visaged as their commander, always hating Germans, German arrogance and German treachery, in the triple-column march order that can be converted into a line of battle by a right or left face. The baggage was dropped behind, archers came up to cover the advance in lieu of the shaken horsemen.

In the morning watches, as the troops got under way, there was a commotion up ahead and the scouts came dashing in with news that a big deputation of Germans was at hand. They were the tribal elders; when they saw Caesar they began a long-winded speech about how difficult it was to restrain the impetuosity of young warriors. The youth alone were responsible . . . Caesar, his eyes sparking heat-lightnings, snapped them short with an order to hold these chiefs in bonds. Double-quick, forward march!

The eight miles to the German camp were covered so fast that the legionaries arrived before news of them. The Usipetes and Tencteri were about their various occupations, thinking of everything but attack. They had no leaders and before they could snatch up their weapons the Romans had burst in upon them, slaying right and left. The women and children began to scream, a sound which always unnerves even the stoutest. The Germans threw down their arms and fled. Caesar flung his Gallic cavalry into the rout, hot for vengeance, and terrible was the vengeance they took, for the Usipetes and Tencteri were penned in the angle of the Rhenus and the Mosa and those who escaped the sword perished by drowning. Out of that huge migration, 430,000 people (they were counted after) only those got away who had gone out on the cavalry raid of a week before.

The blow sent a shock of fear even through the dark forests to the east and it was felt as a stain on Caesar even in Rome, where Cato, back from Cyprus, proposed in the Senate that he be turned over to the Germans for punishment. The motion found no second; a stain the massacre may have been, an act of sheer terrorism and violence, born of angry impatience or unwillingness to work out the problem by the long way. But it was wrought upon men who lived by terror and violence and for whom the best could find but little sympathy.

4

First Adventure to the Isles—There was a delegation of Ubii in the Roman camp, coaxing for swords against the Suebians, who were pressing them hard. Moreover, the nation that marched with their territories on the north, Sugambri, had sheltered the wreckage from the massacre of Batavia and were working up through the verbal stages toward a war of retaliation. A campaign in Germany was no part of Caesar's plan, but he felt he must cross Rhenus long enough to give a pat that would disconcert this stroke.

The Ubii offered boats. He refused, ordered out the choppers and in ten days produced one of the masterpieces of Roman engineering —a forty-foot bridge across the river, stout enough to bear the transit of the army with wagons. (Curiously we meet the Spanish expert, Cornelius Balbus here once more, as an engineer on the project, along with Caesar himself.) The Ubii were transported with delight at this unexpected arrival and the Suebi with fear, which impressed the uneducated Germans about as bridging the North Sea would impress their descendants today. The latter tribe retreated to the heart of the Hercynian Forest and devastated a belt a hundred miles wide around them.

The Sugambri hid in swamps. Caesar burned out some of their fields and a few villages, then repassed the river again and pulled down his bridge. He had a more important project in mind, now long overdue—that reconnaissance of the Tin Isles of Britain which had first stirred his interest two years before. There were persistent reports that the Venetan revolt had been abetted from that quarter, and it would be worth while knowing how much truth there was in the story and to what extent it might be done again. Who were these people of the mists? Had they much silver, as legend was? Pearls?

There is a port at the narrowest point of the Gallic strait, Portus Itius. Caesar led the legions thither and ordered up the fleet that had been used in the Venetan war. The vessels, being green wood, were crank and required much repair; while the artisans were at work he sent out a full-armed trireme to spy landing places along the British coast. Caius Volusenus, an officer who had proved himself of good courage and mind in an exploration among the perilous summits of the Alps was in command. Himself he gathered a convention of Gallic traders and quizzed them sharply about the land he was to visit.

On certain points the commercial men were clear enough—the Britons were half wild still, living on milk and flesh, and their only clothes beasts' skins, beneath which they painted themselves horridly with blue. The upper lip they did not shave; their strength in war was mostly of chariots, from which they leaped to fight on foot, like the princes before Troy. Brothers held wives in common; their Druids wove men into wicker cages which had the form of ancient monsters and burned them alive as sacrifices. But when Caesar asked of the political and geographic complexion of the islands and inquired whether they produced wares of value the traders lost voice and memory. There was some mystery here; to clear it up and prepare his way the Proconsul sent over Commios,

High Chief of the Atrebates, a good Romanizing Gaul who had guesting friendships with certain lords in Britain.

Volusenus came back with word that he had struck the coast at a point where wondrous great cliffs of white stone stood a hundred feet or more above the sea. He coasted along under them to the harbor of the Gallic merchants, but it clearly would not do as a landing point, being set round with steep and broken ground close to the shore, well wooded, where the legions could not deploy. Beyond, the cliffs sank a little; the galley moved slowly under them, taking soundings for a matter of ten miles or more till she turned a towering headland and came on a broad open beach, shimmering white, behind which the ground clambered slowly through dips and curves to highlands far inland.

The landing would be there. Caesar approved, put two legions aboard the transports as soon as the report was rendered, and set out that night, the weather being fair. The formations were the 10th and 7th; a contingent of cavalry was to follow on eighteen horse-transports which had not yet come up from the south.

The wind turned wrong during the night of the crossing. It was the second watch of morning before Caesar's admiral-galley reached the cliffs and there he must needs wait for the slower transports, which had become scattered by the airs and rushing tide. It was afternoon before they came in; the interval was employed in giving copies of Volusenus' report and instructions for the landing to the officers. Meanwhile the Britons had begun to collect on the hills above, advertising their presence by gibbering and casting stones at the vessels. When the united fleet pulled along the coast their chariots could be seen in great numbers, galloping along the heights to keep abreast.

The Roman ships rounded Volusenus' head all together in practised formation. The transports ran in for the beach, but being of heavy draft, took ground while still in deep water. It was neck-high, with slips and pot-holes, a grievous task for armor-laden men with the British blocking the shore in front, driving their chariots into the water, hurling spears and arrows amid hobgoblin yells. The legionaries plunged in gallantly; the fighting became intense, but the Romans, skidding among the stones, could not gain toward the beach, not even when the eagle-bearer of the 10th rushed to the forefront of the fighting. Caesar, surveying the situation calmly from his deck, ordered the warships warped in on the flank of the fighting. The heavy catapults on their decks, the archers in their towers, raked the British line and drove them back a space, but they turned just out of range and kept up the fight in waist-deep water till Caesar put archers and darters in pinnaces which drove through the struggling press and harried the Britons back to shore. Once on firm ground the legions formed line and charged home with a cheer; the Britannics took to their heels.

They began to come in to the camp at daybreak, big men for the more part, ugly and snag-toothed. Of course they all claimed to be chiefs. Caesar questioned them himself, asking particularly after Commios the Atrebate, whose non-appearance was beginning to worry him. Toward noon Commios appeared in person with an escort of thirty horsemen. The Britons had locked him up in a hut after his landing, apparently with the intention of roasting him in a cage as a particularly choice titbit for their gods, and only let him loose after the fight at the beach.

He had much valuable information. There were two main tribes in that part of Britain, he said, Catuvellani and Trinovantes, with the former holding the upper hand, thanks to the ability of their high chief, Cassivellaunus, whom the Britons regarded as the greatest lord on earth.

The situation offered a handhold to Caesar. He spoke fair with all the Britons who came in but particularly with those of the Trinovant alliance. So the army abode for five days; with the country so open and barbarous it could not move without cavalry and the transports that were to bring the horsemen still did not appear.

On the 16th September sails were made out—the eighteen horse transports at last. The soldiers crowded down to the shore to welcome them, but just then a great puff of wind came roaring out of the northeast and spun the ships fair around. The gale rose; some of the eighteen were driven right back to Portus Itius, the rest got into the shelter of Britain for the night, but the wind struck them so hard

they could not hold against it on their anchor-chains and not a one
reached Caesar. This was bad enough but worse came in the night,
for it was full moon, and the Romans, not knowing how the tide-
rips run through those narrow seas, had made no special precau-
tions for the fleet. Tide and gale wrought strong together; the transports burst their moorings and dashed upon the beach. The warships
floated loose, crashing into one another and the sinking transports
while soldiers struggled in dark and pounding wave to save ships
and gear. Dawn showed nearly every ship wrecked and the two
legions marooned on a friendless shore without corn or baggage, for
the expedition had equipped light for a mere exploratory dash like
that across the Rhenus.

Fortunately the day was calm. Caesar manned the soundest of
the remaining galleys with a picked crew of fast rowers and sent it
express speed to Portus Itius for shipwrights and naval stores. He
was too wise to sit still for the return, however; strong foraging
parties went out to get what corn they could from the scant British
fields; at the morning muster all men who had followed the trades
of mechanic or carpenter were ordered to fall out and help repair
ships under Chiefs of Engineers Mamurra and Balbus.

The British, who were in and out of the camp continually, looked
on with sheeps' eyes, not failing to mark the atmosphere of hurry

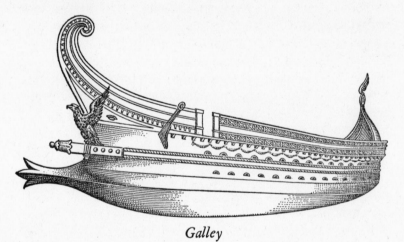

Galley

and fever. They grew chill; no hostages came in. On a day the out-posts reported to Caesar that an ominous big dust-cloud was rising in the direction where part of the 7th had gone to harvest corn from a field. He gathered up the duty cohort with Commios and his thirty, leaving orders for the rest to arm and follow at hot speed. He was right in hurrying; the detachment of the 7th were bunched to-gether in the center of a cornfield, verging on panic, some of them down, with Britons whooping and shooting missiles into the mass from all sides. Commios and his thirty charged in like heroes again and again; the foot formed line, but they were too few to make anything of it but a safe retreat.

The equinox came near, announced by furious storms on sea and land. The messenger-galley slipped through an interval back from Gaul with news that Legate Sabinus, whom Caesar had left in charge, had gone on a campaign among the Morini and no naval stores were to be had, nor ships to transport them if there had been any. That was not so bad as it might be; with bronze and planks from the dozen or fifteen ships beyond repair Mamurra reported that the rest could be patched up enough to reach the Gallic coast if they tried it on a night not too rough. It was as bad as it could be; the Britons were turned complete unfriends, they were gather-ing by thousands outside the palisades, eager to rush the few men inside into the sea and plunder their camp.

They attempted it on the 25th. Caesar had a few light-armed scouts out who gave enough advance notice for the legions to get through the gates and form a line against which the wild men dashed themselves to shreds like storm-clouds on a mountain. Commios performed prodigies with his little squadron; the legionaries hurled themselves into the pursuit all afternoon long, inflicting such loss that the mercurial British chiefs sent in next morning to beg peace and mercy.

Caesar was gracious; told them to send hostages cross channel by trading ships during the winter and next day got his two legions aboard their rickety armada for the return voyage. They made it safely, except for two ships driven up the Gallic coast into the ter-

ritory of the Morini, the soldiers from which had difficulty finding
their way back to Portus Itius.

5

Note in E Major; Second Adventure to the Isles—"Give me colors,"
wrote Marcus Cicero to his brother who was in the marine camp at
Portus Itius, "that I may paint those astonishing islands of yours
with the brush of my poetry. The elections have been postponed
again and the Forum is profoundly tranquil, but with the quiet of
senile decay. Domitius Ahenobarbus failed to get the requisite number of jurors for his prosecution of our friend, young Caelius, so
that business fell to the ground. As for myself, I have been reading
Callisthenes—a cheap and hackneyed writer if there ever was one.
I see you have been wallowing in him, too—are you really going to
try your hand at writing history? If I may say so, you have the
ability and would do better than in tragedy. By the way, may I
recommend to your attention a friend of mine, M. Orfius, who is a
tribune in your army, I do not know with what legion. I had a letter
from your Caesar, brimming over with every sort of kindness, as-
siduous attention and charm. Nothing ever gave me more pleasure
and he has not only found a post for my friend Trebatius, but sends
me a delightfully whimsical expression of gratitude for having
recommended him. I shall certainly make up for my slowness in
paying court in that quarter by galloping, not only with relays of
horses, but with the chariot of my poetry."

Rome was somnolent that winter, which is why the letter was
dated from the orator's villa on the shore at Cumae, where he medi-
tated philosophy in a world of incredible blues. Crassus had mustered
six legions in the Campus Martius and buzzed off for the gold and
glory of the fabled east in a whirl of activity, like some large and
rather obscene fly, chuckling in his stringy money-lender's beard. It
occasioned a scandal that he left on November 15, a month and a
half before his consulate ended, as though the chief magistracy of
Rome were valuable only as a stepping-stone to a province where
he might make money. But tongues were silenced by the arrival of
Publius Crassus from Gaul—gay, gallant, splendid with youth and

the achievements of his two years' commandancy under Caesar, an heir imperial. He would be second and Chief of Staff to his father on the Parthian expedition, and already was rated one of the best soldiers of Rome.

If Crassus caused scandal by going to his province too soon, Pompey caused as much talk by not going to his province at all. He complained that Spain was unhealthy for a man of his years, and was rumored to be drinking a good deal. The contretemps at the consular games had affected him temperamentally as well as politically. As an addition of special magnificence he had introduced an elephant hunt in the Circus, the first of its kind in Rome. The poor beasts were tame; they tried to be friends with the gladiators. When they saw the men meant death they ran around the arena trumpeting in fright and appealing for help with anguished eyes. Cicero was disgusted; Julia, whom Pompey had come to adore with a surprising uxorious passion, left the Circus. The audience sat icy-still through the performance; next day a story went round that the elephants were half human, had been lured aboard ship in Africa by Pompey on the promise no harm should come to them—his luck would be forfeit to the treachery.

Caesar spent the winter south in Illyricum, where there had been a revolt and Roman officers pitched into the gulf of Ragusa. He got things in hand without removing any heads, which was considered highly original of him, then posted back across the mountains at his usual pace to Portus Itius, where preparations were being made for a full-dress invasion of Britain. The sea was the enemy first of might; during the journey down from Gaul he had spent the time in his travelling carriage in designing a new type of ship—galley, for independence of winds, broad-beamed to porter a great cargo, flat bottomed and sturdy like the Venetan fleet that sailed so well among the fitful Atlantic tides. Six hundred of them were built during the winter by the labor of the legionaries.

Occasion also met the Proconsul's arrival, for High Chief Cassivellaunus had warred on the Trinovantes and slain their king during the winter months, and the young prince fled to Gaul to seek Roman aid in regaining his heritage.

There came a check nevertheless. As soon as Caesar was on the ground he sniffed an odor of smoldering antagonism among the chiefs present for the annual great Gallic council and caught a hint of the reason, too—that the strong arm of Roman law debarred them from their old practice of enrichment by raiding their neighbors. From the Eburones and Treveri there were no delegates at all; the other lords said these nations were intriguing with the Germans. Delay would be bad for the British project, but complaisance worse, for these two were the great tribes of northeast Gaul and the Treverian light horse the best in the land.

Caesar hastily put four legions into light order and made a fast exploratory march eastward. The trouble was a faction-fight. Two chiefs, Indutiomarus and Cingetorix, were bidding against each other for support of the plunder-barons by offering freedom from Roman restraints and a warlike raid through the rest of Gaul. Caesar took Cingetorix' part, which straightway made him a fanatic Romanizer, as he perceived he could make more with less trouble by confiscating the goods of the opposite party than out of a war. Indutiomarus was disposed to raise a war at first, and began hiding an armament in the glades of Arduenna wood, but the minor chiefs rounded on him; he bit down his spleen and made submission. It was not permanent; Caesar knew that and knew he would intrigue, but the British expedition was waiting, with summer half gone, and Cingetorix could be trusted to play watch-dog.

See map
facing page 113

At Portus Itius there was more fuming among the Gallic chiefs. Caesar cut the knot by ordering the most recalcitrant to attend him with squadrons of cavalry on the British voyage. Dumnorix of the Aedui refused; tale-bearers said he had sworn to make himself autocrat of Gaul and that he was telling others the Romans had promised their aid to the project. When the Proconsul tried to reason with him he shifted like a snake. "Must!" rapped out Caesar; Dumnorix said nothing but his pale eyes wavered, and when Roman troops and commander were locked in the bustle of embarkation he rode out of camp and away with his retainers, calling the other Gauls to follow. Caesar instantly countermanded sailing orders, made the infantry ready for battle and rushed out a force of cavalry on the Aeduan's trail to bring him back, dead or alive. It was dead; Dumnorix cried he was a free man of a free nation, his escort resisted, and the pursuers had to use their swords.

The embarkation went forward; some light-armed, four thousand horse and five legions, the other three being left under Labienus at the base. At noon on the first August the vessels came to land beyond the strait. The Britons made no opposition, but a few prisoners brought in by Commios the Atrebate said Cassivellaunus had been named High King of Britain to throw the invaders into the sea and only waited to trap them up-country. The spoor of an army was visible through the brush; as soon as the soldiers were ashore Caesar set out on that track with all but ten cohorts and three hundred horse, left behind as a camp guard.

It was a night march, twelve miles. At dawn the Roman vanguard made contact with the enemy, finding them posted on high ground behind a river, with evident intent to dispute the passage behind a work of felled trees. Caesar sent a force to turn their flank and ployed the 7th into a tight wedge of attack; they burst through in the first rush, which made it certain that the enemy were no king's army but local levies and there would be deeper fighting farther on. The force was split into three columns and began a march at all speed to disconcert the British arrangements before they should have time to form.

Caesar rode with his center, sure his swift peremptory action would succeed, but at twilight a fagged and panting messenger, who had galloped on relays of horses all day from the base came in with news of disaster. The moon had shown her horns; wild wind and flowing tide conspired to drive the ships ashore as wind and full moon tide had wrecked them the year before, and nearly the whole fleet was lost.

The columns were ordered in at once. With a small escort of horse Caesar made a fevered midnight ride to the landing-port, arriving with the day to find some forty ships beaten into timber-rafts and the rest sadly hurt. A fast galley went to Labienus in Gaul to have the artisans there build more vessels; Mamurra and whatever artificers the legions could supply were thrown into the work of repair. This was good, but gave no guarantee inconstant Dian might not stir the sea to another fury; nothing for it but get the ships high on the beach, beyond the tongue of any sea, and guard them with a trench and rampart. Time pressed; the whole force, 28,000 men or more, was set to work in relays, with huge bonfires burning through the night to light the toil that never ceased.

In ten days it was done; Caesar turned back to face the Britons, but the delay had cost him the use of his quick paralyzing stroke. King Cassivellaunus was on his front; the tribes were up. In the valley of the same river that had seen the fight a fortnight before, the barbarians clashed with the vanguard of Gallic cavalry. The Gauls broke them, but followed too fast and were in turn rushed back across the stream to the legionary line. Camp was just being built; the Britons swooped down on the duty cohort and working parties, both from the 11th, and gave them a rough time, as they were disconcerted by the novel flash and go tactic of the chariot charges. Caesar rushed in two more cohorts, but the British were fluid as water, evaporating before the onset of the armored swordsmen, then sweeping in to strike their flanks. Another four cohorts with plenty of archers and cavalry were necessary to stop their prancings. Count this battle a draw.

Next morning the Britons appeared along the hilltops, dodging in and out. At noon Caesar sent Legate Trebonius out to gather forage with three legions and all the cavalry, himself holding camp with one. The Britons became bolder and bolder around Trebonius, then suddenly rushed at the three legions with a yell, chariotry, cavalry and footmen, all mixed together. Trebonius had expected just that; he met the wave with a countercharge so fierce the Britons' line blew up and scattered in every direction, their enthusiasm for war melting as fast as it had risen. The cavalry rode into their retreat, giving them no chance to rally—slaying, slaying, slaying.

The blow disjointed the shaky coalition of tribes. Many went home, the Trinovantes sent in a deputation to ask for their rightful prince and Roman help. High King Cassivellaunus held his own nation true to their hostility, however, and Caesar had to turn his march north and west toward their country. Cassivellaunus was a good man of war; by no means downcast at his setback, he turned to a program of small war and ambushes. It was a success; the cloud of Gallic cavalry that hung round Caesar's march was cramped in on the column with heavy loss, becoming so fidgety and racked they failed to scout well.

To counter the new method Caesar speeded up his march toward Cassivellaunus' territories. He was the soul of the resistance, it would go down if he were well beaten, for prisoners said he held his post only through his greatness in war, being hated among the tribes for a harsh and overreaching tyrant. The river Tamesis forms the boundary of his lands. There was only one ford, which Caesar found held by a strong force of the enemy from behind a hedge of palisades, with piles driven into the bed of the stream, sharp points upward under water to make crossing hazardous. The Proconsul sent cavalry right and left to swim the stream. The legionaries went straight in; they had tested these Britons to the marrow and knew they were the better men. Though the water was neck-deep and the spears drove at them, they broke right through the enemy center.

On the march to the river the Romans had suffered many a privation by reason of Cassivellaunus' flying raids on the flanks; they were angry men that spread across his lands to burn the villages and run off the herds in which Britons counted their wealth. Cassivellaunus made a final stand in what passed for a fortification among these islanders—a thickly wooded snout of ground thrust up among a sea of marshes, strengthened round its rim with ditch and rampart. Caesar surveyed the place, decided it could be taken by assault and hurled columns through the mire on two fronts. They broke in; Cassivellaunus himself escaped, but many of the defenders were killed and the bulk of the herds and women belonging to his tribe fell into the hands of the victors. At about the same time a messenger came up from the base camp to say the Britons had made an attack there, but that it had been repulsed with much slaughter and the capture of an important chief.

The double defeat finished High King Cassivellaunus. A day or two later embassies came to make peace in his name and to offer hostages, and they were followed by missions from most of the other tribes. Caesar gave them light terms. Though they did not know it, his own emergency was more pressing than theirs, for word had just come through from Labienus that north Gaul was in a ferment, with the chiefs plotting wars and revenges, lest they meet the fate of Dumnorix separately, and the people, urged on by the nip of empty bellies from a corn harvest failed, willing to listen to any madness.

6

Statement of Theme—Caesar called an autumn council of Gallic magnates at Samarobriva of the Bellovaci, the fortress of the north. It was not satisfactory; as Labienus had said, the air was filled with an itching dust of discontent. The chiefs made piddling complaints and argued every point. The Proconsul sent them home with smiles and fair words, but ordered up a new legion from the Cisalpine province and prepared to winter under the sullen skies of Belgia, his first winter in Gaul. At headquarters he kept a single legion, the 10th, under the immediate command of Trebonius, hero of the British fighting. His intent was to spread the rest of the troops through Belgic territory in a wide circle, where they could both more easily find food and keep down disturbances, but before cold weather two incidents raced up like birds flung before a storm and the arrangement was partially thrown out of gear.

South beyond Sequana River the Esuvii of the coast stirred. Legate Roscius took the 13th Legion thither for the winter. East of them, among the sources of the Liger the chiefs of the Carnutan tribe assassinated their king, Tasgetius, who had ruled his nation in peace and splendor for two years, a friend of Rome. Another legion under Legate Plancus hurried south to lay the murderous chiefs by the heels before they could vindicate their act by combining in an anti-Roman war.

For the remainder of the army the original plan held good. Marcus Crassus, a brother to young Publius, camped with a legion in Bellovacian territory, twenty-five miles from headquarters; Q. Fabius with another among the

See map facing page 113

Morini of the coast. Out eastaway Labienus had a legion where the territory of the Remi marches with that of the Treveri; Quintus Cicero took another to the banks of the Sabis among the Nervii, and finally, the biggest camp of all, a legion and a half, was pitched at Atuactuca, among the Eburones. Five cohorts of this detachment belonged to the old 14th; the rest were the recruit legion that had come up from Cisalpine Gaul, numbered 14 when the five other cohorts of the old legion of that number were distributed among the others to bring them up to strength. Legate Sabinus was in command. He had shown that he possessed a head but no heart, so Caesar gave him as second L. Aurunculeius Cotta, a tough, hard-bitten fighting man whose courage was such that he could and did afford to dispense with brains.

They had trouble. On a bitter cold day a working party had gone out into the black, snow-sprinkled forest to gather wood, when the Eburones turned sour without warning, rushed the laborers and came swarming round the camp by the thousand. The legionaries flew to arms; an ala of Spanish cavalry dashed out one gate and cut a swath through the barbarians, hurling them back with dead men left in odd attitudes all down the snowy slope. They camped among the trees out of bowshot; all afternoon great numbers of them could be seen moving to and fro. Toward evening a man stood forth and began to shout for a parley; Sabinus sent out Q. Junius, his chief of scouts, who knew these people and their country.

He was met by Ambiorix, High Chief of the Eburones. The man seemed much distressed, explained that he had been forced into the outbreak by the under-chiefs, who had been listening to the heady doctrines of Indutiomarus the Treverian. The movement was become national (he said); all the eastern camps of the circuit had been assaulted on the same day and a huge host of Germans had crossed the Rhenus to aid in expelling the Romans from Gaul. His authority over his own tribe had been undermined, but he thought it equal to keeping a promise he would make the 14th of a safe conduct if they would evacuate immediately and retire to Samarobriva. Only the thing must be done quickly; when the savage Germans, the vengeful Indutiomarus arrived, it would be too late. He begged them to make his excuses to Caesar, to whom he owed many kindnesses.

Junius reported; the legates called a council of war in which a hot debate flared up. Sabinus was for accepting—the Eburones were a minor tribe, they would never have embarked on a course so mad unless the other tribes were in it too; Labienus and Cicero had probably perished with their two legions; Ambiorix could be trusted, since he was a good friend of Caesar's.

Aurunculeius Cotta rapped out that they had no right to leave the post without orders. The 14th was well in this secure stronghold, with provisions to last through the winter. Sabinus' lively imagination painted giants across the sky; his temper broke, the centurions had to separate the legates who came to the edge of blows, but most of them voted with Cotta when Sabinus put the question. He went clear mad angry—"Have it your stupid way!" he shouted, "When these soldiers are perishing with hunger, miserably and alone, you will be the one to bear their dying reproaches!"

Cotta had no mental agility enough to stand such fire; he gave way, the trumpet was sounded through the camp and the troops marched with the day, not light and fast, but in a long, loose column loaded with the winter baggage, as through a settled country, so thoroughly they trusted the word of that devoted Romanizer, Ambiorix.

A few miles from the camp the road dips to a valley which becomes a ravine. No sooner were they in the depression than arrows began to fly and with a barbaric shout the head and rear of the column were attacked. It stalled; Sabinus lost his head and went dashing about, issuing useless orders while the soldiers began to grab for their baggage before the Gauls should get at the wagons and steal it. Cotta finally suppressed the other legate and got the men into a hollow square where they could make a stand. For a time they made the defence good, but the Gauls clung thick about them, keeping in protection of woods and overhanging ravine walls, raining in missiles. The legionaries had many hit and gave less blows than they took.

Yet they stood firm till the eighth hour, when Cotta was struck by a sling-bullet that broke his face. As he lay on the ground, desperately wounded, Sabinus caught a glimpse of Chief Ambiorix cheering on the attackers and signaled him for a parley. The Gaul shouted agreement, there was truce for a few minutes as Sabinus went out to meet him, taking most of the senior officers with him to the conference. The opponents mutually grounded weapons and retired behind some trees. Ambiorix started to speak then, lashed himself into a fury with his own eloquence and suddenly tossed up his arm. Down swooped Gallic warriors from the thickets, fell on the helpless officers and slew them every one, then turned against the legion with a shout of victory. Tired, dismayed, officerless, it broke ranks and went streaming back toward the abandoned camp in a disorganized knot that frayed away at the edges as the pursuers trod close on their heels, killing as they ran. With the dark the Gauls went off to plunder the baggage; the remnants of the 14th took stock, found they were too few to defend the place and without leaders, and rather than be burned alive in sacrifice to the barbarous gods of death and night, committed suicide to the last man.

Ambiorix sent runners to Indutiomarus and rode the next day to the country of the Atuactuci with all his horsemen. He had lied to poor Sabinus, the rising was not national—yet; but now it snowballed up fast at the news a legion and a half and two legates had been destroyed. The Roman spell was broke; they were not invincible. The Atuactuci rose en masse, they set the neighboring Nervii alight and the whole lava-flood, 80,000 fighting men burning with victory and enthusiasm, went rushing up the Sabis to wipe out Quintus Cicero and his single legion.

It was a calm day with smoke curling lazily into the slate grey sky of a Gallic winter. The legate had a heavy cold; wrapped in fur, he sat shivering over a fire, trying to hammer out the lines of his latest tragedy, while from a little distance out in the woods came the frosty ring of axes from a working party. Were they alone in the world? No; there was a sudden patter of feet, a clatter of hooves; the forest seemed to split under a vast weight of sound as 80,000 Gauls submerged the working party and came screaming up against the rampart all in a breath. The trumpets sounded through the camp, the soldiers went running to the rampart to plunge into a mad nightmare of fighting. It lasted all day; Cicero, his teeth knocking together in the shivering fit of his malady, was everywhere at once, building up a reserve, hurling it from side to side as the tide of combat ebbed and flowed at one point or another. At night the Gauls drew off; the Legate had bonfires lighted, tore down some of the houses and set every man in camp at work building tall wooden towers of lashed timber. Runners were dispatched through the dark, some to swim the icy Sabis, some to work through the woods, to carry news of the attack to Caesar.

At dawn the fighting began again, more men than before, and fiercely driving home, utterly fearless, right up to the palisades. They got the ditch filled up, they came slugging against the wall in wedge-formation, shields held overhead, chopping at the stakes with axes, yanking at them with hooks. Cicero had his few catapults in the towers, his slender force of light-armed with them; they drove arrows and sling-bolts into the mass below with terrific effect, but mostly it was hard, close cut and thrust work with the sword on every side at once. That day also the defense was made good; that night the camp labored again in shifts, building up the defenses where they had been wrecked, making new arrows, sharpening long stakes in the fire, even the wounded laboring under their bandages.

That next day, and the next and the day following that, with men in four-hour watches, staggering from bed to wall and back to bed. The Legate never slept at all; his eyes sank in, his teeth came out, his voice went hoarse, but still he was the soul of the defense, encouraging, ordering, standing himself in the center of the fight till his soldiers crowded round him and bore him off to take a little rest whether he would or no. The Gauls built a rampart about the camp with a trench, in imitation of civilized siege-works. Every day they rushed the walls and the battle had to be won over again.

On the fifth day the Gauls sent a herald who stood outside and proclaimed to Cicero that all Gaul was in arms and hope of relief vain; the Germans were over the Rhenus, Sabinus and Cotta slain. If he would give up they would offer him safe conduct out of the country. Cicero croaked back that Rome never negotiated with an enemy in arms; if they would surrender to him, he would intercede with Caesar for their pardon. They screamed angrily at him and for reply brought forth the messengers he had sent, tortured them to death before his eyes and flung their heads into the camp.

The seventh day of the siege there was a high wind; toward evening the Gauls began to sling red-hot clay balls and shoot flaming arrows which fell on the thatched roofs of the buildings and set the whole camp ablaze. As the flames roared up, the Gauls came rushing in for another assault, but the legionaries stood to their arms like men, outlined against the sea of fire behind them. At the height of the combat Ambiorix got a wheeled tower against the rampart. It came to the spot where the Third cohort held, but the centurions of that band only withdrew their men a little space from the wall and dared the Gauls to enter. They dared not; the loricated legionaries stormed the tower, hurled the Gauls within from its stages and burned it down, then turned the move into a roaring sally that swept the attackers right back to the shelter of their own works.

On the tenth day a slave from the camp got in among the Nervii as they flowed back from an attack. He slipped through their camp and away with a message to Caesar hidden under the lashing of his javelin. It got through; Caesar learned by questioning the man of Cicero's desperate case, the first news he had had of it. That was the eleventh hour of the day; by midnight the Proconsul was on the march with the 10th. Messengers went out in relays on fast horses; Marcus Crassus and his legion were to close in and hold the great base at Samarobriva, Fabius and his to join the 10th on the march, Labienus and Sabinus to head directly for Cicero's camp.

Before day the 10th had marched twenty miles, moving light, no trains, carry everything on your backs and provision yourselves en route. Near the sources of the Scaldis Fabius came in, but also alas! a messenger from Labienus which said he dared not move. The Treveri were in arms around him, he was himself well-nigh besieged. It also told of the annihilation of the 14th. Caesar for one brief moment gave way to a transport of grief and rage; swore by the immortal gods that he would not cut hair or beard till the massacred men were avenged, then rushed on like a bearded star for the country of the Nervii.

On the eighteenth day of fighting at Cicero's camp a soldier plucked loose a Gallic javelin that had stuck in the face of a tower. He noticed it had something tied to the shaft and carried it to the Legate. Cicero saw it was a message in Greek characters and recognized Caesar's own hand. It was early day, the struggle for existence had not yet begun that morning; he blew a muster and read the message aloud to the weary legionaries, filling them with hope. Three words only—"Courage! Expect succor!" How long had it stood in the tower, unnoticed? No one knew, but as they talked, far on the distant sky beyond the forest they saw a tall pillar of smoke go up, then mushroom out into a dark, wide cloud, so large it could only come from a burning town. Caesar was on the way and taking vengeance as he came.

That day the fighting was less pushed home. Toward eve the Gallic tumult died and a scout, cautiously peering, found the encircling trenches void. The siege was raised; five thousand dead men turned toward life with haggard faces.

Cicero's message that Ambiorix had turned away, probably to strike the relieving army, found Caesar on the bank of a little stream. He had only 8,000 men, the enemy about 60,000, but took thought and action together. Before the Gauls appeared a camp was built, a small camp, not enough for a single legion, with the men doubling up in quarters. As the Gallic cavalry appeared and began to skirmish in the valley below, the Romans, by strictest orders, gave an appearance of breaking and panic flight within the walls. The legionaries began hastily to add ill-built mantlets, men hurried to and fro, Gallic scouts who crept near heard the sound of wild lament.

Ambiorix thought the game won; out of the dark a voice cried that night that Roman deserters would be received with honor; at break of day the Gauls came running disorderly up the slope, each eager to be first in the slaughter and plundering. Then the Roman trumpet sounded, the hidden legionaries leaped up and poured from the gates in a disciplined fury that nothing could withstand. The Gauls yelled and broke; the legions sheared into their disorganized mass, the cavalry rode in loose reined. Through the day there was pursuit, the Roman broadswords pouring a dark libation to the memory of Cotta and the 14th Legion; but at twilight Caesar called in his men and marched on to Cicero's camp.

He gazed in admiration at the cinders of its buildings, the patched and tumbled wall, the shattered towers and the little band who marched out to parade under the bad-tempered old Legate who never would give up. There had been five thousand of them in the beginning, a tenth of whom would parade no more, and four thousand of them had wounds from serious to desperate, mere flesh-cuts not counting. The legion received a tablet to bear forever on its eagles in memory of the great siege, the Legate as warm praise as any man ever heard from Caesar, who was an artist in appreciation.

The battle by the river and the following pursuit had ended at the ninth hour; at midnight the Remi, Rome's friends and Caesar's, raised such an outcry out beyond the barbarians round the camp of Labienus that his soldiers rushed to the wall, but a few moments later they knew the news was good. Indutiomarus and his Treveri were nowhere to be seen in the morning; they had run away to hide in the winter woods, and since corn lacked and the roads were bad Caesar felt he could make no further campaign for the present. He left Labienus where he stood; Fabius went back to the Morini, the legions of Crassus, Cicero and Trebonius were drawn in to finish the winter at Samarobriva and preparations made for a swift campaign when spring should break.

7

Theme in the Strings—Rome's spell was broke; the news spread fast across a land where "it is the custom to halt travelers by violence and not allow them to pass on till they have told some new thing." A legion down, Indutiomarus and Ambiorix free and in arms, King Tasgetius slain—the Gauls stirred chaotically toward liberty through midnight meetings in the Druid groves, brotherhoods of the dagger. Stirred—but formlessly, without set purpose or direction, for the brains were on the other side. The Druids saw, for instance, how Roman law kept the roads safe and the Germans distant and the best they could say for revolution was 'twas pity good men should die in so evil a cause. For there was justice under Rome. Marcus Cicero will write a letter of introduction for his gossip and get him a judgeship in the new province, but warns him—it will be no sinecure as in the East, the fledgling legist must hew to the line, for his sentences will be reviewed by that swift and terrible court, the Proconsul himself.

Yet still Gaul stirred and heaved that winter, inchoate and convulsive as a man in dream. A band gathered out of Armorica toward the camp of Legate Roscius when the news came from Atuactuca, then melted away unseen as evening hoarfrost when the tale of Caesar's march and Cicero's defense came through. The Senones of upper Sequana drove out their Romanizing king, Cavarinus, and refused to send corn. Ambiorix moved behind his screen of northern woods, making alliance with the remains of the Nervii, with the Atuactuci, the Menapii of the marshes, calling in German adventurous bands. Indutiomarus was gathering men round his standard; he also sought to persuade Germans across the Rhenus, but with them he had little success, the Teutons answering stoutly that they had twice made the essay and had no wish to taste the experience again. Nevertheless there was a steady filterage of outlaws and adventurous spirits, some for adventure's own sake, some through the economic necessity of the bad last harvest, northward toward the risings. In February Indutiomarus felt strong enough to move against Labienus' camp once more.

His Treveri were not a unit. Some of them had joined the Roman side and were with the Legate, forming the nucleus of a fine body of horse which he built up, but secretly, keeping them tight in camp, never a skirmish or sally, the old inexhaustible trick of pretended fear. There lay a river between his camp and that of Indutiomarus; the Gallic chief crossed daily with his men, swaggering up and own past the Roman rampart, insulting the men inside with words, hurling weapons and offal over the wall.

It went on for a week or more, or till an evening when the Gauls, having finished their daily sneer, had turned their back to the unanswering camp and were oozing confusedly away. Then the gate sprang open, the Roman cavalry bounded out into the disheveled ranks with the cheering legionaries in line and in very good spirits behind them. The Gauls had no time to turn, they could not abide the shock, there was not even a momentary battle. Labienus had told his horsemen to neglect all else for the person of Indutiomarus; in a rush they bore down the master-plotter's bodyguard, caught him at the ford and split his brain-pan open, which was the end of that Gallic rising.

Now things were outwardly quiet for the remainder of the winter, but there were many masterless men abroad and a running fire of discontents beside Ambiorix. Rude work ahead; Caesar wanted more troops. Spain was quiet, so he borrowed a veteran legion, the 1st, out of Pompey's command there, and had two new ones enrolled in south Gaul and Illyricum, the 14th and 15th. They came up through the mountains to join him at the spring council, but arrived to find he had gone from Samarobriva. With the roads still in a slush he had called in the four nearest legions and gone off on a hurricane raid through Nervian territory, burning towns and driving off cattle. The Nervii broke and submitted; Caesar returned to his base and opened the council in March, earlier than usual.

The meeting was unruly; the Treveri did not come, nor the Senones, nor Carnutes. The fection of the latter tribe was serious; they held the key of Gaul, the central plain that fed the land and contained the Druid holy of holies. Caesar adjourned the council to Lutetia, on the border of Senonan territory, and the legions set out to attend the new meeting by forced marches, but never stopped at Lutetia at all, pushing right on into Senonan territory. Acco, the leader of the Senonan troubles, had advised his people to assemble in their strong places, but the peremptory arrival of the Roman army shattered his plan in the making. He was a high man, high enough to take the blame himself and spare his people. Submission, he told them, was best. Caesar accepted it, but gave them a bitter dose to drink. The lords must attend him through the campaign with their retainers mounted as cavalry, the whole body being placed under the command of King Cavarinus, whom they had just exiled. Then the army spun sharp round on its heel toward Arduenna Wood and Ambiorix.

Labienus had remained in camp, facing the Treveri during this manoeuvre. Caesar dropped two more legions to enable the Legate to take the field against the enemies on that front and hurried on

See map
facing page 113

down the Mosa with five, spread wide in columns for a sweep, the cavalry ahead. He was heading for Menapia, the only land west of Rhenus that had never made a Roman peace, with the intent of turning back south in a long curve, cracking Ambiorix back against Labienus' legions as between the jaws of a pincer.

The Menapii took to their marshes and tussocks as when Caesar had made a first exploratory raid into their country, three years before. This time the defense failed; the Proconsul was determined to finish the thing; the legions marched straight in, laboring like ants behind strong guards of horse. The rivers were bridged, the marshes tamed with a cobweb of causeways, the Menapii mercilessly harried from their retreats, their villages burned, their flocks driven off and slaughtered for meat till they were fain to give up. In a month it was done; Caesar turned up the Rhenus just in time to meet tidings from Labienus of another victory in the east.

The Legate had played the Treveri the same old endless device no Gaul seemed ever to understand. Spies said German aid from the Ubii was coming to them; Labienus wished to fight his battle before it arrived. There was a river with steep banks between him and the enemy. He intrenched a camp, held a council of war and announced publicly, so that the news would be carried across the stream, that he feared such numbers as the Treveri had, and would march away next morning. Sure enough, the Gauls saw his column winding away like a metal snake at the appointed hour. All zeal, they dashed across the stream and ventured on a wild attack from the worst of positions, with a high-banked river at their backs. The legionaries faced round like clockwork and hit them hard in front; Labienus' numerous cavalry swung into their flanks, their line went to wreck and the battle ended in a slaughter.

Caesar turned eastward to investigate the presistent reports of

Legionary Soldier

German crossings, bridging Rhenus near where he had done so
before. He speedily found that the rumor about the Ubii was false.
They remained his friends, reporting that the Germans called in by
the Treveri had been a wandering tribe of Suebian origin from beyond
the edge of the world, and that they had gone home again when they

heard that instead of the easy loot Indutiomarus had promised them they must do battle with the Romans, whom they esteemed of more than mortal kinship.

That cleaned up all the outskirt operations and left only Ambiorix, isolated. Caesar turned into Eburonean territory with his whole force, L. Minucius Basilus going before with the cavalry on a silent swift raid, marching day and night on iron rations and without campfires, straight for the Gallic chieftain's headquarters. He missed his quarry by an eyelash but broke up the Eburonean concentration, such as it was. Caesar's spy system brought word that instead of standing in battle Ambiorix meant to make a small war of assassinations and hedge-hopping among the hills and thickets of Arduenna. He had an answer for that, too; the baggage and trains were concentrated in Sabinus' old camp at Atuactuca, with Quintus Cicero and the new 14th Legion in charge. The rest of the legions cordonned the territory and Sugambrian Germans were invited across the Rhenus to hunt down the Eburones—and ingenious and pleasing method, since it at once extinguished the rebellious tribesmen, spared the lives of the legionary soldiers and amused the Germans, who entered zestfully into the spirit of the thing for the plunder they could get.

The plan had a defect; namely, that the Germans were untutored folk, submissive to no rule but their own caprice. Two thousand of them happened to be cruising in the neighborhood of Atuactuca and the legionary baggage. Quintus Cicero had half his legion out in foraging parties that day, which was unwise of him. The wild men heard of it from a Gaul, and the antic idea possessed them of snatching the camp and its rich booty under Caesar's nose. They turned rein; the first advertisement Cicero had was a chorus of screams from the sutlers' booths outside the ramparts as the Sugambri rode among them, butchering left and right. The next moment they were at the gates and the camp was in a panic. It would have been taken but for the gallantry of a centurion, one Sextus Baculus, who leaped from a sick-bed, rallied a handful of officers as courageous as himself and with them held the portal till the high command could get things straightened out.

Five cohorts were still outside. They came back in two groups, unfortunately divided into veterans and recruits, to find the Germans whooping around the place. The veterans stolidly ployed into wedge formation and cut their way through. The recruits lost heart and head, bunched up together on top of a hill and lost nearly a cohort before the Germans let them alone. Even when they had gone there was a panic Cicero proved unable to quell—Atuactuca was a bad omen, the army must have been destroyed or the Germans would never have dared attack them, they were lost men—and only the appearance of the Proconsul himself put an end to the clamor.

The army never caught Ambiorix. He hid too well in some woodland covert of the Arduenna. But he never raised a war again, either, and it is probable that like the rest of the Eburones, he died miserably and alone of hunger that winter, for the furies Caesar had let loose wiped the tribe from the face of the earth as the tribe had wiped out the 14th Legion.

The work was done when the Proconsul quitted that part of the country for Durocortorum, where he held an extraordinary autumn council and high court of inquiry into the Senonan conspiracy that had overthrown King Cavarinus. A Roman jurist presided; Chief Acco was brought in in chains, found guilty of treason to his king and sentenced to the pain of *more maiorum,* which meant that he was stood up in an iron collar and beaten to death.

"Gaul being thus quieted, Caesar, as he had determined aforetime, set out for Italy to hold the winter assizes."

8

E Major: Full Orchestra—There was a man named Vercingetorix. He was an Arvernian, a son to that Chief Celtillus who had staked his life on winning the principate of all Gaul and lost the throw; yet himself held in honor no less for his lordly birth than for his own winsomeness of character. He had been educated by the Druids for their priesthood and was believed to be not unskilled in magic, but tall and strong and so adept with weapons that there were few to match him in any warlike exercise. Caesar had sought to purchase him to Roman service with the hope of great rewards. He refused and sat quietly at home till the winter after Acco's fall.

The young lords had much unease of spirit by that event. When they debated the matter Vercingetorix ever maintained that the condemnation under Roman law held a surety of Caesar's intention to extinguish the ancient customs of Gaul and make her a mere taxed province. Nor was it accounted the lightest of woes that the Proconsul had made these same noble gentlemen serve in the last campaign under the orders of King Cavarinus, whom they despised as a spineless ninny. They formed committee to meet with the brotherhoods of the dagger who had lain quiet since the movement of the last year aborted. The Druids lent ear—they were no longer checked in by Diviciacus—and Rome trod hard on their religious faith with prohibition of their sincere practice of sacrificing living men, without which they felt at enmity with their gods. The committees sought out the leading lords of Gaul to ask what steps were best to take. Among the rest they consulted Commios the Atrebate, who had led Caesar's cavalry in Britain. Legate Labienus got wind of the consultation and assumed it treasonable. He sent a band of centurions to take Commios, there was a bloody affray at the door of his very house, but Commios slipped away wounded and went into flat rebellion.

That gave Vercingetorix text and occasion. He began to preach that neither innocency nor conspicuous service to the Roman cause could save Gallic nobles from a Caesar bent on destroying them in the interest of his own authority. It were better to die sword in hand; yet there was no reason for death. Let Gaul unite; with one heart and one mind these invaders could be driven back through the mountains, aye, and their own land conquered by the united Gauls as it had been in the days of legend.

Gergovia was the name of the chief city of the Arverni. The lord of that town was one Gobannitio, an uncle to Vercingetorix. When he heard of his kinsman's project he pronounced it raving madness, for honest men lived long under Roman rule and revolution would only bring scoundrels to the saddle. The young lord held to his effort and raised such a storm that Gobannitio had him banished from the town.

Vercingetorix ceased his labors never a whit for that; rather he spent his considerable substance hiring a gang of vagabonds to win the rule of Gergovia by force, but before it came to an open armed clash, a long ripple of rumor rolled in tidings from the south that filled the insurgents with hope and the Romanizers with dismay. Rome was in ferment, her streets rivers of blood, the travelers said, her temples flaming to the skies and that Clodius who was Caesar's own right hand slain. A great Roman army had been defeated and destroyed somewhere beyond the seas; the conquering Republic was tottering to her fall. Caesar stood perched on the Apennines, his gaze fixed anxiously southward and his army in Gaul left without commander or orders.

——Strike now! (preached Vercingetorix) we can thrust a Gallic host between Caesar and his legions and deal with the regiments one by one as Ambiorix dealt with the 14th at Atuactuca.—— The word found favor; with his vagabonds and personal retainers Vercingetorix made a bloodless conquest of Gergovia and banished Uncle Gobannitio in his turn. At the turn of the year he summoned a council of young lords as light-valiant as himself; of all the Celts only the Aedui were unrepresented there, and the assembled chiefs chose Vercingetorix as captain-general for an universal rebellion.

He accepted the charge with the counsel that it would be useless to meet the Romans in pitched battle. Gauls could never hope to match the legionary foot. The great war (he said) must be made up of many small wars like that Ambiorix had raised, with a vast murk of mounted men hanging forever round the legions, denying them any ground but that on which they stood, choking them in a blind cobweb, destroying all food and abandoning towns before their path.

The chiefs roared huge approval of that device; they preferred riding to walking; it was more noble, and only the peasants who grubbed the soil would suffer from this form of war. The levy began at once, every tribe but the Aedui sending up its quota. Vercingetorix imposed the old stern discipline of the ancient Celts under which the last man at the mustering was tortured to death, for every blow a life taken and for every other offence an eye gouged out. The army assembled among the forests of winter. To the Carnutans, because they held the sacred grove, was given the privilege of the first blow.

Cenabum was their central town, a place of much commerce, whence the Roman traders long before Caesar's coming had kept a factory; now an army commissariat was there as *See map* *facing page 176* well, with stores of grain for the legions. At a signal the gates were opened; the vagabonds of liberty entered in, shouting "Kill! Kill!" and raced through the streets at flush of day, slaughtering everything Roman, man, woman, child or beast. By sunup it was done, the corpses thrown to dogs and the booths plundered; by the eighth hour swift messengers and men shouting from hill to hill had carried the tidings through all Celtica and Gaul was a sea of flame.

The first essential for Vercingetorix' plan was to sever Rome's army from its brain. The old Roman province of Ulterior Gaul is shaped like a reversed L. He dispatched a bold and high-born chief named Lucterius to rouse the Ruteni, who live in the angle of the L. They were to make a menace of invasion that should hold Caesar at bay in the province with the local levies. Himself Vercingetorix went north with the main cavalry force of the revolt into the land of the Bituriges, who, as clients of the Aedui, hung indecisive. Drappes, chief of the Senones, had the duty of paralyzing the legions where they lay encamped at Agedincum.

All went well for the rebels. Drappes had only a band of brigands to start with but they so thoroughly raided the corn convoys that Labienus and the legions were fixed to their base. They could not interfere. The Bituriges hesitated delicately for a week, pull devil, pull baker, then tumbled over among the insurrectionaries.

Thus stood affairs when Caesar heard the news—the Province invaded, the legions separated from their commander by a sea of flame. Rome to her fate; Gaul was the immediate necessity. He came pounding over the mountains at a pace that foundered horses, with some young recruits for escort, groping through the stinking smoke of rumor for facts on which to found a campaign. The safety of the Province was the first care; he headed for Narbo in the west, or flat part of the L, ordering the recruits out to the eastern slope of the Cebenna range and some Spanish cavalry up to Vienna on the Rhodanus, lest Vercingetorix should have the inspiration to strike down the wide valley behind him. The legions should stay where they were; he would get through to them somehow, for drawing them south meant they would have to cut their way through; and more important it meant a tacit abandonment of the conquests and an actual abandonment of Rome's truefast friends, the Remi.

At Narbo the militia were called out; with a stiffening of time-expired veterans the town was strongly garrisoned. Parties of horse were pushed forward to patrol the banks of the Tarnis river which makes the border; blockhouses with artillery covered the fords, and so strong a front was made that Chief Lucterius and his Ruteni dared not cross to try conclusions at close range.

He waited for a Roman advance. Caesar, before the arrangement was even complete, was hurrying up to where his recruit army-group stood amid the roots of the Cebenna mountains. These heights are steep at all times; now it was late winter and the steeps covered with six feet of snow, but the indefatigable Proconsul drove his little army straight through, amid incredible exertions, ice forming on helmets and greaves, men dropping from exhaustion—no matter, press on, press on, till they slid down the farther slope straight into the Arvernian homeland. Their tiny force of cavalry spread out like a fan with fire and sword. Vercingetorix, a hundred miles away, was recalled by an urgent and startling appeal for aid from his own people. He dropped the half-formed project of besieging the legions in Agedincum and came flying south. As he did so Caesar left his recruit army-group behind, picked up the Spanish cavalry he had left at Vienna and went flying north by the valley of the Arar to make contact with his main army. Young Decimus Brutus, most intelligent of the legates, was left in command in the Province, with instructions to move the few cohorts he had restlessly and fast, at no cost hazarding battle against Vercingetorix' main army.

The marching cavalrymen with Caesar looked amazed at the leader who fretted because they could not all ride as fast as he. The juncture was made, but barely made, before Vercingetorix discovered how small a force was with Decimus Brutus and came marching north again. He laid siege to Gorgobina of the Boii, that tribe out of the old Helvetian invasion who had settled as clients of the Aeduans. If he could ruin them it would be as useful as downing a legion for its effect on the Gauls and particularly on the Aeduans who still held the Roman alliance. His chances were excellent; it was still February and he in a friendly country, while Caesar was beset by difficulties of supply.

The Proconsul marched to meet him anyway with the eight veteran legions, not straight south toward Gorgobina, but southwest on Cenabum, a move that must shake Vercingetorix loose from his siege, since he would not dare leave the holy city of Gaul to be captured for the credit of his enterprise. Gallic cavalry was untrustworthy now; to cover the flanks of the marching legions a few Germans had been brought in, and recruiting agents went to the Rhenus to bring as many more as could be hired. They were to rendezvous at Agedincum, where the 14th and 15th were left in charge of the base and some new soldiers from south Gaul brigaded into a legion, the 5th, Alauda, from the lark-badge their helmets bore.

The first day's march brought Caesar to Vellaunodunum of the Senones. The gates were closed; to mask the place and pass around would further complicate the painful problem of supply-lines, to siege it would take time. Caesar ordered assaults in relays, day and night. There were none too many defenders and the constant drive kept every man within on the walls. After forty-eight hours they became too weary to care for liberty and surrendered at discretion. Legate Trebonius stayed behind with a few cohorts to disarm the prisoners while the army instantly took the road for Cenabum, moving through the great forest of the midlands with silent speed, hooded close in cavalry to prevent news of their coming.

The Carnutes had heard of Caesar before Vellaunodunum. They estimated the place would hold for weeks, and were struck dumb with horror when the legions came pouring through the forest outlets only two days after leaving it. Caesar marked the confusion in the city by unmistakable signs and held two legions under arms

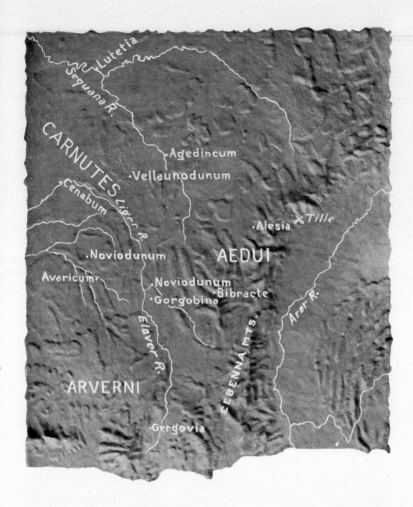

VERCINGETORIX' REVOLT

A general map to show the various points important during this campaign. The Roman Province curved around the foot of the Cebenna Mountains and westward.

when the remainder of the weary troops camped for the night. Toward midnight the wind bore a murmur and gush of movement; a cavalry patrol said the folk within were escaping to the south over the bridge that spanned the Liger. The duty legions rushed to the gates and beat them in; the sound of the trumpet roused the other troops, they grabbed up their arms and fell onto the panic-stricken Gauls. For light they fired the town; in its tortuous streets many were slain and many more captured to be given into slavery. Next morning Caesar spun eastward to face Vercingetorix, who had raised the siege of Gorgobina and turned west to save the holy city, but too late.

The armies met near the Carnutan Noviodunum, in a brush of cavalry vanguards. The Gauls were ridden down by Caesar's new German troopers, and that gave Vercingetorix so poor an estimate of his chances in a general battle that he sat still while the town was taken under his eyes, then moved off southwest to hold a diet of chiefs from the rebellious tribes.

It was shot with stormy dissensions. ——The campaign is a failure (cried the chiefs) this Caesar overbears us as always before.——

——No failure by my fault or will, (said Vercingetorix) I have told you you will never beat these Romans from behind stone walls; Caesar will eat Gaul like a dish of filberts, cracking nut by nut, if we try to hold cities, whatever their value. Burn the towns and granaries! Take to the road, rove round his flanks!——

They agreed he had foretold the fate of the cities. In the future they would follow his advice.

That night the marching Roman columns saw the horizon flush like a rose as town after town, twenty of them, were given to the torch. Yet there was one town they would not burn, the one toward which Caesar was even then marching, Avaricum of the Bituriges, the fairest city and strongest fortress in Gaul, rising like a castle from a circling net of marshes.

It could be approached from only one side, the southward, where a ramp of hill sloped up toward the walls, to end a hundred paces short in a gully like a great fosse. Above the gap's base the wall stood eighty-five feet high, with towers reaching beyond that it seemed to heaven, and the marshes round the other sides stretched too far to permit a blockade. Caesar built a ramp, earth, stones and timber piled together humble-jumble by men bearing materials through long lines of sheds roofed against burning darts with tile or hides. At the front of the ramp were mantlets; along it wheeled towers progressed slowly, a few feet a day. The labor was immense and deadly dangerous, there were forty thousand men in the town who kept up a hail from shot-weapons, day and night. Vercingetorix hovered round the skirts of the Roman army, waging his small-war, with success so good that the Aeduan corn convoys could not get through.

Grain ran out; the Romans had to slaughter cattle and live on the meat, which they considered a beastly diet, fit only for dogs and Germans. Their bellies pinched, their faces grew thin; Caesar assembled them and made a speech, saying that if they wished he would give over this siege. It was a small thing whether or no they had this town, there were other ways of winning the war; but a great thing that he have his soldiers' good will. They answered with a loud shout, crying they would never give up the siege while there was breath in them, and ran forward the more fiercely against the wall.

The towers moved in, but the wall was stout, made of logs laid endwise in rubble and earth, so that it would not burn, yet was cushioned against battering-rams; the only way of handling it was to pick the logs out with hooks and then hammer away with the ram. Daily there were sallies and savage fighting among the timbers and pits. One night the end of the ramp began to cave in, mined from within Avaricum. At the same moment watchfires broke out redly along the battlements and the Gauls came storming forth in a rally, set fire to the ramp, set fire to the sheds and almost captured the moving towers. Two legions on night duty sustained the shock; the others rose from sleep and plunged into the fighting, the sally was beaten back, but it was days before the cave-in was filled and the ramp repaired.

Vercingetorix tried diversions on the outside, tempting Caesar to attack him by shifting his camp, but when the Proconsul closed in he found the place protected by a screen of marsh and would not attack across it, since he held Avaricum secure as matters stood and a failure would waste that advantage. He turned back to the town; the walls began to go, the Roman artillery cleared the towers, and the Gauls decided to abandon the place.

Their men ranked silently in the streets one night to break away across the marshes, but the women heard of the plan and made so noisy a lamentation at being left behind that the Romans were warned of the attempt and the idea had to be dropped. Next day it rained bitterly; as evening drew on and the wall-guards took to shelter from the pelting, Caesar saw his opportunity and massed men for a surprise. Dark came early; one trumpet sounded, the soldiers dashed to the wall and up. They won a tower, another, and the entry was gained, but the Gauls were still of heart. They massed in the squares of the town in gloomy dark knots of armor under the streaming skies for one last desperate stand. Arrows began to fly; it looked like a hard street-fight of doubtful issue, but Caesar, survey-ing the scene calmly from the top of a tower, ordered back his legionaries and bade them spread around the crest of the wall. That took the heart out of the Gauls; it meant they would soon be utterly cut off. They began to melt, to run, and as they ran the Romans leaped down after them, shouting "Remember Cenabum!" Streets and gates jammed to death by suffocation, the arrows kept falling out of the dark, the Roman swords spared none and the sullen sky of morning found a bare eight hundred escaped from the bloody wreck to Vercingetorix' army.

He turned south and away, but drew strength rather than weakness from the disaster, since he had predicted towns would not hold, and henceforward he was better obeyed. The chiefs brightened up when they found their leader took the loss of Avaricum without despair. The sap of spring stirred many young adventurous warriors to join his moving bands, and Caesar faced a hostile army rebuilt, with spring just breaking around.

The Proconsul spent a week among the abundant corn-supplies of Avaricum, planning his campaign. Thus: base on Agedincum,

facing south, make a bold stroke straight into Arvernia to hammer
the Gallic main army back against the Cebenna chain in the angle
of the L and there compel it either to fight a battle or take to earth
in another fortress. His own flanks he meant to swing so far westward that the Gauls could not escape that way.

A strong plan—but before it could be put to execution there came
a messenger with the worst news in the world, which was that of
disunion to the edge of civil war among the Aedui, with two men
claiming election to their high magistracy and their state wavering
in its old alliance with Rome. Caesar instantly turned east to see to
the matter; the Aedui were his base, his connecting link with the
Province, the source of his corn supply.

He found the two chiefs, Cotus and Convictolitavis, moiled in
one of those garbled barbaric political causes where it is beyond the
wit of man to find any reason or justice on either side. Inquiry established that Cotus was technically ineligible for the magistracy;
Caesar summarily declared him disqualified, pronounced his rival
elected as the sole legal candidate, and then turned back to his war.
The Aedui were to help him with a great force of cavalry under two
of their high chiefs, Eporedorix and Virodomarus, and ten thousand
infantry to guard his supply lines. Grateful Convictolitavis swore on
his head that he would stop at nothing to benefit the man who had
awarded him the election.

But the mischief had been done; not even the Aeduan help could
compensate for the loss of time. Vercingetorix used that gap to complete the reorganization of his forces. Northward the Parisii of the
middle Sequana set on foot an army under their King, Camulogenus.
They marched against the friendly Remi, who had to be saved for
the sake of morale. Caesar split his strength; Labienus with four
legions went north to deal with the new revolt; himself south and
west with six to carry out the original plan against Vercingetorix;
the new 5th Legion remained to hold Agedincum.

The clash of the main armies came along the banks of Elaver
river, a stream swift and deep, where the Gauls had shattered the
bridges and stood to dispute a passage, doubling to and fro to meet
Caesar's moves on the opposite bank, not sure of his plan, but mean-

ing to clog his footsteps wherever he might move. The Proconsul
could find no way through, but one night he camped behind a fold
of ground and next morning sent four of his legions, grouped in
six parties with baggage sandwiched between, upstream at hot
speed. The watchful Gauls followed. As soon as they were beyond
sight the other two legions broke from cover, hastily built a bridge,
intrenched a bridgehead on the far side. It was proof against assault.
Vercingetorix recognized the fact and retreated, as the six legions,
united, came swinging across. Caesar dropped the hostages, his prisoners, war-chest and magazines back to the Aeduan Noviodunum
with the cavalry of that nation and grateful Convictolitavis on guard
and stripped down for a fast-moving campaign.

Vercingetorix' flank was turned by fast marching. He could not
get away west, north or east, and he feared being thrown back into
the foothills of the Cebenna where things might go hard with him
among the rocks, his army being mostly horsemen. As lesser evil he
chose to make a stand in Gergovia, a huge fortress
built on a mighty quadrangular rock that jutted

See map
facing page 193

twelve hundred feet straight up from the plain, with outcast beetling
spurs.

Caesar arrived before it after a five days' march and camped
southeast of the place to make a survey while a rattling cavalry
skirmish went on round the foot of the castle. On the north no
chance, only stiff precipitous terraces were there, so wooded an infantry advance would go to smash among the trees. On the east,
sheer glacis unclimbable; on the west a complex of lesser hills (now
called Risolles) connected with the fortress by a saddle, but covered
with the tents of the huge Gallic army and protected by a loose-rock
wall; on the south another flanking eminence, the White Rock, itself ending in a precipice that overhung a little stream, and reaching
a long arm back to the foot of Gergovia hill. The whole was too
wide in sweep to besiege in form with blockade and contravallation
with only six legions.

There was a Gallic outpost on the White Rock, but it was small.
Caesar recognized the rock as the key of the fortress, controlling
the garrison's inlets of food and water. He lulled them by unenterpris-

ing small cavalry fights for a few days, then in the silence of night fell on the place with two legions, threw the Gauls over the precipice and had a fortified camp run up by morning. The Gauls rushed down to break the line between the two Roman camps; Caesar promptly drew out all six legions and behind the screen of a battle-order which Vercingetorix would not attack, intrenched a com-munication-line between the two posts.

Check for the Gauls whose forage failed without the egress by the White Rock, but Caesar had little joy of his victory, since the Aeduan corn-convoys were failing to come. He sought the reason; Eporedorix gave it to him, straight from the shoulder. Grateful Con-victolitavis was a scoundrel, he had taken a bribe from Vercinge-torix and become his man, the Aeduan state was in a wild turmoil, internally warring *pro* and *contra* Rome.

Bad enough. It changed to worse with the next morning when news ran in that the ten thousand Aeduan infantry left to hold the communication lines were marching to join the enemy, crazy with rage over a lying tale Convictolitavis had given them that all the Aeduans with the Roman army had been butchered by Caesar's or-der. Caesar instantly paraded his troops, told them emergency de-manded their supremest effort, and set out on a frantic march toward the onrushing Aeduans with four legions, leaving Legate Fabius with only two to hold the lines.

The men marched half the night and half the day, twenty-five miles in bad country. Caesar gave orders to surround the ten thou-sand Aedui but not to harm a hair of their heads on pain of death. When they had been rounded up, he brought forward Eporedorix, Virodomarus and the "murdered" horsemen, safe and healthy. The Aeduan infantry, plunging from one extreme to the other, threw down their arms, burst into tears, and offered to submit to any pri-vation if Caesar would only forgive them for having assassinated the Roman officers who had been serving in their ranks a thing they had done in the first flush of resentment at Convictolitavis' tale. He gave them a gracious pardon as honest men deceived.

While he was about it a runner came from Fabius to say he was desperately beset with continuous hard assaults like Quintus Cicero the year before and he could not answer for the issue beyond the fifth hour as he had too few men for the lines. The four legions turned and went back faster than they had come, no stop for food or drink, men gasping for very breath, but they made the trenches in time, and the Gallic thousand that had been boiling round since the hour Caesar left on his march melted back angrily into a flaming red dawn. Stragglers who had been unable to keep up with the terrible pace of the march kept coming in all day.

The day had to be spent in refit and rest for the men, and two days after that, with Aeduan refugees among Vercingetorix' men in Gergovia coming down near enough to the lines to hoot at those who stood with Caesar, and every message from Bibracte telling of new troubles in the rear. Caesar must work fast. He rode out past the White Rock for a reconnaissance; to his surprise the hill of Risolles behind the wall seemed bare and he rushed forward scouts to ascertain the reason.

The report was that Vercingetorix, alarmed by the loss of the White Rock, had summoned all his force to fortify the saddle of Risolles; if that were taken Gergovia would be cut off from any source of provision rich enough for so large an army as held it.

Before day Caesar had his men in motion from the big camp down the lines to the White Rock in small parties with standards lowered so the Gauls might not spy the movement from their heights. He had a plan, a complicated, daring, dangerous plan, to cut the knot of his difficulties with battle, thus: throw the main force up the denuded heights, right through the Gallic camp as though to assault the southern face of the fortress. Vercingetorix would be forced by his own fears or the urging of the chiefs to attack the Romans as they stood on the heights; there would be a general combat and then the Roman broadswords would tell the story.

The plan had concords and variabilities, like a trill of music. At earliest day a few horsemen went out, westward down the valley, with rush and clamor, as though to make a long circle and assail Vercingetorix up the saddle of Risolles from the west. With them went the muleteers, decked out in bright new helmets that from afar made them look like more cavalry, a whole army of cavalry; behind marched a legion in order of battle. There were some woods along the stream. The legion halted there, out of sight from the town, as though in ambush for some enterprise.

The Gauls took the bait, rushing out along the saddle and its dependent hill to see what the legion might be doing. On the other wing the ten thousand Aeduans were sent forward against the lofty eastern scarp of the fortress, not to fight but to frighten. Between, the main legionary body made its rush up the hill, with Caesar holding the 10th in reserve to fling it against Vercingetorix' flank and sweep his line into rout when he attacked.

All went well, so well that it went ill. The 13th and 8th, who led the storming party, went in with a valor so outrageous that they surged over the hill wall as though it were not there, through the Gallic camp, and up against the base of the fortress itself before the Gauls had time to turn toward them.

Caesar from the White Rock saw them ramp up against it, making human pyramids to ascend, hammering at the gate with their swords, crying encouragement to one another, while women within the town, sure it was about to be taken, wailed and threw valuables from the top of the wall with pleas for mercy. The Proconsul blew a recall; across the intervening vale and above the shouting the men failed to hear it. He hurried toward the spot, followed by the 10th, but it was too late; Vercingetorix had thrown his big masses not against the 13th and 8th, but through the western gate into the town. They hurled weapons and stones down on the luckless legionaries, who had no ladders, and were beaten back with heavy loss. The Gauls began to shout then, and more of them poured round the foot of the wall to complete the rout. Caesar and the 10th barely covered the retreat and held the valley in front of the White Rock against the counterstroke that developed as soon as Vercingetorix saw Gergovia was safe.

That night there was misery in the Roman camp. The storm was a failure, the siege was a failure, they had lost a battle for the first time in Gaul. Nothing now but retreat. The Aeduan foot had begun to desert as soon as the battle was over; as the army set out on its cheerless retreat toward Agedincum, Eporedorix prayed Caesar that he too might leave "to bring the Aeduan state back to the Roman alliance."

Caesar saw through the plea, but held it safer not to show qualms. He gave the permission and the Aeduan cavalry rode away. They were next heard of at Noviodunum, where they released the hostages Caesar held for the surety of the few states and chiefs not yet in arms, released the prisoners, stole his funds, burned his grain-depots, killed his officers and threw his military machines into the river. That stroke turned the Aeduan state; grateful Convictolitavis murdered all the Romans in Bibracte, raised his standard and marched to join Vercingetorix.

The game was up; Gaul lost and the world lost, all the blood and treasure spilt in vain. Nothing now remained but to make junction with Labienus in the north and fight a way back to the defence of the Province—if, indeed, that much, for the Liger was held at all its fords by powerful forces of now hostile Aeduan horse, the Roman army penned in a narrowing triangle without provisions or scouting service, a hundred thousand triumphant enemies behind and wilderness ahead.

9

Finale Fortissimo—Agedincum stands near the headwaters of the Sequana, on the left bank. The Parisii are along the middle reaches, with their great town, Lutetia, on an island in the stream. When Labienus left Caesar he marched straight ahead down the left bank, but was halted by the marshes of the Essona, where King Camulgenus, an old man and a feeble, but very skilled in war, had taken situation. Labienus tried to slash straight through on a built causeway. The effort broke down against the king's strong front and a well arranged archery screen. But the Legate was not beaten; he spun quickly round, letting the morass that had halted his advance protect his rear, while he seized boats that carried him across the Sequana, then marched toward Lutetia down the right bank.

In the morning the Gauls saw the tail of his column moving past; when the Romans reached Lutetia they found the bridges gone and the town in flames. The same afternoon runners came in with dread-

ful news—the Bellovaci in arms and coming down with a great host
on their rear, the Aedui joined to the revolt, Caesar defeated under
the walls of Gergovia and in full retreat toward the Province, therefore the army cut off there in wildest Gaul. Labienus summoned a
general meeting of his soldiers, stating the case soberly and without
exaggeration either of optimism or despair—"and now there is no
hope but in your own courage, industry and fortitude, and so we
will to battle with them tonight."

It began to blow as the general was speaking; twilight came in
gusty with pelting hail that speedily changed to a huge storm of
wind and rain. Through the weeping dark by torchlight five cohorts
moved upstream with the boats, making much noise as though they
meant to effect a crossing above the island of the city. Five more remained in the camp opposite the island. Labienus, with three legions,
went downstream to a bend, slipped a few men across a narrow spot
in boats, surprised the guards on the far side and managed to get
his legions across.

The manoeuvre was more of a success even than Labienus intended.
Old King Camulogenus, when he heard of Romans moving upstream, Romans moving downstream and a party still in the camp,
could think of nothing but that they were trying to fly in three
parties. He split his own forces to make sure of smothering all three.
Only a small guard was set opposite the island, where crossing
would be most difficult. Half the Gallic army went hurrying upstream after the five cohorts and barges that had gone thither; the
other half, the best troops with the king in person, swooped down
on Labienus through the grey dripping dawn.

The Romans had formed line; they charged home with a cheerful
resonance that bore no trace of fear and the Gallic left cracked under
the stroke. On the right the old king led; he made a hard fight at
the river's brim against the 12th Legion, but the 7th from the other
wing swept down the Gallic line, surrounded the Parisii and cut
them down to the last man. Camulogenus was among the slain, and
when the parties that had gone up river came back in disorderly
haste, too late, they likewise went to smash.

Labienus rested his victorious troops for one night only, then marched fast for Agedincum, where he picked up the army trains, 5th Legion and German recruits for the cavalry and found—blessed news!—that Caesar's defeat was not as bad as first reports had made it. The Proconsul had made a long, exhausting march on short rations, but escaped from the trap in which the Gauls held him by forcing a passage of the Liger at a spot they never imagined possible

Vercingetorix

—a half-ford where water stood to men's breasts. The cavalry formed a line above the ford to break the current, another below it to catch men swept from their feet; the legionaries toiled through, holding their packs overhead, and the two forces made junction three days' march from Agedincum.

The Germans were at hand to the number of four thousand, powerful men with vacant faces who would follow the devil to hell for pay, but their horses were small Transrhenane ponies, no use against raw-boned Gallic cobs in a shock. Caesar made his officers go afoot and took the horses from the baggage carts to mount them. He could do without baggage, but horsemen he must have if he were to make the long retreat through a country infested with enemy cavalry and yet arrive in shape to save the Province.

For that was his problem now. Vercingetorix, with all Gaul at his command but the Remi and the tribes made tributary to them

(Lingones, Suessiones, Treveri) was swinging from his Fabian system to an energetic offensive into the old Roman borderland beyond the Arar river. He held a great diet at Bibracte. The Aedui claimed the leadership of the united armies of Gaul, as the largest nation and the one whose reinforcement had turned the scale of war. It was refused them; they looked sour over it, and had to be consoled. Vercingetorix mollified them by assigning to their levies the task of most profit—ten thousand men to harry the borders of the Roman province and to rouse the peoples of Gallic race who lived there. The peoples of the western Cebenna were to cross the mountains during the summer and strike into the angle of the L; Vercingetorix himself would deal with Caesar.

Men in any number to the hundreds of thousands were ready to follow him, but he remembered the failure of the Belgic alliance through inability to provide food for a large army and took a force more light and handy. Every man of the 80,000 foot was a picked man, the 15,000 cavalry were nobles odal-born, the choice and pride of Gaul, a regiment of officers.

The new method of fighting was to be a bolder variation on the old—hang round the Roman column as it went marching toward the Province holding every defensible position with the foot, forcing Caesar to deploy and manoeuvre daily on short rations, wearing out his troops; peck at the column with swift cavalry strokes here and there, chip off bits of it, make the long march a Via Dolorosa, a retreat from Atuactuca on the grandest scale. The plan needed a base of operations from which the Gallic army could be fed. There was just such a base in the land of the Mandubii, a clientfolk of the Aeduans—Alesia, a mesa-stronghold, a pocket Gergovia. Vercingetorix had it fortified and provisioned, then sallied out just as Caesar took up his march, to make the Gallic horse ride down the Roman wolf forever and a day.

Caesar had a kinsman named Lucius Caesar. He had been made Legate and officer of the Province when he left it behind in the winter. Lucius raised twenty-two cohorts of recruits; they held the line of the Arar against the Aeduan movements, but things were going badly farther south along the Cebenna front and Lucius sent up a message to Julius for help.

The message arrived just as the Proconsul was setting out on the great retreat, with each legion in the column followed by the clumsy train that bore its food, since no dependence could be placed on living off the country. Vercingetorix had the march scouted, saw the long ribbon of men and wagons moving slowly down the vale of a little river (today called the Tille) and determined to strike it a heavy blow in that close strait. He addressed his noble horsemen in a fashion that made them take fire; with a great shout they swore together that they would ride twice through the Roman ranks or never look on home again. The Gallic foot were drawn up on a hill in support; another hill concealed them from the view of the Romans so the cavalry attack would come as a surprise. Vercingetorix trotted slowly down past the shouting tribesmen at the head of his squadrons, rode up the reverse slope, then launched himself and his men like arrows against the Roman array.

The light cavalry screen round the head of Caesar's column blew away like smoke. The legionary soldiers had just time to halt and form hollow square, baggage inside, stern set faces under the round helmets, incurious fatalistic eyes fixed on the yelling thousands careering round them. Last stand!

Last stand; but no flinching. The Gauls swept past and back again, swinging long swords from the saddle at the men below. There they stood in hopeless isolated valor, hoping for a miracle. Along the wings the Germans bore up against the storm, holding the sky suspended on their broad shoulders and stupid heads; if they went the army went and Caesar was lost and perhaps Rome itself.

The Germans held. They did more, they crept a tiny advance. Caesar, looking on, objective as ever, noted how the Gauls on his right began to shake under the blows of the Teutons. A little eminence looked down a low grade to the battlefield on that side. He ordered the Germans through to the crest. They massed, they broke through, they made it, turned and came thundering down in a headlong gallop; the whole left wing of Gallic cavalry tattered out and spread before their stroke. The Proconsul swung up his arm, the legions abandoned baggage and formation, and with clenched teeth launched a desperate charge, infantry attacking cavalry in an incredible reversal of the laws of war that the courage of Gallic nobles could not withstand. The whole Gallic line went to pieces; the whole Roman line followed, fast and grim. Eporedorix the Aeduan was taken, Cotus was taken, hundreds were slain, the rest went pouring in onto the Gallic foot and carried that too away into a retreat that became flight as night closed down and the Germans rode into the fugitives with the legions hot behind.

Nor did night check that pursuit, nor anything. Caesar, with a sudden hope of ultimate victory dancing before his eyes, dropped the baggage, rested his men only for relays of an hour or two, then flung them into the pursuit again. They marched like madmen, pausing only to fight down what resistance the rearguards offered. It went on for a day and a night and a day, thirty-six hours. Vercingetorix had no chance to build up a rally, no chance to choose his route; he was driven irresistibly back toward Alesia, his base. He reached it at the second twilight; before the evening meal Roman campfires began to leap from the darkness round the foot of the fortress-mountain.

When he looked from the battlements next morning the whole eleven-mile circuit round the base of Alesia was covered with the little men from the south, working like ants. With a shock of horror the captain-general of the Gauls realized they were shutting him in for a siege. It could never be borne; the town held the entire baronage and leadership of Gaul, without which the populace were so many masses of dough to be baked into whatever form of cake Caesar might design.

There is an open plain, three miles wide, west of the fortress, leading out and away by a broad valley. Toward noon Vercingetorix See map facing page 208 rallied his whole strength of cavalry and sent them to the spot to smash the Roman lines before they could form. Caesar had his Spanish horse covering the construction work on this side; the Gauls drove into them with a will, and beat them back. The legionaries had to stop labor and form an infantry line, but before Vercingetorix could go through to strike the foot, Caesar put in the invincible Germans. The Gauls were beat; they broke, they galloped out of the struggle, they lost many a head as they tried to get in first through the narrow gates of Alesia with the Germans whooping and striking them down from behind. Next morning, when Vercingetorix looked forth again, there were redoubts all round the town; the indefatigable legionaries were already beginning to dig long connecting lines of trench to join up the posts.

The Gallic chief summoned his brother leaders to a council. ——Break through in the night tonight (he said) as many as can make it on horseback. Tomorrow will be too late. Cry a rescue; rouse all Gaul, in its thousands and hundreds of thousands, for one supreme effort. If these eighty thousand here, the picked men of our race, are captured, the spirit of Gaul will be captured with them and we shall never be free.——

One by one the chiefs made choice whether they would go or stay; those who were to leave rode out the gates in phantom bands with muffled hooves, out and away through gaps in the closing teeth of steel. They had a month; Vercingetorix estimated the corn in the city would serve his men that long on half-rations. Next morning he had the grain all brought to headquarters and stored there for issue under his own superintendency. Across the long neck of land that slanted up to the stronghold from the east he let build a wall of loose stones, double crotchetted at the ends, to guard against an escalade on that side, where alone it would be practicable. On all other fronts Alesia would be proof against assault by the huge scarp of its situation.

Caesar had the news of the escape of the chiefs from deserters the next morning. Already he was trying the incredible task of shutting in well over 80,000 men with few over 50,000, and an eleven-mile circuit to cover. The riding of the ghost-cavalry meant he would have Jupiter alone knew how many thousands more on his back.

Skill must do the work of strength. Engineer Balbus was in Rome; himself with Mamurra must trace the parallels and see them dug, a giant task, for Alesia was no isolated peak, but sheared up from the heart of a bowl of jagged hills like a lion's tongue between his fangs. North and south of the fortress two little streams coursed westward past—Lutosa on the north, Osera on the south—emptying both into the River Brenne, which splits the plain of the cavalry battle midway. South of Osera is a tall, three-pronged hill—Flavigny today; on it were placed two infantry camps fully fortified, one of them the headquarters camp. Northeast of the fortress is another three-pronged mountain—today Bussy; it received a third infantry camp. Northwest a higher, steeper, longer spur, Mount Rea; at its foot went another camp for infantry. Three cavalry camps spaced across the western plain from Mount Rea to Flavigny; another shut the gap between Rea and Bussy. All round the circle and among these camps were *castella,* petty castles, redoubts, twenty-three of them, built stout and furnished with artillery. Inside the redoubt line, close to the Osera on the south, on the bank of the Lutosa on the north, swinging across the low plain on the west, wherever possible filled with water from the streams, ran the line of ditch that had frightened Vercingetorix, eleven miles of it. Above it towered a palisaded rampart; every eighty feet was a three-storied tower.

Inside the main lines another trench, twenty feet wide, twenty feet deep, hugged the foot of Alesia's spurs on the west to slow up sallies on that side, where alone a large body of men could rush the lines. This would keep the garrison in, but not the relievers out. A second rampart was run round the outside of the camp line, sweeping up the summits of Flavigny and Bussy, across the jutting promontory of Mount Rea and along the western plain, fourteen miles in circuit with the same elaborate furniture of ramparts and towers.

The labor was enormous and few men could be spared to do it, for the Gauls sallied forth in the energy of despair, time after time, so there was daily hard fighting along some part of the circle, a constant whirr of arrows and clash of steel all round the beleaguered fortress. In the Roman lines men ate where they stood, their weapons in their hands, slept on their feet like horses, leaning against catapults in the towers, or woke to the ring of metal and drove javelins into the torchlit dark with numbed fingers.

Yet they persevered. The line was made good, it was completed all round, inside and out, and when it was completed, tireless Caesar was not yet satisfied, but must double the ditch across the western

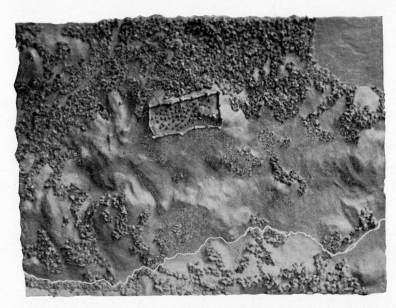

THE SIEGE OF GERGOVIA

In the upper illustration the north is at the top. North and northeast of the city are visible the wooded heights and marsh which prevented operations against it on that side. Caesar established his camp on the hill at the extreme east and ran his siege lines from that point to the White Rock, as shown in the lower illustration. The saddle of Risolles is visible immediately at the west of the city; along this saddle and on the relatively steep but open ground just west and south of the city the Gallic army was encamped, and the attempted storm took place across the slope at the south of the town. Lower down, southwest of Gergovia, and connected with the saddle of Risolles is visible the height around which Caesar's feinting force circled to attract the Gauls' attention.

plain, and when that was done, add further obstructions to the whole circle, inside the ditches toward Alesia, outside them where they crossed field and hill in the lines of circumvallation.

Five rows of shallow trenches went in on both faces, filled with tree-tops whose butts had been sunk in the ground and whose branches had been sharpened, pointing up. The men called them *cippi,* a soldier's pun, for *cippus* is equally a tombstone or a mile-stone. These tree-branches soon bore a dreadful fruit of dead men, as the Gauls stormed into them in their sallies and were impaled on the sharp points. Nor was this enough; inside the cippi, conical pits were dug, five feet deep, at the bottom of each a deadly, long impal-ing stake, and then the whole covered with branches and light earth so that men in a charge would tread through and stick themselves on the stakes before they could gain their feet. The men called these "lilies." Nor was this enough; the blacksmiths in the Roman camps fashioned monster fishhooks of iron to Caesar's prescription; inside the row of lilies toward Alesia, outside it toward the relieving army, the ground was sown thick with these devices, each in its little pit, fixed to a stake of its own so that the man caught by one would be held painfully fast. The soldiers called these "stimulators."

And now it was six weeks since the day when Vercingetorix rode down into the Vale of Tille to crush the beaten Roman. The shoe was pinching in Alesia; Chief Cirtognatus of the Arverni proposed they butcher and eat the townsfolk after the custom of the ancient Gauls with useless mouths in a siege. The council agreed, but Ver-cingetorix said no, they could not afford to do that for the credit of the revolution. As a compromise the townsfolk were driven out to the Roman lines. They came wailing up to the rampart, men and women staggering with hunger, begging to be body-slaves, to do anything for food, but the Romans would not receive them either, food was as short in their camp, and the helpless folk were driven back up the hill of despair to the men who had rejected them.

And now it was six weeks and a day and the mountain southwest beyond the plain was black with the relieving army. They had a quarter of a million men, eight thousand of them cavalry, under the leadership of Commios the Atrebate. Every tribe had sent its quota, even the Helvetians of the Alps, silent since Caesar's first campaign. The generals were Vercassivellaunus of the Arverni, a cousin to Vercingetorix, and Eporedorix the Aeduan (how had he escaped? we do not know); they had a committee of noble Gauls to aid them, not the best of arrangements in military matters, but none of the tribes would trust any other with full command.

As they drew near down the long slope, they raised a universal shout. The besieged in Alesia set up an answering cheer and came running toward the lines that crossed the western plain while Commios led his cavalry down in instant attack. Along their ramparts the Romans stood to arms, the long-range catapults on the castella-roofs began to open up, and from the cavalry camps, Caesar's horse streamed out to meet charge with charge. In a few minutes the plain was a boiling tumult of riders. Clever Commios, with a memory of Britain in his mind, had supported his horse with a force of archery. The Roman cavalry were worsted and began to break up, the battle front swayed back toward the siege-lines. For the sake of morale Caesar dared not lose this first encounter. He hurried more men from the camp on the north, rallied the unconquerable Germans, and ploying them into one solid column, hurled them back into the fray. Commios had his men all in, with no reserve to meet a new impact; the Germans burst through, rode down the archers, cut them to pieces and sent the vanguard of the relieving army reeling back in prone rout. First blood!

That night the Gauls were quiet but for bickering archery skirmishes, the next day likewise, but spent their time in making a huge quantity of fascines to bridge the ditches, mural hooks and ladders for the palisades. At midnight they came down silently from their mountain top; raised a simultaneous loud yell to advertise Vercingetorix, and dashed for the rampart under a cloud of stones and arrows. Through the dark the Roman trumpets sounded; reinforcements dashed down the line from Mount Rea and Flavigny and a tumbling struggle began, the bloodier because of the dark which brought stones and arrows whirling down out of nowhere and rendered shields useless.

On the outside face the relievers stumbled into the stimulators, lilies and cippi, losing heavily among the death-traps they could not see nor avoid for the press behind. The catapults cut heavily into their packed masses; when they rushed the wall the Romans smothered them under volleys of heavy pikes or clove the heads of the few who struggled up through ditch and obstruction to the battlements. Legate Antonius was the heart of the defense, a big man, all hairy and rough, who shouted furious curses as he brandished a sword like any private in the thick of the combat, yet kept an eye to note every development and appeared with reinforcements for every emergency.

The attack from inside was a failure; Vercingetorix spent the precious time getting across the twenty-foot ditch and then the moat. His stroke fell strongest only with the first light of day, when the relievers, soundly beaten now and fearing a cavalry charge into their flanks from the camps where bonfires showed the Germans astir, had begun to flow back. Full day shone; Caesar, from Flavigny, ordered a column into the field as though for a counterstroke. The Gauls let go and foot-slogged dejectedly back to camp and castle.

All three armies were eating themselves to death, the relievers fastest, and their men beginning to mope for ill-success; whatever they were to do must be done quickly. Vercassivellaunus made the new plan and led the new attack. It was to be a surprise along the slope of Mount Rea where the lines were weakest and the slope lend momentum to assault—at high noon when bright light would befriend the bigger battalions—with 60,000 picked men in the spearhead of the attack—with Commios the Atrebate leading a cavalry advance across the western plain supported by the rest of the army—with careful preparation in fascines and baskets of earth to smother Caesar's wolf-traps. The 60,000 marched by night to concealment in the gullies behind Rea's hill, paused there for a long rest, a good meal and an exordium from the Druid witch-doctors.

Vercassivellaunus gave the signal; the 60,000 stood up and shouted, then rushed down the slope toward the Roman lines. Commios in the plain below swung forward with his cavalry and the remaining foot. Vercingetorix, from the fortress gates, caught the flicker of movement along the skyline. He had been waiting for something like that and had his 80,000 massed and ready. Now the gates were thrown open and they came streaming out to strike the lines along Mount Rea on the inside as Vercassivellaunus hit them from outside. The crisis.

Vercingetorix was not caught by the twenty-foot ditch this time; had told off sappers to bridge it. They had materials ready, in a trice they filled it up and his thousands came rushing at the rampart. The front rank of Vercassivellaunus' men threw fascines and dirt on the stakes and stimulators, tore down the cippi, and in a few minutes had had a causeway right up to the rampart, and locking shields overhead hurtled against it in a flying wedge, while their comrades from behind hurled missiles over their heads into the defenders. Caesar, watching from the crest of Flavigny, saw his men holding on both fronts at once, a nerve-racking experience for them, for they could hear a roar of battle from their rear and only wonder whether the men who covered their backs would stand firm.

Antonius was locked in a struggle of his own in the lines across the western plain; the cavalry were hotly engaged with Commios— no help from them. The Proconsul ordered Labienus in from the camp on Bussy with six cohorts ——Hold as long as you can (he said); if overpowered at the lines, make a sally and fight it out in the open with the shortsword—— then rode himself to the spot, calling on the men by name. They responded, they fought inspired; Vercingetorix' assault was beaten off at the inner wall, but he turned his forces and flung their full weight against Flavigny in a grand climacteric, right across the Osera under such a flight of missiles that the Roman artillerymen were driven from their towers, and with such a fury of assault that the nearest wall was torn down and the Gauls burst right into the lines.

Caesar turned back; Decimus Brutus and six cohorts were drawn out of the Mount Rea battle and sent to hold Flavigny, then Legate Fabius with seven more, but still the Gauls came on, and the Proconsul had to drive into the battle with some of Antonius' men before the point could be held and Vercingetorix driven out. It was a nightmare; no sooner had the tide against Flavigny ebbed a trifle than a messenger came from Labienus. He was again hard pressed, the soldiers' missiles were all exhausted; they were fighting now with the sword against Gauls in front while sheets of arrows dropped out of the sky on them. Labienus had let the redoubts go, called in every man for the defense of the Mount Rea camp and was not sure he could hold that.

There was only one force left unengaged, the cavalry in the north camp between Bussy and Mount Rea; Caesar sent them in a frantic uphill charge into the flank of Vercassivellaunus' attack, and himself galloped down the lines again into the thick of the Mount Rea fighting. He arrived just as Labienus made his sally, no more holding the lines now, make it a field battle as the last chance. The weary legionaries caught sight of Caesar's scarlet robe blown behind him like a banner, lifted once more their battle-shout and charged home with unexampled fervor; at the same moment the big Germans came blown but unexpected against the Gallic flank. It broke; Vercassivellaunus, in the front of the battle, cheered his men on to hold up, but their supports were gone, man for man they were no match for the Romans with Caesar's fiery drive behind, for a few minutes only they bore the double blows, then the hope of Gaul went to wreck on the hillside and when the Romans looked round from their battered lines they could see nothing but enemies flying in every direction.

It was twilight; the hard game had lasted a good seven hours. Caesar let loose the Germans onto the skirts of the flying relievers—no need for cavalry in his camp now, his lines were proof against anything that remained—and moved slowly over the battlefield in the dark with his clerks, taking count. Of the 60,000 picked men most were slain; seventy-four tribal standards, the sacred totems of the Gauls, had been left on the field, Vercassivellaunus was a prisoner, the other chiefs down—glory enough for one day.

Next morning the Proconsul sat on the seat of judgment in his praesidium, issuing rewards for valor. There came a shouting that died to a rumor of sound. The soldiers who had been standing round fell back to right and left with the instinctive dramaturgy of Latins, and down the lane they formed, riding alone and without arms, head held high, glittering with gold, came Vercingetorix. He rode to the foot of the judgment seat, made his horse do a caracole, then leaped off and knelt in the dust at Caesar's feet without a word.

Gaul was conquered.

"Caesar now returned to the country of the Aedui and recovered the rule of that state, and the Arverni sent deputies to him there to make their submission. The legions were sent in to winter quarters. He himself spent the season at Bibracte. When the dispatches of the campaign were published in Rome a public thanksgiving of twenty days was voted."

HEARTBEAT; HEARTBREAK

Julius Caesar

The fiction writer is hampered by the necessarily unchanging characters of his characters; for fear of inconsistency he dare not imitate life to the extent of making personality the most unstable of natural phenomena. It is impossible, for instance, to conceive an invented Julius Caesar, including all the contradictions, the radical changes in idea and thought process that took place in the actual Caesar during his conquest of Gaul. The tremendous tumult of Vercingetorix' rising was but the prototype and shadow of an inner ferment; its projection, as it were, into the objective world. During those years his ivory tower of aestheticism came down with a crash, plunging him into a raging sea of uncertainties through a night starless with tempest.

He had been ambitious before Gaul, but with the romanesque, undirected ambition of youth (one can still be a youth at 40) to "do something worth remembering." The governorship in Spain had left him with a hint that ambition might drink deep of military renown. But the early experience of the Gallic war, the battles of the Helvetians and Germans, soon surfeited Caesar's ambition with this type of glory. He was an engineer and an aesthete; the sight of dead men offended his sense of economy of effort—so many years to make these machines useful to the world and there they lie, smashed beyond redemption.

And Caesar had not a trace of the cruelty on which so many great military reputations are founded. He had not even the normal Roman quantum of cruelty; at the gladiatorial shows which he attended by social necessity he masked a distaste for the spectacle by immersing himself in writing letters (it was made a cause of complaint against him as womanish and finicking), and he never attended an execution if he could avoid it. Finally, the excitement of war, of danger, of battle, had so little appeal for him that it failed to excite him at all. He never plunged into a fight, sword in hand, like Legate Antonius; when he plunged in at all it was, as at the battle of the Sabis or at Alesia, with only a shield and his commander's cloak, a thought-out movement performed for the effect it would have on the soldiers, not to be construed as an enthusiasm. Every observer noted that he was always the coolest man in a battle; the reason was that the battle left him cold, one more repetition of an experience long since drained of emotional value. It was held a thing incredible that Caesar conducted one battle (the ancients do not say which) from his tent, hearing reports and issuing orders while he caught up on his correspondence in the intervals. There is nothing astonishing in it, nor was it a piece of delicate exhibitionism; it was simply the act of a man more interested in letters than in fighting.

It takes a genuine affection for any art for a man to become expert in it, and his dislike of war as an art-form is the most probable reason why Julius Caesar, to whom all other arts were one, never became great as a soldier. This statement has an odd ring to a generation accustomed to thinking of Julius Caesar as one of the greatest soldiers who ever lived, but it is simply the truth. He was never a great soldier, he was not even a good soldier, in the technical sense. His strategy was bold, but hackneyed and obvious; his tactics positively infantile, consisting of nothing but placing his army in contact with the enemy on reasonably good ground under reasonably good conditions and letting Roman discipline do the rest. The single device he employed in Gaul was the time-worn ruse of pretended fear. He handled cavalry like every amateur captain, timorously, using it only for scouting and pursuit, the one exception being in the Vale of Tille, where a real battle charge was forced upon him. He got himself surprised again and again in situations where only Roman discipline and his own cool head saved him (at the Sabis, by Ariovistus, in the Vale of Tille), which is something that almost never happens to a good commander. Most indicative of all, he avoided battle rather than seeking it, where your true captain, your man who delights in the art military, is forever building up to the climax of a great swinging battle that will end the war. In all the nine years in Gaul there were only three open-field battles—with Ariovistus, with the Helvetians, at the Sabis—only one of the three provoked by Caesar, and that one at the beginning of the war.

How then did he achieve military results that have been the admiration of soldiers for twenty centuries? He achieved them because he was a great soldier at every point where military life impinges upon civil, or rather political life. Being a good civil engineer and architect enough to make a large plan and see it largely carried through, he was doing no more than apply acquired knowledge to a variant on a familiar problem when he undertook military engineering. His scouting service was poor, for scouting is a matter of military technique, but his espionage service, which is the securing of information undertaken from the political and psychological side, was unrivaled in history. He always knew the enemy's strength, what they intended to do and when they intended to do it, and he usually knew these things by information straight from the opposing general's tent. As he kept his own plans locked in his skull, not even trusting lieutenants as able as Labienus or as devoted as Balbus, this gave him an initial advantage of the first order.

Professional soldiers call the business of feeding their men "logistics" and treat it as a mysterious business divorced from "higher" military considerations. It would be unjust to blame them for the attitude, since the best professional soldiers are devotees of nervous excitement, who find counting boxes and bales a bore. But Caesar found nervous excitement wearisome and thought logistics a matter of elementary necessity, not unlike that of keeping up the corn dole for the voting populace of Rome. The whole Vercingetorix campaign revolved on the food question as on a pivot; it was lack of provender that brought down the huge forces of the Gauls, and we find the Proconsul offering to abandon the siege of Avaricum that his men might fight on full bellies or marching back to the Province for rations.

Hardly any professional soldier would so cheerfully have sacrificed his precious plan of campaign to the full dinner pail, yet it is not surprising in Caesar, who knew nineteen hundred years before Napoleon that "in war the moral is to the material as four is to one", and that the fulfillment of the elementary necessity of food is the foundation of *morale*. And of all Caesar's excellences as a leader his attention to *morale* was perhaps the greatest. No officer was ever more beloved by the rank and file, just as no politician was ever more frantically applauded by the rank and file of the populace—and the method of attracting devotion was in each case basically the same. Superficially it was the old trick of remembering each man's name and something about him and showing an interest in each man's physical well-being. Yet such a trick is effective only when there is sincerity behind it, an intelligent interest in people for their own sake.

Yet this is not all, it cannot be all. Men have taken such qualities into war before and since and have not been numbered among war's supreme masters. L. Atilius Regulus had most of these qualities and ended up in a Carthaginian torture chamber; Cornelius Sulla had most of them and had to bring in Pompey to fight his battles. There was something more, the thing that made friends and enemies and even Caesar himself believe in "Caesar's Fortune", the mysterious emanation that led his opponents to pile blunder on blunder when they faced him in the field. King Ariovistus was a good captain but let Caesar catch him in a battle just when he did not want to fight one; King Cassivellaunus was a master of guerilla war, but abandoned the method he knew best for the defence of a fortified position, which he knew least; Vercingetorix was the ablest military man Gaul ever produced, he spent a winter warning the Gauls against being caught in besieged towns, yet was himself trapped in a siege; Ambiorix—no matter, all the campaigns are variants on the same theme, nobody could fight Caesar without making fatal mistakes.

The fact is that not even Caesar recognized the strength of his method. He was, in the language of the prize-ring, strictly a counter-puncher. He brought his army into the presence of the enemy and stood still. The mere fact that he was there produced an intolerable psychological pressure. The opponent was bound to move, to lash out at this menacing presence, and whatever move he made would leave some opening, for in war as in the prize-ring a movement to strike unfits one momentarily for defense. Whatever movement the enemy made Caesar instantly turned into a fatal mistake by throwing the whole weight of his well drilled, fast-moving army into the opening.

The difficulties of this method are two; to recognize the opening and to trust one's whole strength in the counterstroke, holding nothing back. Both demand intelligence and cool headedness, the abstract point of view. No, Caesar was not a great captain, the method is not that of a military man, with reserves and lines of retreat, a system which can be followed—but rather the application to war of a prodigious intelligence, an intelligence not indeed infinite, but a reflection of infinity with only those minor refractory defects which separate the reflection from the original. An intelligence possessing that calm confidence in its own ability to detect any slightest faltering from perfection which is the attribute of infinity.

And this calm confidence, this arrogant optimism, lies at the base both of the difficulties Caesar encountered and of his resolution of them. He embarked upon the conquest of a nation of some millions with barely 50,000 men. He was careless about his marches, careless about his cavalry, about the assignment of his legates. Yet no surprise could ever really surprise him, for the value of surprise in war lies in its effect on the mind, and his mind was never affected. He considered every problem in that unearthly blue light of rationalism in which all difficulties sink to insignificance. We feel him never so out of character as when yielding to the impulses that beset ordinary mortals, as when he swore vengeance for the massacre of the 14th or when he ordered the extinction of the Usipetes and Tencteri. Even so, it is difficult to say that impulse had not ceased and calculation begun—was he playing on the morale of his own troops when he cried out in wild rage over the fall of the 14th? on the morale of the German people when he ordered the massacre?

With such an intellectual equipment it is astonishing that anything ever stirred the man. The picture furnished by the Gallic campaign and by the Pompeia-Clodius episode is that of a thinking machine from whose makeup the emotions have been deleted, or in which they have been sublimated to furnish motive power for exercises in intellection. Yet the picture furnished by the Gallic campaign is not the whole picture, it includes an indigestible element, the explosion of grief and anger after Atuactuca. The picture furnished by the Pompeia-Clodius affair is not the whole picture, it does not include the earlier Caesar who stepped back from the threshold of a great career to fly to the Greek sea with the girl he loved, nor even the Caesar who dedicated a book to Cicero. It is all Caius-Jack, not Julius.

And it is the existence of these other avatars that explains the spiritual turmoil, the frightful mental pressure under which he labored during the last years of the Gallic campaign. For optimism, Caesar's type of optimism is rooted ultimately in a confidence of the inherent reasonableness, honesty and ability of the human race or (in terms a Roman would understand) the justice of the Fates. Men and Fates had dealt hardly with Caesar. He gave the Gauls a regime which insured them—all of them but the unbridled young nobles— more comfort and more self-government than they had ever enjoyed, yet they went careering off in the train of the first flibbertigibbet adventurer who appeared. The rising was a blow; still Caesar was patient with the lower orders in it, he could forgive them the more easily as honest men ill-led. The defection of Commios and the stupidity of Labienus in sending an armed guard after him were harder to bear. Both men were leaders, whose business it was to think. Yet Caesar could and did forgive even this. He was loyal to his friends as he expected loyalty from them; Labienus was not only pardoned but assured of the regency of Gaul when it should come time for his chief to return to Rome.

In fact, the whole Gallic uprising was liquidated and the conquest assured by a general amnesty after the capture of Alesia. The soldiers each got one captive to be sold or kept as personal slave (they deserved no less for their efforts) but these slaves were carefully chosen from the Carnutans who had taken part in the Cenabum massacre. Neither Aedui nor Arverni received the slightest punishment; even those taken in arms at Alesia were fed, clothed and sent home to wonder over the generosity of a conqueror who violated all the then known laws of war in the interest of mercy. The people of Gaul as a whole found the Roman yoke lighter than before the great rebellion. The Proconsul reserved his punishments not for the men who fought wars against him, but for the men who fomented them, for the thinkers who should have known better. Vercingetorix and Vercassivellaunus went to Rome in chains, there to be executed— strong men, noble men, but not good men, who had sold their abilities to a fatal cause and led the poor dupes of their eloquence to a ruin which Caesar turned back on the heads of its authors.

After this there were no more revolts in Gaul, not ever. The embers of Vercingetorix' war persisted for a year among the Bellovaci who, with characteristic Gallic particularism, had refused to come to the relief of Alesia, declaring they were a free people and would fight Caesar in their own way. They were easily crushed; and so was the minor trouble round Uxellodonum in the south, where Drappes, the bandit-chief who had cramped Labienus in the first months of the bigger rebellion, gathered the refuse of the wars round a hill castle for a career of organized brigandage.

Gaul was conquered—not merely in a military sense, for the spirit of the Gauls remained so little broken that under Roman leadership and without the aid of the legions they thenceforward did what they had never done before, beat off every attempt the savage Germans made to burst their frontiers. It was a conquest begun with the sword, for the Gauls would understand no other argument, but it cannot be too much emphasized that the true conquest was not military, not achieved at Alesia, not by Caesar the soldier, but of the mind and heart, so that when the Proconsul left their country they quarreled over which should ride under the standard of the man who had less subjugated them than united their free spirits under his presidency.

Yet the success of the great enterprise only threw into sharper relief the failure of the other achievements to which it was subsidiary. Caesar's heart remained in Rome—and now these four years he had been forced to sit idly by, watching as from beyond death, while the brave new world he had built there collapsed into a hell's twilight of contending greeds. The conference of Luca had left the triumvirate in the saddle, with such scoundrels as Clodius and Milo outside the law, but it could not quench the determination of the old Senatorial aristocrats to see the world in flames rather than yield an inch of their hoarded privilege.

2

For the first year, indeed, there had been that somnolence "of senile decay" which Cicero had observed from his villa, only faintly punctuated by certain bitter crawings against "the Dynasts" from sweet poetic voices. Poets of the age before printing were always conservative in politics; they could exist only in societies where accumulations of unearned funds were diverted to provide them with an easy way of life in return for the useless beauties they created. There was in Caesar's radicalism, with its ceaseless demand for strained effort, something particularly ant-like and horrifying to the sweet singers. They resented his existence, it was an embodiment of the energy they despised.

Beside, Clodia was the pivot on whom the literary world revolved just then; she and her brother were intensely bitter against the triumvirate since the Luca conference had cut away the pedestal from which Clodius sought to school Rome to his own wild humor. Catullus and Calvus, greatest of their day, were her lovers; she urged them on to satires of unpoetic viciousness as they reclined on the dining benches under the blue skies of the Gulf, drinking Opimian sweet wine or fumbling delicately with the meat of an ortolan's breast while Caesar's shield bore the shock of Gallic spears that they might live. "Every man's woman and every woman's man," cried one and they laughed, and Catullus wrote a poem which (complained Caesar) "has marked my name with an indelible stain" and read it aloud amid drunken applause while naked slave-girls threw rose-petals.

Perhaps this lay near the root of the tree of agony on which Caesar was crucified in those years, that he had given the best of his life and mind to art and art turned on him as a Philistine materialist. Perhaps rather the dawning realization that "Caesar's Fortune", that invisible intimate genius in which he had placed his hope of a life without pain was a myth. For the Forum soothsayer spoke true when they said Caesar's luck was out. The success of the Luca conference dazzled over, but only temporarily, the fact that whatever aid Caesar had received without himself could be counted on no longer.

The message announcing his mother's death found him at the shore as he embarked for the first adventure to Britain, and the blow it brought is not to be measured on any facile basis of immediate reaction. It struck too deep for that, the reaction would come slowly, for the bond between mother and son was deeper than the masculine-conscious ancients tell us. Old Gorgon she might appear to others; Caesar found in her a quality of mind overcoming heart, or better abetting heart in heart's determination not to let temporary convenience for herself or affection for the boy turn her from her strong resolve to discipline him into the rounded man. It was a quality he had learned to appreciate the more since growing to intellectual competence, for he could recognize the difficulties his own high and sensitive youth must have presented. It is not improbable he had leaned heavily on old Aurelia's wise counsel during the years in Rome, for there is discernible in his transactions there a certain gentleness later muted if not missing. All gone now—she had passed and he separated from her by a thousand miles of wild Gaul, not even a comforting word or message at the last. Shoulder pikes, forward march.

Yet this was only the prelude to a tragedy deeper because less a part of the natural order of generation. One expects (however the conscious fixation of the thought be shrunk from) to lose one's parents some day; but the message that Caesar read by the cheerless firelight while unfamiliar seas beat on the sands where lately they had strewn his wrecked armada, told of the loss of his Julia. Julia— we know so little of her, only her romantic birth and that the two greatest men in the world loved her with quiet full affection, Caesar as father, Pompey as wife. She moves through the twilight of the old Republic like a bright Hesperian shadow who might have led it to better days. While she lived the friendship of the triumvirs endured and Pompey laid aside ambition to taste the pleasure of her presence, and when she died the son she bore him went with her. All gone now and Caesar is a childless man—fall in, fall in, we must embark for Gaul and face the swords of treacherous Ambiorix' rising.

[Caesar himself gave no sign of the wound, it lies clean beyond the frontier of speculation whether there were not some tiny flicker in the intellectual flame at this moment, some wavering that led to faulty distribution of the winter camps, some miss of the sure political stroke that brought on the disaster at Atuactuca and up through it the great revolt of Vercingetorix.]

Gone—and with her the strongest bond of the affection uniting the dynasts who must henceforth be a tripos of mutually opposed forces holding equilibrium only by interest and exterior fears, always subject to easy irruption. The last tie had disappeared and the tripos become a bipos not long later, for young Publius Crassus was gone now, too, the darling of the three, son to old Crassus by blood, to Pompey by courage and high heart, to Caesar by intellect—gone to the golden East in the train of his millionaire father in a tragedy

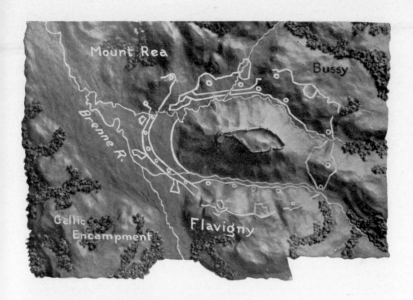

THE SIEGE OF ALESIA

In the schematic map Caesar's intrenchments are shown as heavy lines
and the redoubts as small circles, excavation having shown they were
circular in trace. The twenty-foot ditch curves round the foot of Alesia
mountain, just west of it; the Gallic wall is at the opposite end of the
town. The Roman camps are shown as enclosures, that in the center of
Flavigny being the headquarters camp.

that became the greatest of all those that attained the triumvirs, for it was the tragedy of thirty thousand homes as well.

Old Crassus, eager to make his reputation, would not play the indulgent father so far as to take his son's advice against beginning a desert campaign in summer. The Parthian horse-archers danced out of the heat haze around the dusty columns; young Publius fell in a brave futile rally and his father died next day when the army went to pieces, "an example to the wise of inconsiderateness and ambition, who not content to be superior to so many millions of men, being inferior to two, esteemed himself as the lowest of all."

The news came up from south in the black winter when the traders of Cenabum fell under Gallic swords, along with letters from Balbus and Marcus Cicero that must have told how Caesar had become the butt of all the versifiers of Rome. The shock was heavy; not only had Caesar hitherto lived free from the sharpest pangs that afflict existence, but he had always been able to retreat from any blow into the sanctuary of his aestheticism. Consider: a man who has spent his life reading the latest books and cannot now pick up any new book without finding it a burning denunciation of himself—"every man's woman and every woman's man." As though a friend of many years had turned and struck him—nor could he ease the hurt with the obvious avoidance that these were butterflies, for they were men whose talents he had respected and continued to respect. On their part the butterflies could not but regard their Caesar as a traitor, who had been a butterfly himself once, and now turned to sordid politics from divine aestheticism.

Well—was it these repeated shocks that made the Proconsul cling so desperately to the two young Bruti, the last of the golden friends of his heart? Balbus, Oppius, Aulus Hirtius, Asinus Pollio, these were friends of the mind and guest-board, whose thought might meet his but in whose emotion there was no delight. Young Decimus Brutus and his kinsman Marcus were surely not of these, rather in them Caesar found the mirror of his younger self, with a curious disinterested strain running through of—Puritanism? patriotism?— some ancestral inheritance. Marcus Brutus' mother had been one of the Catos, a sister of the priggish Marcus Porcius. Her name was

Servilia; Caesar had been her lover long ago and in the general chorus of literary scandal during the triumvirate days there were not wanting voices to declare that Caius Julius' affection for this Marcus Brutus might be more paternal than friendly. It was not true, being impossible by the time-table, for Caesar was fifteen when Marcus Brutus was born. His affection for the young man was, in fact, only paternal at the second remove, an outgrowth of the singular explosion that had made Cato his enemy forever and a day.

It was Cato's own fault, whose narrow suspicious mind trusted no man's probity but his own, and dated from the time of the Catiline plot. Scene—the Senate House with Cato just accusing Caesar of being privy to the conspiracy. A slave slipped among the benches and delivered a note to Caius Julius' hand. Cato spotted the movement—"Even now he is receiving notes from his fellow conspirators!"—and shrieked a demand that it be handed to him, as arbiter of public virtue. Caesar passed the note over with cold disdain; Cato glanced, then bit his lip. The rest of the Senators, scenting monstrous involvements, cried "Read it! Read it!" till Cato had to . . . It was a note from his sister Servilia, making a rendez-vous with Caesar, so passionately endearing as to leave no doubt of their relations, and therefore doubly bitter to the self-righteous Cato, for his sister was married to another man. There was a scandal and a divorce; Caesar took young Brutus as his special protege, since the boy was overyoung to leave his mother and both her family and his father's cast her out.

3

Now Cato was back in Rome, back from the municipal commission of Cyzicus and the annexation of Cyprus, having acquitted himself with more credit in both than anyone had believed possible, for he was an expert accountant and had cut right across all questions with iron justice in the old swordstraight Roman way. Cato was back and become the façade of the Conservative opposition, its concession to virtue, tolerated in this company for his great hatred of Caesar.

Their time seemed ripe with Cato back and the bond of the great coalition become one of mutual interest and exterior fear, not of affection any more. And now if interests lose their community? Pompey lived in the heart of a society never weary of pointing out that his partner had gained at every exchange in their alliance. ——Pompey the Great sitting at home among his empty honors while the Radical upstart erases his name from the tablets of memory.—— While he had Julia he did not care; nothing mattered but Julia's sweet self and the child she was to bear him. In the year following his and Crassus' consulate Domitius Ahenobarbus, the hereditary evil genius, got himself elected to the chief office, but he was frozen powerless, he could accomplish nothing against the triumvirs but a few ranting proclamations, for Julia was still alive. So the silence of senile decay gripped the political life of the city and Cicero sat down to write a treatise on the ideal republic.

——It needs more than the concord of all good men (he wrote) more than the good will of high-born men, in which I have hitherto mistakenly placed my confidence. There must stand behind universal right opinion a *rector* or *moderator,* strong and fearless enough to wield the military sword for the righting of wrongs, philosophic enough to use it justly.—— Did Pompey read it as a call? see himself mirrored there? for the treatise was widely read and talked on, as Cicero's treatise was bound to be, and the author had once called Pompey the greatest man who ever lived—surely he must be meant the ideal *rector.*

Whatever the impulse the greatest man who ever lived began again to inject his infinite wisdom into the consular elections for the year—gently and without so much opposition to the other member of the compact as would invalidate his bond. Caesar's candidates were Caius Memmius and Valerius Messalla, the Senate's one candidate L. Domitius Calvinus, and Pompey had promised his interest to a man named Aemillius Scaurus. The election itself was not a matter of high moment except to the participants, Caesar and Pompey being assured in their commands, merely having promised friendliness to deserving lieutenants anxious for place. But it turned into a flaming scandal when all four aspirants, less anxious about the election than about the juicy provincial administrations they hope to obtain in their proconsulates, made formal contract with Consul

Ahenobarbus to pay enormous sums for an assignment to provinces, an assignment the outgoing consuls must make before election. The bribes given to voters were enormous; Scaurus' purse was not deep enough, he perceived he would get the worst of it, and complained to Pompey. The Infinite Wisdom suddenly perceived a way to match Caesar's Gallic splendors by getting the Senate to declare that constitutional government had broken down and only his appointment as Dictator could save the world. He persuaded Memmius to rat on the other place-hunters; the shameful contract was read aloud in the Senate House amid crocodile tears and groaning imprecations from members who had mostly been parties to the same sort of manoeuvre at one time or another. Cato foamed at the mouth; the whole town rang with the story; there were riots and disorders that roared on for weeks and months, with no elections at all till near the end of the year. But it did no good to Pompey; Domitius Calvinus and Valerius Messalla got the election in the end and were declared consuls without assignment of any provinces, so they spent their money for nothing after all.

And where was the new proletarian democracy for which Caesar had toiled, the party of all-men-equal? Alas, they were following Clodius and Milo, Milo and Clodius through the paces of the old Pyrrhic dance of knife and knuckle-duster. Milo wanted to be consul for the next year; Clodius did not want him to; the Senate wanted a candidate of its own, and the Infinite Wisdom did not want anybody to be consul lest the government of laws work, however lamely and he lose the chance for the dictatorship on which he had now set his heart. In riot and confusion Domitius Calvinus' brief and shameful consulate ended; the Senate piped useless flatulencies, there were no elections because no time for them and the new year broke over a Rome without executives or judges, the government offices closed, sheer anarchy, in the full sense of that misused term. Milo and Clodius clashed in a pitched battle, with their bands; Clodius was slain and the riot sheared on into the Senate House, where Clodian partisans tore up the benches and burnt Rome's Capitol over the body. The fire spread, with riot and pillage running behind the flames; for days, weeks, the imperial city was one wild valley of turmoil and hunger, while Pompey sat in his suburban villa, counting his thumbs and fingers till such time as the Senate would come to its senses and name him absolute dictator, while Caesar frowned sadly across the ranges with the earthquake of Vercingetorix shaking Gaul behind his back.

So the Infinite Wisdom got his wish in the end—not Dictator, the title was suspect since bloody Sulla used it—but sole Consul with proconsular powers, which was the same thing. His Word boomed out; the streets resounded with the iron tramp of legions; as though by a sorcerer's spell all the hideous things disappeared back into their holes and the noble lords yawned as they returned to the congenial effort of inducing a greater spirit of friendliness among the carp in their fish-ponds.

Milo was laid by the heels and put on his trial for murder. Our little gossip Cicero came in to defend him, as the enemy of his enemy, but did it badly, for the Clodians in court set up a clamorous shouting, threatening to have the orator's entrails if he persisted, so he stammered and sat down. Milo was condemned; Cicero consoled him in jail with a copy of the beautiful speech he had meant to deliver and Pompey rejected the offer Caesar made him of a new matrimonial alliance between their two families. He was sole Consul now, Infinite Wisdom by decree of the Roman Senate, too big to ally with one who was merely one of the Republic's generals. Would honor his bond to do nothing against Caesar, but would take no step toward him.

4

Could C. Julius Caesar maintain his confidence in a guardian Fortune under such a succession of shocks? Could any man? He was one of the supreme optimists of history; he continued to believe in the fundamental friendliness and honesty of men when the evidence ran against such a confidence; he forgave the Aeduans of Alesia and gave them new clothes, he forgave Cicero his bitter words, he even forgave Catullus the poem of indelible stain in a letter full of gentleness and warm appreciation. When the Infinite Wisdom, with Rome and Spain already in his hands, asked back the legion he had lent during Vercingetorix' war (he needed it no more than he needed a third leg), Caesar sent it without a murmur and added a money present for each soldier, equal to the man's salary for a year.

Sublime self-confident optimism—the Conservatives were certain now it was the outward signet of that inner madness the gods throw round those ripe for destruction. Every letter eagerly was scanned for hint of disaster—"There are strange whisperings; one says Caesar has lost all his cavalry, which I suspect is sure fact; another that the 7th Legion is destroyed; that he is surrounded among the Bellovaci, cut off from the rest of his army. Domitius Ahenobarbus whispers the news behind his hand with an air of triumph, an open secret."

Clearly the man's luck was out, Great Pompey was turning in his orbital movement round the sun of his own splendor, no longer Caesar's friend. He had even permitted a discussion in the Senate of who should succeed to the government of Gaul when Caesar's term ran out. It came about in the most natural way in the world as a pendant to the discussion of a new law extending for five years Pompey's command "in Spain" which allowed him to keep six legions as a kind of private bodyguard.

"What about the command in Gaul during this period?" inquired someone.

"The authority of the Senate," remarked Pompey loftily, repeating his own words of ten years before, "in such matters is paramount."

Everyone knew what the authority of the Senate would be. The Senate would decree that Caesar lay down his *imperium* and return to Rome a private citizen, therefore an impeachable citizen. All the little Conservative hacks felt a thrill of joy and Cato's thin lips writhed with pleasure at the thought of getting the strong Proconsul into a prisoner's dock where he could be made to answer for the high treason of thinking the lords of the fish-ponds unfit to rule the world. Why, the whole conference of Luca had been based on the avoidance of this very event, foreseen by Caesar from five years' distance! The arrangement had been then that his term in Gaul was to extend five years from the end of the first five-year term so he would be legally eligible (by a ten-year interval since the last) for a new consulate, could be elected to it and return as Consul, clothed with a Consul's inviolability to nagging political prosecutions. But Pompey himself had fumbled the matter and passed the bill too soon; the two five-year Gallic terms overlapped, leaving an interval now one year ahead, after the time when Caesar must give up Gaul, before the time when he could be elected. Or at least so claimed Pompey; Caesar held the wording of the bill gave him the full ten years. We have not the worded bill to decide, but Pompey said there was a gap, and through this gap, without one whit deviating from the legal obligation of his bond, was striking to keep Caesar from the first place in Rome.

Could Caesar maintain a faith in his special Fortune with so outrageous thunderbolts of death and desertion crashing into the garden close he had built round a happy life? No—nor did Caesar. The old optimism, the old self-confidence, the old surety of a familiar genius suffered a mountain change as he spied beyond the ranges, turning to something ice-cold and glass-hard, as though the man himself had become a globe of crystal, refracting the beams of some ulterior light. No bitterness; ice is not bitter, it ejects impurities as it congeals. No selfishness; for he kept nothing for himself. Only he drove on and on, like the prophet of some evangel, with his full intellectual powers unchained in the service . . . of what? He may not himself have known.

Some sense of which penetrated the more subtle intellects at Rome, leaving them horrified and foreboding. "I shiver," wrote sensitive Cicero, "at every word of Caesar and his legions; I seem to foresee a terrific struggle, such as has never been before." "When you see the swarming legions strengthened with reserves and a great force of mounted men," sang poet Lucretius, "Religion, hope and peace fly panic-stricken from the mind—" then despairingly—"Ah, what does it matter? the whole of life is a struggle in the dark." And Servius Sulpicius Rufus, the great jurist, named Consul to follow Pompey, when the question of the Gallic succession came before the Senate, could only beg for reason and delay. ——You are making a civil war (he said) the most frightful of all civil wars. Draw the inference yourself, from how every such struggle has been worse than the last, with the combatants progressively showing greater ruthlessness, so that this time will crush the Republic itself and whoever wins will set up a tyranny permanent and intolerable.——

For this Caesar in his new avatar was become a portent terrible to all thinking Romans, since no dogma of their pantheism or polytheism was more firmly settled than that which held a lucky commander better than an able commander; yet there stood the man whose luck was out with nine terrible and victorious legions at his back, hovering like a thundercloud above the Alps. His luck was out; but he had taken Alesia, he had conquered Gaul. Could it be he was superior to the only supernatural force they knew?

But the lords of the fish-ponds would take no warning and the Infinite Wisdom wished none. The Senate rushed on toward the Apocalypse, certain as ever that the spoken word was master of the world, and Pompey stood aside to let them, calmly waiting for the hour when they would pull down Caesar and leave him *rector* and *moderator*. However fast the sands ran out they slipped too slow for Caesar's enemies: M. Claudius Marcellus, for instance, Sulpicius Rufus' partner in the consulate, found a man of Inner Gaul to whom Caesar had granted citizenship wearing a Roman toga and had him stripped and scourged—"since the acts of Caius Caesar are illegal" —but it was not enough. "How slow and inefficient Marcellus is!" exclaimed Cicero's correspondent. "He merely dawdles. Here it is June and he had brought in no motion yet to deprive Caesar of his command."

Well, Marcellus would satisfy them yet. He did, in fact, bring in the motion at the next session and the fish-pond baronage discovered to its surprise that Caesar was not altogether without defence even on the battleground of their choosing, for no sooner had it been voted that successors be appointed to the command of the Gallic provinces than up leaped a couple of tribunes crying "Veto!" Voted then that "the soldiers now in the army of Caius Caesar shall be entitled to their discharge if they have served long enough, and their pleas for discharge shall be investigated by a Senate committee." "Veto!" "That no subject but the Gallic provinces shall be debated at the March term of the Senate." "Veto!"

So the year wheeled on to its close and the new consuls were another Claudius Marcellus (Caius, cousin of the last) and L. Aemillius Paulus, great names out of the noble days of the Republic, better than the men who bore them. They brought in a bill of recall against Caesar, but Pompey, still watchful of his honorable bond, cried that it was premature and illegal. ——We cannot honorably settle anything about the governorship of Gaul till the March Kalends, but then I shall not hesitate.——

"But what if Caesar wishes to keep his army and stand for Consul too?" prodded someone, speculatively.

Pompey's face suffused with blood. "What if my son tries to beat me with his stick?" he shouted angrily.

The Senators smiled secret smiles, they saw the way now. Pompey was honoring his bond, to stand by Caesar till the time came for the legal appointment of a successor, but he would not stand with him a day beyond that date. They passed a motion that the eastern frontier was in a dangerous condition and that Caesar should send a legion from Gaul to face the Parthians. Caesar sent it fearlessly— the 15th; it marched down to Capua and there inexplicably failed to embark, being brigaded with some of Pompey's troops.

But Caesar was not altogether without resources. Cornelius Balbus had been in Rome for a year, buying brains with the spoils of Gaul, and first among his purchases stood Scribonius Curio, one of the new board of tribunes. "A man of noble birth, eloquent, intrepid, prodigal alike of his own fortune and reputation and of those of others; one ably wicked and brilliant to the injury of the public, whose passions and desires no dignity of wealth or gratification could satisfy—" said one of his ill-wishers, and though Curio could not have been quite as bad as that (for the affection in which he was generally held does not meet this picture) he was head over heels in debt and for sale to the best bidder.

It was a good investment. The end of Caesar's proconsular term was now only a year away, but when Consul Marcellus brought in a bill that he should give up Gaul Curio vetoed it. Pompey, affecting the moderator, offered a specious compromise—let the man keep Gaul till November, six months beyond term. Veto again—November left a gap of two months for prosecution, whose very existence would keep Caesar from another Consulate.

"You see the point—Gnaeus Pompey has made up his mind not to allow Caesar to become Consul unless he first hands over his army and his province"—or in other words lets the Senate make its drive at him, bring him to the prisoner's dock, where he could take his chance on acquittal or crawl before Pompey for mercy—"Caesar is convinced that there is no safety for him if he quits his army. He proposes, however, as a compromise that both he and Pompey should give up their commands."

He had done exactly that. Legate Antonius, Marcus Antonius, the big, coarse, hairy man who split Gallic skulls in the fight round Alesia's hill, came down from Gaul to stand for election as a tribune and brought with him the offer of compromise exactly as stated. ——No, no (said Pompey) it is not so nominated in the bond. By law I am captain-general of the Republic's war in Spain for three years more and Caesar is a private citizen after next March—— (A protest with its humorous side, there having been no war in Spain for nine years and Pompey not having visited the place for sixteen.)

No compromise; the year turned slowly on, with the aedile Marcus Caelius giving a most recherché exhibit of black panthers. Caesar held games and a lustration for his soldiers in the territory of the Treveri. The elections came off in the usual turmoil of corruption and riot; Antonius got his tribuneate, and the new Consuls were a pair of Conservative puppets, another Marcellus and Lentulus Crus, who had been Clodius' prosecutor in the sacrilege case. Cicero discussed with his wife the advisability of affiancing their daughter Tullia to P. Dolabella, and made a trip to Athens; when he reached Rome again he found the city seething with a rumor that Caesar had offered Pompey a new composition through the mouth of his secretary Aulus Hirtius, and that Pompey had rejected any compromise, and was preparing for a struggle.

"What am I to do?" wailed the orator. "Each of them counts me as his friend. Me against Caesar, imagine it!—after having pledged him my word! Besides I owe him money and it is bad form to be in debt to your political opponents, yet I believe in Pompey. What am

I to say?"—and posted off to drink wisdom from the infinite fount of it near Cuman villa from which Pompey had once slipped out the back door when he came to call.

"Pompey thinks the constitution will be subverted," he reported the conversation next day, "even if Caesar is elected Consul after giving up his army, and is of the opinion that when Caesar hears of the energetic movements against him he will abandon the idea. Still, if Caesar should play the fool and come on, Pompey expressed a hearty contempt for his military ability and a firm confidence in his own and the state's resources. 'I have only to stamp my foot and the earth will spawn armed men,' he said. I own I was relieved of my anxieties when I heard a soldier and a strategist of such capacity discuss the dangers of a hollow peace. In a word, he appeared not only to seek peace, but even to fear it."

No compromise; Scribonius Curio, ablest of the lieutenants, saw it. In the last days of the year he rode up to Ravenna, whither Caesar had come with a few cohorts of the 13th Legion. ——Up standards, shout trumpets, march on Rome! (he urged.) Nothing will satisfy these men but blood.——

But Caesar would not, they were his friends and relations who had sat at his table, he did not hate them, and it seemed to him a horrible thing that the blood of poor soldiers should be spilled in a family argument that might be settled with the bleeding of wine-skins. So he sent down yet one more offer of compromise through a discreet messenger; he would bow before the Ineffable Me, accept the second place or no place, give up seven of his legions and all Gaul but the old Cisalpine province, keeping only two and the name of an office to save his own safety. When the letter was read in the Forum the populace crowded round the messenger, crowned him with garlands and threw roses at him till he stood like a pillar of flowers, but ——No, (said the implacable Senate) we will have nothing but flat surrender and Caesar on trial for his life—— and ——No, (said Pompey) it is not so nominated in the bond.——

——One lone legion then and mountainous poor Illyricum, begged the messenger, only that for safety, only let us keep the peace.——

——No, it is not nominated in the bond.——

No compromise. The new year dawned with a fierce debate in the Senate, for Curio had come down from Ravenna with a letter from Caesar, his last word. ——Stand up (it said) be men like the Senates of old, decree that all extraordinary commanderships shall cease, make Pompey give up his army. I will willingly do the same and we be private citizens together.——

Senator Calidius, a Liberal, followed the letter with a motion that Pompey go to Spain and govern the province assigned to him; that would avoid all quarrels. The House burst out in screams; over the tumult rose the voice of Consul Lentulus Crus, a dark-faced, fearless man, bellowing that the Senate should take a strong line ——We need arms, not votes against this robber!—— An emissary from Pompey declared that if the Senate only held firm they would have the greatest man who ever lived to command their armies. Calidius' motion was howled down. Lentulus Crus offered one that Caesar should be recalled immediately—"Veto!" shouted Tribune Antonius, and the sun went down on a tossing sea of words.

That night the streets were full of soldiers and hurrying emissaries; Pompey had sent out a proclamation calling his Eastern veterans of ten years back to the colors. The consuls and praetors went through

Chariot

the streets with their red military cloaks round them, the temple treasures were called on to arm for war. When the Senate met again Caesar's legate Roscius made one more plea for delay to let him send a deputation to his chief, some last moment plan might be forthcoming. Lentulus Crus refused to put it to the vote and offered one instead declaring Caius Julius Caesar a public enemy. Antonius, imperturbably courageous, rose to veto, oblivious of the screams of hatred that rose around him, but at that moment some of Pompey's soldiers in the portico flashed weapons and began to shout "Slay! Slay!"

——Fly for your lives—— whispered someone to Antonius and Curio. They fled; at the city gates they were joined by Legate Roscius, Senator Calidius, Calpurnius Piso, Q. Cassius and a few others, but word of the exodus had gotten out, a posse of hired gladiators was hunting for them, and they had to stop among the tombs and dress as slaves before they could get into chaises bound north.

With the Caesarians gone the Senate suddenly found harmony. Without debate a law was passed recalling Caesar from Gaul and naming Domitius Ahenobarbus governor there, effective at once. Without debate the "Ultimate Decree" passed—Rome and Rome's possessions under martial law, constitutional guarantees suspended, all officers of the state to bend their efforts against the public enemy. Without debate a rider was attached naming Pompey the Great captain-general of the Republic; without debate a *levée en masse* decreed.

At Ravenna the carriage from Rome came in late in the afternoon. Caesar had invited some friends for dinner and had barely time to hear the news while he dressed, carefully as usual, in the elaborate fringed toga with the loose girdle. At the table his conversation held the sparkle and gaiety of old, but when dark came he begged indulgence for an hour. Outside, the anxious lieutenants were waiting, eager for orders. They had Caesar's two-toed horse. He mounted and rode wordlessly with them south through the town to the bank of the little stream that marked the boundary between Gaul, where he was constitutional governor and the Roman homeland, where he was an outlaw unless a suppliant. There was a long, low-voiced conversation, Caesar hesitating, the others urging him on, you can imagine their arguments ——Not for yourself, but for the work, you will not be a traitor to a high destiny and those who trust you, you cannot abandon the plebs whose hope you are—— till he took fire on a sudden, whipped out a sword, crying *"Jacta esto alea!"*—Let the die be cast!—and rode forward across the Rubicon with the blade gleaming frostily in starlight.

He was Rome's enemy on Rome's soil and the Civil War had begun.

GREATNESS IS A RELATIVE QUALITY

~~~~~~

Roads to Rome—The great north road is the Flaminian Way; it
drives straight as an arrow-flight down the peninsula's eastern face
from the Padus valley, pausing to throw two long veins across the
Apennine backbone, via Arretium and Iguvium to Rome. When
Caesar pushed his vanguard over the Rubicon he heard both places

See map	were held by strong Pompeian outposts, either
facing page 225	flanking an advance through the other and both

one along the Adriatic coast. He had only one legion, the 13th.
Four of the remainder were with Legate Trebonius in Outer Gaul,
and the 5th, 8th, 9th and 12th wintering at Bibracte under Legate
Fabius. For messengers to go and troops to come would take weeks,
and there might be snow in the Alps further to delay matters. Besides Pompey had seven veteran legions in Spain, which would
infallibly fall on the rear of such a movement or steal Gaul with its
defenders gone.

Ahead seemed worse. The 1st and 15th were still at Capua, under
the enemy's orders, the Senate's levy en masse had brought not less
than ten legions to the colors, with men trained in war to lead them.
Defense? No, 'twere fatal, the scattered Senatorial enlistments, given
time to concentrate, would come roaring up the peninsula like a wave
of war with ever-victorious Pompey riding on the crest. Attack? A
lunatic enterprise by every military canon—but Julius Caesar was not
a military man, only a politician in deep trouble who considered fact
lord over figures. He knew the hidden weakness of his foes; they had
good fighting hearts and heads, but too many, a parliament of generals who would clog the strong command with disputation on fine
points of strategy—or being given a wing, lead it to their own greater
glory and the overthrow of the cause. He knew the 1st and 15th,

two years in his own service, would fight half-hearted against the master who had always been generous with them and their old comrades of Gaul; knew Pompey's veterans would not soon quit the rustic farms Caesar's land-law had given them; knew the voiceless plebs of Rome were heart and soul with the champion who had been driven to the sword because he stood their friend, knew the Senate's levy was half made, with many cohorts in many places and no large organization nor drill at movement in large units.

He knew; so that it did not even disturb him when Titus Labienus, his best legate and familiar companion, for whom he had set aside the reversion of the Gallic command, served him the last and scurviest trick in the round of treacheries, by first distributing the cohorts of the 13th where they would be most difficult to assemble, then flying to Pompey.

——Why, the man has done me a service!—— exclaimed Caesar, in inextinguishable generosity sending the vanished legate's papers and possessions after him under a flag of truce. The remark was no more than truth; Labienus lulled the Senate into a false security by carrying them a tale wrought of the tissues of his own fevered mind, that Caesar's troops were half disaffected and wholly scattered, unfit for combat.

Nothing was less accurate; as Labienus fled the first maniples of the 13th were right on his heels down the great north road. They took the fortress-post of Ariminum the day Caesar passed the Rubicon and that night pushed through Fanum on Ancona, with Legate Antonius flung out on an eccentric to seize Arretium and guard the flank. Messengers to the north were riding hard; six of the Gallic legions were to assemble at Narbo under Legate Fabius and hold off Pompey's seven from Spain, while the 8th and 12th came through by forced marches to join the Proconsul in Italy.

C. Scribonius Libo was recruiting in Arretium for the Senate, entirely occupied with his muster-rolls and with no conception of an enemy anywhere near him when Antonius came pouring into the streets with his veteran cohorts. Antonius dropped a guard in the town and turned back to the main road. As soon as he arrived Caesar sent Curio with five cohorts along the other road to Rome against

THE CONQUEST OF ITALY

Fanum (not shown) is a little town on the road between Ariminum and Ancona; Alba is just north of Corfinum. The Rubicon is an insignificant brook falling into the Adriatic just south of Ravenna.

Iguvium, where the Senatorial Minucius Thermus had five cohorts of his own and was fortifying. Minucius' troops were green; the townsfolk curdled on him and began to throw bricks from the rooftops when they heard Curio was coming, so the Senatorial leader retreated. That did him no good either, he could not keep his men under the standards and most of them drifted off to their homes or deserted to Caesar.

In Rome dwelt panic; Pompey, by a simple computation of miles and marching speeds, made out that Caesar would be at the gates with the 13th before he could call up any experienced troops to defend the capital, and had given orders that all loyal men should evacuate with him to Luceria in the south. "Better to die with Pompey than live with Caesar," moaned Cicero, as he fled the town, "but Pompey has no policy, his alarm and confusion are boundless, he is nothing but a miserable rag-doll of a general", which is an odd change of tone on Cicero's part from a month before—then he adds as an afterthought— "Not that I am afraid, you understand, I'm only bursting with indignation. Shall I commit myself to the good cause, after all? Or turn my coat and join the big battalions?"

A question which many another was asking in heart and conscience as "the monster" out of Gaul strode down the coast through Pisaurum, Ancona, Auxinum, gaining recruits at every step, rumor magnifying ten thousand times his strength. Senatorial Legate Attius Varus held Auxinum with six cohorts; he essayed a stand against the advance, then a retreat, but Caesar's van drove in on him so fast he had to pull up and rank for a fight. Before the weapons met Attius Varus' men threw down their arms and began to cheer for Caesar; they all joined his standards, bringing Attius Varus to him as a present and asking to have the man boiled in oil, but Caesar let him go.

Asculum was the next town before the advance, a great stronghold from the days of the old Samnite wars. On February 5 the Senatorial Lentulus Spinther encountered "the monster" there. Lentulus Spinther had ten cohorts, a legion in numbers, but not in heart, for they ran away or deserted before the shock. The Senatorial headquarters near Capua was full of babbling confusion, with two or three hundred armchair strategists offering Pompey advice or orating on his supineness, trying to rule in war as in peace by the spoken word. "Now stamp your legions from the ground!" cried Favonius, Cato's ape, in a fine sarcastic rhetorical passage, but could offer no definite plan for stopping Caesar's rush when asked to do better himself.

Pompey at least had a plan, not so bad a one in a military sense—delay, delay in Italy, concentrating troops and holding out a strong front. The Spanish army would come through south Gaul eventually to fall on Caesar's rear; fifteen or twenty veteran legions could be gathered from garrison duty or recalled from farms in the East, enough to overwhelm the lunatic enterprise, though all the peninsula should declare for Caesar. Time! Gain time, that was the essential, for the pieces in this grand concentric attack to move.

But the Pompeian generals were dolts who wanted to bake cake before mixing dough under spur of the Senate's ceaseless urge for immediate battle and expulsion of the usurper from the peninsula—why, he interfered with the normal business of life! Three of them, Lentulus Spinther, Vibullius Rufus and L. Hirrus, managed to concentrate thirteen cohorts on Caesar's front, but their minds were so shaken that instead of fighting for delay they fell back precipitately to the fortress of Corfinium, where Domitius Ahenobarbus had twenty more. Redbeard Domitius was senior commander and anxious for battle. He had counted noses, discovered he had a numerical superiority and determined to fight, which was against strict orders from Pompey.

Corfinium was a good place to make a battle, the bed of a bygone mountain lake, with glowering sharp hills around, immensely strong. Domitius threw parties out to Sulmo on one flank and to Alba on the other, holding the passes, then sent a letter to Pompey; ——Join me here with the 1st and 15th legions, and we will break Caesar to pieces with our united armies.——

——Impossible (Pompey wrote back); the men I have here are old Caesarian soldiers, unfit for battle against him. I cannot imagine why you fail obedience. As a far-seeing commander you are bound to consider not how many cohorts Caesar can oppose to you at the moment, but how many he will be able to assemble. He has gathered many recruits and has another legion at least on the march from Gaul. You will be caught in a trap if you fight him alone; we are both helpless unless united. Fall back here with your whole force as soon as possible.——

Possible! That was the rub, for even as Pompey penned the letter the possibility was doomed. Caesar's vanguard clashed with the Senatorial outposts at the bridge of the Aternus river that very evening; won a passage and next morning led the invading army in toward Corfinium. Domitius from the walls noticed rusty armor among the blockaders, sent a scout to find the meaning, and before noon had the tidings that he was attacked not only by the 13th and at least a legion of Caesarian recruits, but the 12th and 8th as well, which had joined up during the night after a fast march all the way down from Gaul. That made Caesar's army superior even by a nose-count. The balance tilted still deeper when Antonius appeared before the Senatorial outpost at Sulmo and the seven cohorts Domitius had stationed there, instead of fighting, joined him.

Next morning a messenger worked his way through the lines from Pompey. ——Escape at all costs (it said); cut your way through.—— It was not possible at any costs, Caesar's men had labored as before Alesia, and Corfinium was closed in on every side by trench and wall. Domitius' courage ran off him; he called a council of war.

Were they resolute enough? he asked the other Senatorial leaders, to float down the river or sneak through the sentry-line? The town was surely lost and if Caesar caught them inside he would put them to death. They agreed to premise and conclusion, but some privates overheard the discussion, spread the news through the ranks that their leaders were deserting, and the men called a council of war for themselves. They had no will to fight Caesar, poor common men who had been pressed by Pompey's crimping-agents. At day they sent a bugler out to blow a parley and in unanimous mutiny surrendered bodies, arms and leaders. Some of the aristocrats tried suicide to escape the tortures they were sure they would get. Before they accomplished the matter the mutinous soldiery fell on them and frog-marched them into Caesar's camp with blows and curses.

In high, disdainful scorn "the monster" sent them free with a
military guard as far as Capua to see the angry people did not break
their heads or take their purses. Caesar's under-officers protested.

"No," said the Proconsul, "I have no quarrels but those forced
upon me. Let us see if by moderation we cannot win all hearts and
secure a lasting victory, since by cruelty others have never been able

Coin of Pompey

to establish anything permanent, with the single exception of L.
Sulla, whom I am not the man to imitate. Let us adopt a new method
of conquest; to fortify by mercy and generosity."

The loss of Corfinium broke Pompey's front; he saw he would be
penned against the Tyrrhenian Sea if he remained and before the
place even surrendered, was marching rapidly for Brundisium and
the gate of the East, with his unsteady legions dissolving en route.
The Senate went with him and held a meeting, very sour and peev-
ish, to discuss methods of raising funds, since in their haste to quit
Rome, they had left the public treasure behind. Pompey, now far
from the days of the triumph of magnanimity, suggested proscribing
the Caesarians of Brundisium. It was a rich town; the Senate agreed
enthusiastically and the next ten days were spent in lopping off
wealthy heads (for the moment the test of Caesarianism was the size
of a man's bank account) and confiscating all the portable property
that could be found.

That trick finished the process Caesar's clemency had begun.
Praetors Manlius and Rutilius deserted to the Proconsul, taking nine
more cohorts with them, and not a few of the Senators slipped from

Brundisium by night to go back to Rome. More had stayed behind in Campania, including our old friend Cicero—"Do you see what manner of man it is into whose hands the Republic has fallen?" he wrote to a friend in the city about this time, doubtless hoping that the letter would be exhibited in the proper quarters— "How clear-sighted, how gallant, how thoroughly prepared!"

No matter, let them trim, these sprats were not the game Caesar hunted, he was off for Brundisium, driving his army twenty miles a day to catch Lord Whale himself, and nearly did, for when he camped outside the town Pompey was still within at the head of twenty cohorts only. The remainder of the Senatorial army, three legions, had left with the consuls for Epiros, there to raise the big army from the East.

Caesar rode round the walls of the city and found the place too powerful to storm, but it lay at the end of a long bottle-neck harbor which he thought he might cork by one of his astonishing strokes of engineering. Lines were drawn round the city and camps planted at the shore on both sides of the bottle-neck, from which two long moles of stone and rubble stemmed outward from each other. That brought on fighting, the first in this strange war. Pompey embarked men in big, decked-over merchant ships and sent them down the harbor where they grappled savagely with Caesar's men on the moles. The Caesarians won and closed the gap between the moles with huge rafts moored side by side, with a causeway and towers built across them to form a floating bridge.

It held for nine days and things began to pinch within Brundisium. Then the Pompeian fleet returned from Greece, fell on the floating bridge with their heavy rams, and night and tide aiding, cut through. Pompey was ready; had spent the nine days loophold-ing the houses of the town and barricading streets. When the fleet came in, he dropped a rear-guard of archers and artillerymen and began embarkation in the dark. Caesar could tell by the sounds that something was toward and sent his men at the walls; they broke in, but made slow work of the street-fighting in the dark. When they got through to the water's edge the Pompeians were already afloat and nothing could be captured but two ˎtransports which fouled the moles in the dark.

And so the war escaped from Italy to set the world afire, and Caesar turned back to the Rome he had not seen in nearly ten years.

2

MATIUS AND TREBATIUS TO CICERO, GREETING:

As we were leaving Capua we heard that Pompey with all his forces had left Brundisium on the 16th day before the Kalends of April; that Caesar on the next day entered the town, made a speech and went off at full speed to Rome, to remain there a few days before setting out for Spain. He will stop at Beneventum on the 8th day before the Kalends, at Capua on the 7th and on the next night at Sinuessa. This we consider certain.

The Proconsul moved like a flicker of lightning. He could make out Pompey's grand strategic plan now, and see how its framework stood firm in spite of the whirlwind of marching men he had blown through it. The real peril for him and Italy was not the sword but hunger; Pompey, as ancient admiral of Rome had the fleet and the men of the fleet, with squadrons out patroling the routes between the peninsula and the corn-lands. The old soldier meant to starve the peninsula by blockade, while he raised armies to complete the overthrow—Ha! let the fickle populace cheer the usurper now, they'd pipe another tune when lean hunger pinched their gorge.

There was a counter. Not the blow direct at Pompey in Epiros, for Caesar had no method to cross the straits without some semblance of a navy. No—rather the attack oblique. The 8th, 12th, and 13th legions were dropped to rest in garrison at Brundisium, Tarentum, Sipontum, under trusty legates. That would keep off any clutch at the east Italian ports from the sea. Sicily was a corn-land; Scribonius Curio went there with the three legions who had changed allegiance at Corfinium, slipping across the strait by night. Sardinia was a corn-land; Valerius the Legate took there the legion won in the tearless victory of Asculum. Legate Dolabella (whom Cicero was decided upon as a son-in-law) went to the Adriatic shore of

Picenum to build a fleet; Legate Hortensius to build another for the Tyrrhenian Sea.

Caesar himself was to take the long route, the land route to Spain, there "to fight an army without a general so that later I may fight a general without an army." For the seven Spanish legions were Pompey's best and truest soldiers; without them he would be hard pressed to find sure men.

So much for the military situation, and that was the easiest part to plan, merely match counterstroke to stroke. But politics hung more dubious, for while the Senate was of Pompey's persuasion he held the official reins of the Republic, with all that unto these appertained of tax revenues and the aid of subject kings around the fringes of the world. More yet—Caesar's lieutenants and administrators were wild spendthrift adventurers like Scribonius Curio or beardless cavalry captains of Decimus Brutus' stamp. Such men would never make the backbone of an empire, he must have men of sense and merit, solid citizens, or there were nothing permanent in what he did.

CAESAR THE IMPERATOR SENDS GREETINGS TO CICERO THE IMPERATOR
Though I have only had a glimpse of our friend Furnius and have not been able conveniently to speak to him, being in a hurry and on the march, yet I could not neglect the opportunity of writing to you. I beg you, since I trust that I shall quickly reach Rome, to let me see you there and employ your advice, favor and help in every direction. Pardon my haste and the shortness of this letter. By the hand of Furnius.

The two men met at Formiae on the 28th March. Caesar clove straight through to the heart of the question between them.

——Come to Rome (he said) and attend the session of the Senate which I am having called. With good will and honesty to help it the old Roman Constitution will march yet.——

——No, (said Cicero, knees quaking but mind firm) No, not while the consuls are in Epiros and there is no check on a Radical revolution.—— The slant of his mind shone through; radicalism was no solution of the Republic's troubles, he would not be co-architect of a new order.

Caesar: "Yet I beg you to come. Servius Sulpicius Rufus will attend. You know him for the best legal mind of ours or any generation, and he is with us. Volcacius Tullus will be there, and he is a sound intelligent man, too. In Epiros, the Senate's but a rump; the best are here. Surely you can see that your failure to attend is equivalent to a vote of censure on me, and your voice is important. If you fail the others will hold back."

Cicero: "My case is very different from theirs. I owe a debt of gratitude—"

Caesar: "Come at all events, if only to discuss how to make peace."

Cicero: (slyly) "In my own way?"

Caesar: "Do you want me to dictate what you should say?"

Cicero: "Well, I shall have to contend that the Senate cannot legally approve your Spanish expedition, nor your invasion of Greece, and I shall sympathize with Pompey."

Caesar: "I certainly don't want you to be talking like that."

"To be sure," said Cicero, the wild horse of his eloquence now unreined, "but neither do I want to be in Rome, and if I must come I shall have to say these things—and quite a lot more, too."

No deal; they parted, Caesar to Rome with the final word that if he could not have Cicero's advice he would take his own and rule unchecked; Cicero on the next ship that sailed for Greece and Pompey's camp, quite sure that the Proconsul did not like him, "but I like myself," since integrity had triumphed over terror. He was received in vinegary silence as a coward and a trimmer and set himself to compose nine questions of casuistry "which bear upon the duty of a citizen and also relate particularly to the present crisis. By employing myself with such question and debating both sides in Greek and Latin, I divert my thoughts and also throw a good deal of philosophical light on matters important at the moment."

Philosophical light? Pompey's hurrying squadrons bucked against the blue combers round the shores of Italy; Caesar's legions raised a marching song and on the Kalends of April he met the Senate in a temple outside the city gates. The debate was senseless and interminable— An idea, oh, a most desirable excellent idea this that the Proconsul offered of sending a peace deputation to Pompey, but who'll bell the cat? Answer—none; Pompey having sworn to make shorter by a head anyone who did not join him when he left Italy. So they turned to the consideration of other matters, and like Cicero, having discovered that it was a mild monster they had for a master, spoke what they thought, which was that his measures should be obstructed to the bitter end. It was inadmissible that the inhabitants of the Padus valley should receive citizens' rights; it was undesirable that money from the state treasury should be used to purchase corn for the people or to furnish the prosecution of this war . . .

——Enough! (cried Caesar) I am foolishly wasting my time.—— On the fourth day there was no session. Tribune Antonius jammed Caesar's proposals through the assembly of the people, and the Proconsul strode in person to the door of the Treasury with a file of soldiers behind him. On the steps stood a Conservative tribune, young L. Metellus. ——I veto the people's bill for the use of the public funds in this war,——he said.

——Stand aside (ordered Caesar) or I will have you put to death.——

A gasp of horror rose from the milling crowd; this was impiety at its highest, the person of a tribune was sacrosanct. Metellus went pale but stood his ground, crying "You dare not!"

Caesar drew his sword—"Young man," grimly, "it is even easier to do it than to say it."

Metellus dared not put it to the proof; Caesar mounted the steps, and finding the doors held fast, summoned an artificer from the Gallic legion to strike off the locks with his hammer. The next day he took the road for Spain. Marcus Lepidus was left behind as Prefect of the City, the judges having fled with Pompey; Legate Antonius was named commander of Italy while Caesar should be absent.

3

War Without War—Massilia, the seaport of the Gauls, was held for Pompey. In the fading days of March Domitius Ahenobarbus, set free by Caesar after Corfinium, had come up the harbor with a squadron of galleys and a reinforcement of troops to make it secure. He had license from the Senate, the old Senate, Pompey's Senate, as Governor of Gaul; beside, Pompey, as an old sea-fighter and the man who put down the pirates, was a great favorite in the city that lived by the sea.

Caesar checked his march long enough to discover that the place would not be won by any easy attack, dropped three of the new Italian legions under Legate Trebonius to blockade the place, with young Decimus Brutus in command of a naval force yet to be built up the Rhodanus river, then hurried on toward the Pyrenees.

Fabius the Legate had preceded him, pushing out from Narbo at the beginning of the month, six legions strong, forcing the passes before the Pompeians could get enough men up to them to hold them in strength. They had troubles of their own, chiefly with organization. Lucius Afranius held West Spain for Pompey with three legions, Marcus Petreius South, or Baetic Spain with two, Terentius Varro Ulterior Spain with again two. They were men widely different; Afranius an adroit, fencing tactician, Pompey's high lieutenant in the old eastern wars; Petreius a bulldog, slugging fighter, Varro an essayist, theorist in agronomy and government, interested in breaking the Greek olive monopoly, white-haired and irritable, less concerned with war than with ruling well the turbulent province Caesar had held before him. They arranged it that Varro should govern Petreius' district and his own; Petreius came up to join Afranius with his two legions and they raised enough of native levies, some armed in the Roman manner, some after their native fashion, to give them a total strength of about 40,000 men.

Below the Pyrenees the next great barrier to invasion is Iberus river. The country between is harsh and rugged, covered with deep woods and poor in food. A stream swift and un- See map facing page 305 fordable splits it from north to south, falling into Iberus at right angles. The name of this river is Sicoris; midway of its length a huge nipple of stone overhangs the right bank and on its crest is a citadel called Ilerda. Here Afranius took his station to hold off Caesar's men, but as the town was too small to hold 40,000 additional bodies, he used it as a base, building his own camp on another nipple-hill close by. Fabius came swinging down with his six legions and pitched camp some two miles north and on the same bank.

Fabius was weaker in numbers, but stronger in cavalry, having brought down some six thousand Gallic horse. When he had been there through a month of outpost skirmishes Caesar rode in with a personal escort of nine hundred more cavalry, and things began to happen at once. On the morrow of arrival the Proconsul drew his forces out, marched down to front the town and offered battle. Afranius would not fight; a rumor had come through that Pompey in person was on the march across North Africa to aid him, and he conceived it his duty to present a mere impenetrable defense till, with the aid of his principal, he could crush Caesar.

Defense is a bad system for any general when he had the odds on his side, and doubly so against Caesar, for it surrendered the moral superiority to the world's greatest master of morale. Yet to apply pressure to the doubled hill-forts Afranius held was a problem.

On the second day Caesar drew up for battle again in the plain, then had the rear rank of his line fall out and dig the trench of a new camp, only seven hundred yards from the enemy's position. At night his men lay on their arms; at dawn the fighters formed again, with the rear rank digging as before, and so till the third day, when new camp and rampart were complete, but Afranius, having made his plan was too sound a tactician to change it for a threat. On the fourth morning, he only drew his men up in order across the steep hillside, where it was folly to attack them.

Caesar, surveying the ground, felt something might be made of a small knoll midway between Afranius' camp and Ilerda—if he could gain and hold it, the bread-route from camp to town would be cut and the Pompeians must abandon one or the other. He tried it out of hand, the antesignani, forlorn hope, *corps d'élite,* of the 14th Legion dashing from the line in a sudden rush for the hill.

Afranius had remarked small premonitory shiftings in the line opposite him, however. He hurled his own men for the same spot, and having less distance to go, they arrived first. They beat off the antesignani of the 14th in a sharp tussle, followed up behind the recoil. The whole legion, unsettled by the novel open-order tactics of the Pompeians, bunched, heaved and then reeled back and broke. Caesar himself was down in the center of the line with the 9th. He wheeled it round, ployed into column, and thrust the column through the center of Afranius' loose bands at the charge. Afranius' men went back in turn, right up the steep slope toward Ilerda's gate, but rallied under the wall and came back again.

The 9th, with the hill so steep against them could not gain. Their front was excessively narrow, room for only three cohorts between the rocky walls; weight and the slope told as the Pompeians charged. They could not retreat, either; if they tried it the Pompeians would come down onto their backs at the run and tear them to pieces. So they stayed and fought it out, with fresh men being fed up the files to the front on both sides. The combat lasted five hours, or till the 9th, under Caesar's personal direction, made one more desperate uphill charge, drove in the front facing them and disengaged.

They were fortunately out of what might have been a disaster, but the day was pure loss, for next morning Afranius had the knoll between town and camp heavily fortified.

Caesar gave the soldiers a forty-eight hour rest before trying anything new, but before it was over the weather took charge of operations, with a great storm tearing across the mountains in the north, melting the winter snows and bringing the Sicoris down in such a spate that "it was agreed none had ever seen so huge a flood." The bridges across the river went out, all but the stone bridge connected with the city of Ilerda, and that was a disaster, for it left Afranius with a connection to the east bank, where alone food and forage could be found, while Caesar had none.

The Proconsul could not rebuild his bridges, either; Afranius was conscious of his advantage and kept sharp watch, with patrols moving along the east bank and concentrating rapidly wherever Caesar's engineers showed— "It was no easy matter at once to avoid darts and work in the swirling water." Food began to fail— "The price of corn rose and the want of it diminished the strength of the soldiery"—and worst of all a big convoy from Gaul, six thousand slaves and officers with a chest of treasure and only a few cavalry for guard, was on the way, coming down the wrong bank of the stream, quite ignorant of the bridge trouble.

Afranius took three of his legions across to attack the convoy. The Gallic light horse with them made a good stand, skirmishing so effectively that at the price of a few hundred casualties they beat off the legions for a day, but they were in bad straits and being driven into the river on the second morning, when they saw Caesar's blessed eagles come riding into view over a cloud of dust.

The Proconsul had marched fast and far, twenty miles up the river, beyond reach of Afranius' patrols, during the night. His men bore with them boats of a novel type he had seen in Britain and now imitated, ribs woven of withy work and hides for cover. In the night they launched them on the hurrying torrent; a cohort won over, then a legion, and spent the hours before dawn fortifying a bridgehead. Under this cover the engineers worked; before the second night they had a bridge across, and so the convoy was saved.

That was good but not good enough; it gave mere safety, and the bridge was so long a distance from the camps that it offered no scope for offensive action. But Caesar's busy brain was not drained yet. Lower down, close by Ilerda, Sicoris splits round a double island —what if this could be turned to account? Caesar thought it could; put his laborers at the spot, dug, canaled, installed a huge system of drains thirty feet wide, leading out of Sicoris above the islands and back into it below. Sicoris flooded into the new channels. The tripartite stream ran shallow enough for cavalry to ford it.

While the work was on good news came in, news of a great sea-fight off the capes of Massilia and Caesar's men victorious. Young Decimus Brutus had floated his new fleet down the Rhodanus on the spring tides, green-timber ships, jerry-built, with inexperienced rowers and seamen out of the merchant service who did not know one warship's rope from the other, but the fleet was manned with the choicest soldiers of the legions. The fast Massiliote craft raced round them, crushing oars and lancing in with the ram, but the legionary soldiers threw grapnels at every approach, locked with their foes, one against two, and leaped across the staggering bul-

warks to play it out at hand to hand on the enemy's decks. Ship
after ship they cleared, with their own sinking beneath their feet;
when nine Massiliotes had been won Redbeard Domitius tore down
his standard and fled. Brutus was master of the sea and rode at
anchor blockading Massilia.

The legionaries of the Spanish army gave a cheer for Brutus and
the news. Their ford was finished, the Gallic horse poured through
and scoured the countryside on the east bank. Afranius' foragers
could not bear up against them; they moved too fast and far and
charged too firm when it was a fight. The Pompeians began to go
hungry; they had so long avoided battle that they had an inner conviction now it would be fatal, and could take no counsel but the
wild one of abandoning the position and moving south of the river
Iberus to lay the stones of a new defense.

They dared not go by the west bank of the Sicoris, where the way
was easy, through flat plains. The dreaded Gauls would eat them up
if they tried that. Instead it was to be a quick crossing by the stone
bridge, a quick march through the small belt of broken lands till
they gained protection of the rugged steep hills a few miles down,
along the other shore. Well enough a plan if they could steal a
march on Caesar.

But that was not an easy thing to do. He had word of the move
from his Gallic scouters. Half an hour from the time they started
in the dead watch of the night, the Pompeians found cavalry all
round them, shooting arrows and spears out of the dark. The missiles
from nowhere never missed; they themselves were shooting at
ghosts or shadows. At day Caesar's soldiers could see the column
from across the river, retreating slowly, their passage clogged in dust
and circling horsemen. The legions clamored to pursue, to fight,
clashing their weapons and shouting at the officers. Caesar addressed
them; there was no bridge, he said.

——Never mind (they cried) we'll go by the ford.——

It was neck deep in water and a fast current, hard for men loaded
with war-gear. Caesar, as he had in Gaul, posted a line of horsemen in the stream to catch those swept from their feet, and not a
man was lost though many stumbled. The legionaries came up out

of the cold flood burning hot with enthusiasm, made a rapid-fire march through the hot hour of the day and caught up Afranius' faltering army about three in the afternoon.

Afranius must fight or fortify. The latter was the lesser evil, his men being weary with eighteen hours' running battle with the cavalry and much out of heart. He swung off the road to a high hill and laid out lines, a Camp Despair, in a wan, savage land, all colored dun, slate and red without a speck of grass and little water, with the friendly mountain gorges that would save him from the attentions of those infernal Gauls still five miles distant. Caesar camped also, close by, and northward.

That night there was a council of war in Afranius' camp. The men were broken with fatigue, but something must be done—how about a surprise night march? Caesar would never expect it two nights running. Good, approved the subordinates; the men were stealthily gotten under arms, silently they began to move—when sharp and clear a trumpet rang out from the opposite camp, blowing the assembly.

The move had somehow been seen; that meant cavalry in among the ranks as soon as they moved, chopping and stabbing, a dreadful thing at night. Afranius gave up the effort and sent his men back to bed. The next day he had to rest them, and used the time to ride out for a reconnaissance. Straight south, some distance from the Sicoris, lay a defile; though it led to nowhere its walls would protect them against the Gauls and give them a rest. When the Pompeian leader returned from his trip it was with the resolution to march for the defile with the daylight, no doubt losing part of his army on the way, but saving the rest.

Again good if it had been done earlier, but Caesar also had spied out the land and guessed Afranius' intent. Before break of day he was in motion, out the back gate of his camp. The Pompeians, taking their breakfast, gave hoots of joy; they imagined Caesar was being driven back across the river for lack of victual, which made their wakening more painful when they saw the long column swing round abreast, then ahead of them, rising and dipping among the sharp, treeless hills. Afranius hastily dropped his baggage with a few

cohorts to defend it and rushed out in light marching order to get
to the defile. It was a race, a mad, scrambling race, with Caesar's
men clambering among crags where they had to pass their weapons
to one another and pull up or let down by helping hands, but the
Pompeians were as severely handicapped by the Gallic riders, who
now charged fearlessly right against their ranks, since they feared
no counterstroke. Caesar had a start and more energy; he won the
race, his men filed from among the spires square across the path.
With the legions of Gaul in front, the cavalry of Gaul round flank
and rear, there was nothing for the Pompeians to do but come to a
stand again, which they did on a tall ridge of many colors, naked in
the burning sun.

One more hope. Two miles west was an outcrop. It connected
with a higher ridge cavalry would never be able to climb. If Afranius
could reach it he might save at least part of his army by marching
along the crest till he reached the Iberus, where there were friendly
cities. He sent forward 500 Spanish targeteers to seize the outcrop;
small, active men, moving at the keen run. Caesar flung the Gauls
at them; the targeteers were surrounded in the valley—"nor could
they, with their small shields, hold out for the least time against the
cavalry charges, but were slain, every one, in the sight of both
armies."

The Pompeians huddled together, unnerved and horrified, no
water, no food, nor hope of safety, a pudding of an army that the
slightest blow would crush. Centurions and tribunes flocked around
Caesar, begging him to order the charge, it would not be a fight
but a massacre, they could kill them all by sunset and with the slightest loss. But the Proconsul would not.

"Why should I lose any men at all, even in a successful battle?"
he cried loud enough for the privates to hear. "Why should I suffer
any of the men who have served me so well to be wounded? Especially as it is as much the duty of a commander to win by policy
as by the sword. Let us have compassion; these are fellow-citizens,
Romans, whose slaughter appears inevitable. I prefer to gain my
object without loss to us or harm to them." The officers retired,
grumbling sourly that he might not find them so ready to fight next

CAMPAIGN OF DYRRACHIUM

Buthrotum (on the larger map) was the main Pompeian naval base. On the smaller map, Caesar's doubled lines near the seashore are shown at the base; the little square just above them is Pompey's secret camp, connected with his main lines by a rampart crossing the brook Lesnikia.

time, but the Proconsul's stone face was inflexible, he drew back his lines a little space and let the harried Pompeians return unharmed and wondering to their camp.

That night he set guards on all the outlets from Afranius' position and moved his own camp south of the enemy's. They were in trouble about water, the Gallic horse kept attacking the watering-

Coin of Caesar

parties. Afranius and Petreius decided to draw a palisaded rampart from the camp to the valley were most of the reservoirs lay and went out to superintend the engineering details. While they were about it, Caesar sent his men forward, not to attack but to fraternize. The conversations began with the Pompeian soldiers thanking Caesar's for sparing their lives the day before, and expressing the feeling, which must have been pretty general in their camp, that they were fighting on the wrong side. They were, however, afraid that if they surrendered now they would end up in the arena or on the block.

——Oh, no (Caesar's men assured them), Our general is the mildest of masters—— and doubtless proved the point with tales of how he had spared Domitius Ahenobarbus after Corfinium and sent traitor Labienus' personal papers after him. The incredulous Pompeians sent a deputation of centurions to hear the truth from Caesar's own lips. He confirmed all his men had said; promised he would not harm even Afranius or Petreius. That made things simple; they went about the detail of arranging a capitulation, with old friend visiting old friend and townsman townsman throughout both camps, amid much jollification, when Afranius and Petreius rode back in with their personal bodyguards.

Afranius was for accepting the situation as it stood, but Petreius was stiffer in the backbone. He sounded the trumpet, paraded his guard and an ala of barbarian horse, cut down all the Caesarians he could catch and ordered the rest to be given up. Those whom he caught he killed; but Caesar gave to the Pompeians found in his camp a present of money and sent them to their homes.

Now the war began again, with the Roman habit of discipline reasserting itself among the Pompeians as Petreius took hold in place of Afranius, who was completely unmanned. The new chief's one idea was get back to Ilerda. He started in the morning, marching in hollow square, and it was a horrible march, with the Gallic horse persecuting the marchers unmercifully. They had to stop a dozen times to drive off these pests and when they charged too deep into the shifting ranks they ran into Caesar's legions, rebounding each time with losses heavier than they liked to take. When night came they camped once more, still seven miles from the temporary safety of Ilerda citadel and two from water.

Morning brought no respite. Indeed it made matters worse, for the Pompeians were able to observe that Caesar was fencing them round with a long ditch and rampart. They threw away their trappings, slaughtered all the beef and baggage cattle, and thus lightened, tried one more push, but it was no use, the same old story— cavalry all around slowing the march to a dragfoot crawl, with Caesar's legions stiffening the resistance, so they could not even get beyond the trench line.

Petreius rested one night more, then came out in line, offering the battle his party had been so anxious to avoid while they held Ilerda. Now he could not have it on any terms; Caesar merely formed in a way to protect his growing line of forts and kept the men digging. The Pompeians went back and endured for two days more, without water, firewood or any food whatever; then Afranius blew a point of parley and sent in to ask a private interview. Caesar refused, but offered one in eye- and ear-shot of both armies.

The Pompeian leaders came out and humbly confessed they were beaten men, begging Caesar not to be angry with them for having been faithful to Pompey and their duty; if there were mercy in the world he would at least spare their lives.

——Nobody (said Caesar) has less right than you to complain of the hardness of war or to make appeals for mercy—and rolled on into a little oration on the justice of his cause and how ill they had guarded Spain for the Roman people, at the end of which he set his terms at this not extravagant figure: Afranius and Petreius to resign as governors in Spain, their army to be disbanded and sent home, themselves to give paroles not to fight against him again.

Men and officers accepted with a wild joy, as though reprieved from the gallows, as indeed they were, for it was the custom in these civil struggles to treat beaten enemies hard. Caesar gathered up his legions and began a slow march for Gades and Ulterior Spain—slow to let news of his victory and coming precede him and do the work of more victories. He reckoned rightly; Varro the botanist-governor had been clucking around like some bad-tempered barnyard hen, trying to raise money and a fleet during the fighting in the north, but when news of Caesar's approach arrived, he dropped the effort and tried to throw himself into Gades for a siege. One of his two legions mutinied and deserted to Caesar; the Gaditanians closed their gates in his face and declared for their old governor, and Varro had to surrender at discretion.

Caesar sent him home to watch his forcing-bed and book-shelves, gave back to the provincials the money he had taken from them and left Q. Cassius Longinus as governor of Spain. Cassius was not liked well in that country but he was a knowledgeable man and could be counted on to do an intelligent job. He had the two legions which had been in Varro's service.

4

Indicative—Massilia had fallen and the summer worn away in a changing dance of war, now dark, now light. Caesar had the news from the packet of dispatches he found waiting in Narbonnese Gaul under the drooping leaves of autumn.

Light: Massilia was taken after a hard, bruising siege by land and sea. Legate Trebonius heaved up a mound against the wall but those within were not feather-pated Gauls to take fear at such a sight; Phocaean Greeks, rather, masters of the science of their world, who lined the battlements with giant catapults that drove twelve foot steel-tipped lances through mantlet, shield and mail and three men behind from a quarter of a mile distant. Trebonius roofed his works in timbers a foot thick; the Massiliotes set them on fire with blazing arrows. He bricked them over and covered the bricks with rawhide; the defenders hammered them with huge stones that cracked brick and timber alike. He plated the bricks with layers of matted anchor cable, and now there was nothing to be done, the moving tower marched in, the battering rams began to beat and the walls crumbled. There was yet hope for the besieged; Pompey had sent from his eastern headquarters Lucius Nasidius with sixteen ships, who ran swiftly through the strait of Messana, up the Italian coast and camped near the beleaguered city. When Admiral Brutus turned against him the Massiliotes brought out their fleet, resurrected for one more battle. There was another fight off the harbor, more desperately carried on than the first, but the end of it was that Brutus had the best of the battle, Nasidius fled, and the Massiliotes lost ten more ships, with the last remnants of their fine navy crushed back to the quays. The town surrendered not long later; but with Domitius urging, the people had a try at treachery, making a sudden rush two days after the surrender, and burnt out the siege works. Trebonius rebuilt them huger than before, of brick and masonry; he hammered great gaps in the walls, brought down two towers and forced an entry. The town capitulated again; the soldiers wanted to sack it, but Caesar came in time to stop them, though not in time to catch the arch-villain Domitius, who had run through the blockade and away on the wings of a howling gale in the last days of the siege.

Light: Scribonius Curio landed in Sicily with the three Corfinium legions. Cato held the island for the Senate, but with no force to combat such an army. He abandoned his charge with the characteristically Catonian gesture of summoning the leading merchants to a meeting at which he told them that Pompey was a scoundrel who left his lieutenants helpless after lightly raising a mad war that would devour them all ——However (he continued), he represents the cause of constitutional government. I shall leave to join him at once and I advise you to do the same.—— The merchants laughed, stayed and sold their grain to the Curio. Through the summer it went up the peninsula in long wagon caravans that freed Rome from the fear of famine and blockade.

Dark: Curio transported two of his legions to the African province. He was opposed by Attius Varus, a kind-hearted, generous great gentleman, much loved by all the slaves of his vast estates, a failure at Auxinum, but a good captain for all that. Varus had an ally, King Juba of the Numidians, who would join any party against Curio, hating the man because he had once offered a bill in the Senate to depose the king. Curio had no experience in the field, yet approved himself a good man of war in the beginning by surprising a landing on the coast. He marched inland; near Utica he won a battle by virtue of his own impetuous drive and the fire of his Gallic cavalry, who broke the light Numidian lancers in a thundering charge, then rolled up the Pompeian line. But Curio was self-satisfied, Curio was arrogant, he must play the little Caesar, a part he conceived to mean reckless dash without scouts or flankers to his column of advance. He made a furious pursuit march through a thirsty land, so fast his soldiers wearied and the cavalry could not follow. At the end of the road Numidians came flying through the heat-haze from the rocks on every side, it was too far back and the length of the Sahara forward, and there died Scribonius Curio and all his men.

Dark, light and dark, light, dark, but darkest from the Adriatic shore, where Dolabella's new Caesarian war-fleet clashed with Pompey's navies and lost a disastrous battle with a score of vessels sinking among the flailing oars. Caius Antonius, a kinsman of the fighting legate, came round the boot of Italy with Caesar's Tyrrhenian fleet to repair the wreck, but came too late and was cooped up in Black Corcyra with fifteen cohorts of men. The place was bare of corn, the Pompeian squadrons caught up his messengers and sank his best ships when he strove to cut through. His vice-admiral,

Titus Puleio, turned Judas on him—and Caius Antonius must surrender with fleet and army, a deadly harmful stroke to Caesar, for
how could he now win over the Tarentine strait to reach Pompey
in Greece?

The 9th Legion, at all events, were sure he could not; at Placen-
tia on the march south they mutinied, declaring they were tired of
war and fearful of the future. (Better say tired of war on Caesar's
plan, for the grievance, as privily reported, was that they had been
appointed to guard the captured legions from Spain on the march
home, and never allowed to plunder a man or steal a slave.) Caesar
was in the north when the mutiny broke out: he descended on the
9th like a god of wrath, with more faithful legions grouped round
him, clove to the marrow of the dispute in one day's questioning,
and declared his intent of decimating the recreant legion; that is,
cutting the head off every tenth man, the old Roman punishment,
not used for ages.

Coming suddenly to a sense of their position the 9th begged mercy
and hard service. Caesar so far relented as to execute only twelve
ringleaders, then marched to Rome for a brief delay before hurrying on to Brundisium to mobilize for the advance on Greece and
Pompey. When he left the city a deputation of men of all classes
followed him down the road crying that the world wanted peace;
but it was observed that in the mock combats between "Caesarians"
and "Pompeians" among the urchins of the slums the Caesarians
always won.

5

Sword and Trident—Cicero, whose counsel seldom wanted candor
when he could lard advice with an epigram, was taken by Pompey
to see a grand review of the army soon after arriving in Epiros. His
face must have expressed misgiving, for the captain-general of the
Senate was moved to ask what the orator thought he ought to do.

"Make peace," grunted Cicero, and when Pompey, with some
heat, pronounced his intention of going on with the war to the last
extremity, added grudgingly, "Well, then, make it last as long as
possible."

What Pompey replied, the orator failed to state and the retort would probably not have looked well among the decorous verbosities of his published correspondence if he had recorded it, but the estimate of the senatorial army he had expressed was shared by both men. A rag-tag and bobtail host, impressive in name and number, with archers from Crete and Lacedaemon, from Pontus and the Cyclades; with Deiotarus, Tetrarch of Galatia and six hundred horsemen; King Ariobarzanes of Cappadocia leading five hundred more, and the same number from King Cotys of Thrace; from Macedon, two hundred, under Lord Rhascypolis, a man of particular valor; eight hundred slaves and mounted shepherds from Pompey's own estates; two hundred horse-bowmen of the desert—a parade of strange names and battle-cries. Nor could their numbers hide the fact that they were Oriental and mercenary, the East in arms against the eagles for pay, as it had been in the old princely days when Rome won the world under the Scipios and Aemillus Paulus. Caesar (trust him!) had not failed to emphasize the point by securing election as Consul of Rome when the old year faded out; now he was authorized general of the Republic against her enemies from oversea.

Of legions, Pompey had nine, five that he had brought from Italy, one garrison legion from Cilicia, three of re-enlisted veterans from Asia and Macedon, but the Italian troops unsteady and shot with desertion, their cadres filled out by pressed captives from Caius Antonius' force, who wanted to fight on the other side. Interspersed among the whole were Thessalians, Acarnanians and other impolite peoples armed after the Roman manner. Sixty thousand all told, but no homogeneity, no cohesion, no drill. With right good military reason Pompey might hold a low opinion of Caesar's soldiership (——Why, the man's a lucky blunderer only, he used to say, incapable of arranging a battle in form!——) but anyone would hesitate before attempting Roman legions with such a patched-up array.

No—Pompey was not contemptuous, however the young senatorial magnificoes might tot up thousands and laugh as they diced for the property of rich Radical A, fat tax-farmer B, whose names would be on the proscription list . . . when they returned to Rome. Not contemptuous; Cicero's advisement ran with the very teaching of his own experience—prolong the war, hold the seas and drill these ragged bands to conscience of their high mission.

The old general took his part in good spirit; his fifty-eight years sat light on his shoulders, so that he was again almost the young triumphant Pompey of splendid enthusiasms whom Sulla had saluted as Great. When old Tidius Sextius, lame in a leg, came into camp, champing his toothless gums, and the heartless young aristocrats laughed at him for a figure of fun, 'twas Pompey left his seat and ran to embrace the aged man, exclaiming for all to hear that the cause of justice was well served when men of such infirmities chose to be there in danger rather than in peace at Rome. In the morning Pompey was first from bed; he rode at the front of the headlong galloping cavalry when they drilled; at teaching infantry to wield sword and shield he was the best sergeant of the army, and few of the young men could match the skill and force with which he hurled the javelin.

So the autumn passed and winter storms began to blow down the Adriatic. The drill went on, the seas were tightly kept, for here at least Pompey held the strong hand, with five hundred men o' war and Cornelius Bibulus (Caesar's one-time partner in the consulate) as high admiral. He split his force in five fleets for the winter, keeping them in base harbors with only light cruiser squadrons out to run down any scouts Caesar might send.

On the 4th January there blew a gale. The night was calm of wind but held a long queasy swell that tired the rowers fast. Lucretius Vespillo and Minucius Rufus, in charge of eighteen light galleys based on Oricum, judged it prudent to keep port till fairer weather shone, but toward noon a countryman came in all hot with tidings that there was a flotilla on the sea. Vespillo and Rufus put out at once and ran down past the Acroceraunian peaks; as they rounded the promontory that shelters Avlona's gulf, they could make them out—a great navy of transports rocking on the tide, their decks black with men, their sails gleaming in the cold wintry light. It was Caesar!—the madman actually daring the strait in the teeth of wind and Pompey's fleets,

See map
facing page 240

Alongside the transports were galleys; one—two—three to twelve Vespillo counted as they swung prows and massed for a fight with white foam bubbling beneath their rams. Not as many as their own eighteen cruisers, but though the transports behind were lumbering slow, they would hurl their cargoes of invincible legionaries into a close action with terrible effect. Vespillo and Rufus dared not attack. Bibulus was their nearest help with a hundred and ten warships, but he lay under the shadow of Corcyra, fifty miles away, and the Caesarian armada was already close in. The Pompeian admirals did what they could—their fastest two ships sent off by a circuit to warn the high admiral, themselves retiring on Apollonia northward, to ask troops to be sent down. Too late at both points; Caesar had his landing unopposed at Palaeste.

He had only seven legions, all much under strength, with shortage of arms, supplies and many things needful, the lack of ships at embarkation having pinched so sore, and there was no cavalry to speak of. Yet they formed on the beach with right good heart, climbed panting up the precipitous steep slope above, then plunged down a long scaur of a pass between piney overhangs on Oricum. Manlius Torquatus held the place for Pompey, but his troops were local; when Caesar summoned the place they said they would not contend with the Consul of Rome, as good an excuse as any to keep from fighting the seven grim legions with their own slender numbers. Just at twilight Caesar marched into the town under the pall of smoke from some grain ships Vespillo had fired in the harbor, with a secure base on the Epirote side won eight hours from landing. Legate Fufius Calinus went back with the transports that night; within two days' space he was expected to rejoin with four more legions, supplies and cavalry.

That hope turned sham; Vespillo's scouts had warned Bibulus. He put to sea with his whole armada at the coming of the news and the night being fair and windless, caught up the Caesarian transports off Brundisium, going home empty. Thirty he captured and barbarously burnt, ships and crews, "hoping the rest would be deterred by the severity of this pain." Thence turning back he made good his defect by setting so keen a watch along the coast not even Amphion's own dolphin could have pierced his sea-guards. Caesar must live or die by what he had carried in that first secret dash.

Yet it was no thought of despair for the blockade that made the Consul send a new offer of peace, for that was done the first night, as he lay in Oricum, before Bibulus' raid. The embassage was Vibullius Rufus, the old Pompeian officer taken with Afranius in Spain and guarded for such a purpose. The terms: all armies to be disbanded within three days, Senate and Roman people to arbitrate the quarrel. Vibullius took the charge but with first intent to school Pompey of his danger; he posted night and day across the hills to find his chief marching slowly west from the plains of Macedon, where he had held his autumn manoeuvres, and told him of the fall of Oricum.

Pompey caught the danger at once; Caesar, pushing north, would cut him from the coast, hold the ends of the great lateral Egnatian Way, seize the rich magazines at Dyrrachium and Apollonia, and ruin his sea-power by depriving the fleet of bases. He sent the march-pace up to double and treble-quick, so fast that some of the recruits threw away their arms and took to the woods. At Asperagium, where the highway splits for the two bases, he heard that Apollonia was gone, captured on the 6th, when the townsfolk declared for Caesar and threw open their gates. At Dyrrachium he was still in time; he camped outside the city and while Labienus tried to restore some order in the shaken army, Vibullius broached the mission of peace Caesar had given him.

He did it cleverly enough, persuading to support the cause Scribonius Libo, Theophanes (Pompey's Greek secretary) and Lucius Lucceius, who once stood with Caesar for the consulate but who, like most free-thinking rich men, had abandoned his dilettante radicalism at the clash of arms. Pompey heard barely three sentences, then stopped the deputation with upraised hand. ——Of what use is Roman citizenship (he asked) or even life itself, to me, if I must own them to Caesar's bounty?——

No accommodation, the whole world held too brief space for two such giants, let the sword say which should rule.

Caesar had halted at the Apsus river, throwing supply-roots into

Greece behind him. Pompey marched down and they faced each other across the stream. There was another faint effort to negotiate, aborting when Labienus came down to the bank and bellowed over that "Peace we can have none till we have Caesar's head!"—the truth at last. The armies hung there, Pompey drilling, Caesar desperately anxious for reinforcements. Marcus Antonius had come

Coin of Pompey

down to Brundisium and was in command there, waiting for wind, with four more legions—the last two of the veterans from Gaul, the 5th and a big recruit legion, the 27th.

Bibulus held the blockade against them through two months of storm with lack of food and particularly of water throughout his fleet, a strange situation, for the Caesarian posts held all the shoreside springs and the fleet had to run clear to Corcyra or Dyrrachium for supplies. By time the supply vessels brought back water the load was uneconomic; mostly the sailors drank dew and rain-water caught in awnings.

The admiral suffered agonies from chills, fever and a vindictive hatred of Caesar that would not let him rest. Once he sought to gin the man he loathed with false negotiations for a truce; once he raided Brundisium harbor and lost an amphibian struggle among shoals and islands. In February he weakened and died of combined spleen and pneumonia; there was no one left with such a driving force of malevolence to be trusted with full admiralty, so the squadrons were divided among several commandants and Caesar began to get messengers through. He wrote anxiously to Antonius, urging him to make the passage while the southwest gales were on the water and would carry transports across the straits faster than the Pompeian oarsmen could drive in pursuit.

At the end of March Antonius struck, putting out on the tail of a westering storm that held the Pompeian ships pinned back against the Epirote coast. At noon his ships raised the Acroceraunians and Apollonia's phare, but in such a gale they durst not clew up for the entrance and must run away up the coast. The wind carried them right on past Dyrrachium; Pompey saw them from the heights and so did his vice-admiral of the port, Caius Coponius. Coponius hurried out with sixteen war-galleys; the wind fell light then and they gained through the afternoon, while the legionary soldiers formed on Antonius' decks to make the best defense they could, with not much chance against Coponius' driving rams.

Antonius had a battalion of Balaeric slingers aboard. They were just taking aim with the hope of knocking out a steersman or hortator in the oncoming warships when the wind suddenly freshened in whirling gusts, hard from the south. Straight ahead lay the harbor of Nymphaeum, open to the gale; it would wreck the ships to go ashore there, but save the legions. Antonius headed straight in.

Fortune stood valor's aid; no sooner had the homing transports swirled through the neck of the harbor than the storm shifted southwest again. Coponius' galleys could not bear up against it, the rowers being so weary after the long pursuit, and the ships caught in a powerful current beside the wind. Every one of the sixteen went shivering on the rocks.

Two of the transports also were lost. Dull sailers, they had lagged and went aground south of Coponius' flotilla. Pompey's men held the shore at the point where they came to land. The Pompeians persuaded the 220 recruits of the 27th from one of the ships to surrender and then cut their throats. The 200 veterans of the 5th in the other ship put up a bold front and ultimately cut their way through to Antonius, who wanted to slaughter those of Coponius' crews he had captured. Caesar forbade it, gave each of the captives a new cloak and sent him to his home.

But that was later; meanwhile the messengers telling of the landing had reached Pompey at midnight and Caesar at three in the morning, when Pompey had already stolen from his camp to lay an ambush for Antonius, as he should march to join his chief. The point was near Scampa on the Egnatian Way. Pompey hid, lightless, silent, but country Greeks carried the news to Antonius, who stood fast, waiting. Caesar circled. His messengers reached Antonius and they concerted a plan to fall on Pompey with sudden double shock at daybreak, but the old general had scouted them and slipped the blow back to Dyrrachium.

With Antonius' reinforcements Caesar passed from standfast defense to a campaign of flowing manoeuvre. East in Macedon, Metellus Scipio was coming up with two new legions from Syria to Pompey's help. The Consul detached the 11th and 12th to hold him off under Domitius Calvinus, another bankrupt bought aristo, who had once sought the consulate as the Senate's candidate, but a man of good military experience. South into Aetolia went Lucius Cassius for Caesar with the 27th, part of a new effort to win supplies and barbaric allies in Greece, for Caesar was now completely cut off from Italy by a new disaster on the narrow seas.

It had fallen thus; Pompey had a son, young Gnaeus, the mirror of his sire, who led a cruiser squadron from the Dyrrachium base. He came onto Oricum out of the blue, smothered the guardship at the harbor mouth under a cloud of missiles, kedged up the hulk that blocked the entrance and once in, carried off or burned all the ships there. Next day he showed at Nymphaeum and repeated the trick on the fleet Antonius had crossed in. Caesar's sea-lines were smashed beyond repair, not even news of him came through to Rome, where men lived in ominous excitement and the shadow of death. The only news they had was that from Pompey's camp; they expected him to win and the victorious aristocrats to come with their legions any day and open the proscription lists.

Not yet; Caesar's men and Caesar felt he held the upper hand. He turned from Scampa down the road to Asperagium where the enemy stood, and with his 35,000 flung a challenge to battle in the teeth of Pompey's 60,000. Pompey shunned the encounter; now the armies faced each other on the south bank of Genusus, a little stream that follows the Egnatian Way to the sea.

Next day Caesar turned east out of his camp. Pompey thought he had gone off on a provision hunt, but toward midnight was routed from bed by an officer to interview some peasants who had brought the well-nigh incredible news that Caesar was swinging north along the vaulted rocks of the watershed and was marching like mad to cut between him and the Dyrrachium base. The men were gotten out of bed to the road before daybreak. They had the short line and good paving, but Caesar so much of a start on his exploit that as the Pompeians debouched beyond the white rock of Petra, there stood the hostile army, poised like a lion couchant between them and their food-bins.

6

Ave, Pompeius, Imperator!—It had been a great and a punishing march, sixteen hours among the crags in full kit, but it failed its purpose after all against Pompey's invincible determination not to clutch close till his men were drilled to ripeness. He would not attack; Dyrrachium across the bay was too strong to be stormed by less than an army and impossible for an army with an enemy behind it. Caesar could only stand across the road and watch while Pompey fortified the white rock of Petra and drew supplies across the bay by water.

No—it would not do, Pompey the Great was too good a soldier to throw his weight behind an ill-prepared thrust in a moment of panic or pique. The man had balance, was unashamed to confess himself beaten at chess, looked to the larger issue. No—his mind was walled in granite and unassailable, it was his strength as well as his weakness. To haunt him from his shell a new plan was needed that would pinch with actual and not threatened pressure. And however planned it must be planned hastily, for every hour Caesar's strength trickled thinner through mere waste of war.

Trickled thinner, for he could not call in barbarians and mercenaries as Pompey did, press men, station requisition officers in every hamlet, raid temples for their gold. Caesar was dedicated to a less imperial theory, one that did not treat the world as a private corporation organized for the benefit of senatorial aristocrats or every man who disagreed as a traitor. His case was that large powers subtend large responsibilities, that one could have control of millions in men and money only on condition of employing them for objective purposes. The Senate's tactic of impressment, forced contribution and proscription had provided it with a powerful army, but to imitate that tactic was to admit that the Senate's theory was right to the extent that it was more effective in meeting practical emergencies. And then he had no motive for making war but personal ambition or a mouldy idealism, unrealistic as Cato's. Yet his army was wearing out, the loss of the sea-lines cut him off from reinforcement from the only quarter whence he could accept help, that is, the Roman citizenship; and his only course was to attack his adversary where he stood or similarly to damn him from his fountains of resource.

"On considering these points Caesar took counsel from the nature of the place", Pompey being on a littoral shut against the Adriatic *See map facing page 240* by hills sharp and dangerous indeed, but where an engineer might trace a high commanding line to cut off egress to the inland valleys. The armies rested one night; the next Pompey's men saw torches flashing among the peaks and when day came perceived Caesar had seized those nearest and was beginning to hem their army in with a line of trench and fort.

That brought fight; Pompey's light troops boiled out for fierce local attacks with sling and arrow and a few cohorts in supporting distance. The combats were deadlier than they looked, day-long pounding with every shot aimed, and so many men wounded that Caesar's fatigue gangs spent their free hours making themselves queer bulgy overcoats of rawhide or cut-up bedquilts to turn the missiles. The work went on; there was no way of stopping it altogether but by the general battle Pompey would not risk. Nevertheless he devised a counter by building lines of his own opposite Caesar's, taking in as much ground as he could. As he had more men, the lines ran faster. He pushed the contravallation out so far it swept in part of the ridge Caesar wanted.

The spur of the line was held by the 9th Legion at the time. Pompey launched a surprise attack that carried that legion down hill, across a valley and up the opposite slope in a hot little charge. Caesar himself rallied the legion; Antonius led a rousing counter-charge that drove Pompey's advance in with heavy loss but the spur was not to be regained.

Bad check; Caesar was forced to swing his line wider to the next ridge, and that made his problem twice as hard, for the circuit he built was really too wide to keep with his 22,000 men, being sixteen miles from end to end, a man to every four feet, provided none of them ever slept. Pompey did not make matters easier; he kept up nagging little drives on special points, his archers creeping up draws in the night and loosing flights of arrows at the campfires, so that Caesar's men must camp chilly and eat cold food or run the risk of unseen death.

Yet the lines closed tight, they pinched, they pinched; Caesar got at the sources of the brooks and smothered them, so there was no water in the senatorial camp and the mules all died. The stench of rotting flesh fouled the air; food was bad and scarce among the senatorials, the dandies of the salons had to blister their sweet hands digging wells or gag with thirst, and forage was so much lacking that the cavalry was shipped by sea across the bay to Dyrrachium.

It arrived most opportune. Caesar had a letter from a traitor inside the fortress and was planning a surprise of the gate. The traitor was a double traitor; as the column of attack came toward the walls in the night, out rushed Pompey's horsemen in a thundering onset that smashed up the Caesarian vanguard, while another column struck at flank and rear. The Consul was hard put to it for a while, only the steadiness of the splendid 10th saving a disaster, and as the men slugged back to camp at break of day there came a messenger to say that Pompey was assaulting the lines.

It was true; Pompey had planned it so, a double operation, hurling four full legions through the grey of dawn against a single redoubt at the center of the line where Cohort VIII of the 6th, less than 300 men, held the post. The fight was like a whirlwind, with Centurion

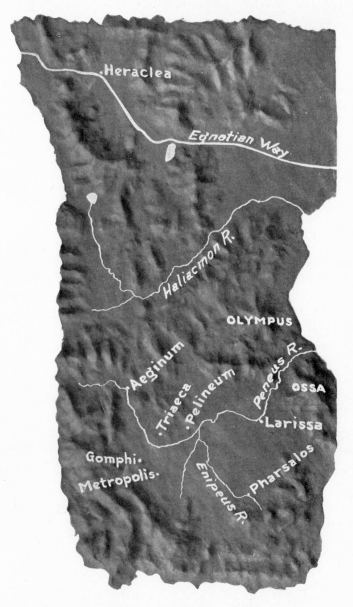

CAMPAIGN OF PHARSALIA

The valley of the Aous, by which Caesar marched to Thessally,
is shown on the previous map.

Cassius Scaeva the hero of the day, standing all alone in the gate, like Horatius the One-eyed, striking down a dozen foes with incredible address, though he came out of it more like Horatius than he cared to be, for he lost an eye in that brawl and took wounds in leg and shoulder, yes, and had a hundred and twenty holes in his shield when it was over. Every man of the three hundred was wounded; the palisades were coming down, when Legate Publius Sulla appeared over the hill with the 7th and 12th at the run. They charged into the Pompeian flank, threw the stormers back down the slope, drove them headlong in torrential rout—and then Sulla sounded the recall, not wishing to call in more legions and make it a full-dress battle without orders from his head.

Caesar heard the news without a murmur of disappointment, even praised Sulla for saving the redoubt, and paraded as much of his army as could be spared from the lines to hear the warm words of praise with which he gave Cassius Scaeva the bays of valor, a purse of two hundred thousand sesterces and promotion to the highest command in the legion.

It was June now and growing hotter. Such vantage as Pompey had won he lost again when Caesar set forts opposite the gates of Dyrrachium and kept the Pompeian cavalry horses from coming out to eat. They had to be re-embarked and now forage was shorter than ever in the senatorial camp, with half the men detailed to feed the starving creatures by pounding up a gruel of roots and bark for them. The animals did poorly on it; Pompey saw he must some or anyhow break the blockade, for his sole strength and advantage was in those horses and the men who rode them, it would be long before he could match Caesar's legionary foot.

Occasion developed with necessity; on a night in June two Allobrogian Gauls, Egus and Roucillus, appeared before his sentry-line. They had been officers in Caesar's cavalry; he caught them cheating on the soldiers' food, a mean crime, and gave them demotion and a public reprimand, which they interpreted as earnest of severer pains to come. To insure welcome when they deserted they sought all they could learn of posts, trenches and routine, whose guard was badly kept, which ramparts weakly held.

There was a spot at the southern end of the encircling line where it curved across a little plain to the sea, just beyond the brook Lesnikia. The lines were doubled here, with a transverse trench along the beach lest men be landed from boats to take them in reverse. They looked stout enough from Pompey's side, but Egus and Roucillus said the transverse trench had gaps, not being finished, and that the 9th Legion, which held the sector, was so few in numbers its night watch was a mere picket. Pompey got his light-armed into boats, all helmed in woven wicker hoods, his own invention to fend the sling and ballista balls that do most of the wounding at night.

Toward dawn of the 9th July the boats went round from his lines and came in onto the beach. The men rushed for the southern end of the trenches with a trumpet screaming. At the sound, up rose sixty cohorts that had taken cover near the inside of the lines, and made a charge. Pompey himself led; he burst through the gap in the uncompleted transverse trench, taking both defense lines in the rear and knocking down the men of the 9th like a row of skittles. There were only two cohorts of them on duty, anyhow, just changing the guard, caught disordered and out of alignment. Caesar's Quaestor Marcellinus roused the other eight cohorts in their camp at the foot of the hills and came pounding down to the rescue, but they were disordered and hasty too, and Pompey had time to form his men, seventy cohorts against eight in that close place, where numbers and pushing pike told heavily. The 9th went to pieces; the Pompeians pressed shouting on to storm Marcellinus' camp and Legate Antonius from the mountain tops arrived with twelve more cohorts only just in time to save it.

Twelve veteran cohorts and those big ramparts were more than Pompey could swallow at a gulp; he halted to reconnoiter and prepare for an assault in form, and while he was doing it Caesar came riding in at the head of thirteen cohorts more, who had seen a black bar of smoke across the morning sky and knew it meant disaster.

The Consul saw the position must be retaken. There was the whole day to take it in, for Pompey, obviously satisfied with his gain, which pierced the siege-lines, had working parties out to fortify the place and would evidently attack no more that day. Caesar dropped two cohorts to cut a line facing the new Pompeian fortification, which would lull Pompey's attention; paraded the rest in a pair of columns, plucked up their spirits with a few words and then sent them forward, quickstep along the bank of the brook Lesnikia to sever Pompey from his main army.

Pompey had a redoubt at the spot where they struck and a rampart running back to his main lines behind a screen of trees. Caesar's men did not know of it till they came against it, but stormed in so fast that on the right they breached the palisaded wall, on the left burst into the redoubt and waged a surging struggle among the tents within. The feat took time; in that time Pompey rushed reinforcements by the sea-face, chiefly horsemen who fell on Caesar's right in a crashing charge, caught this wing at the loose and hurried it back. The men tried to crowd out through the breaches in the palisade; they jammed and there was an unreasoning panic that spread to the left wing as well. Caesar rode in, trying to stop it, seized the flying standard-bearers to make them face the enemy, but they were already so beyond control that one of them tried to strike him down to get away the faster. Pompey's numerous cavalry poured in on the stampede, hacking and shouting, everything was lost—but just then the signal of recall blew in the senatorial camp, the whole raging parade whipped round and went home.

So Caesar got off with his life, but that was all, for his strong lines of Dyrrachium were burst, the army had suffered heavy loss, was routed and in despair, no longer fit for battle against a triumphant enemy of more than three to one. Nothing for it but retreat; the men were drawn in through afternoon and evening to Marcellinus' camp to prepare.

As they marched down with standards and spirits trailing, they could see the lights and hear the shouts of jubilee over against them, where the Pompeians were celebrating their victory. "Imperator!" they called to Pompey, and gave a cheer as headsman's axe fell on the neck of each of the prisoners, whom Labientus had lined up for this curious form of sport. Most of them were from the 9th Legion, which he had commanded in Gaul, so he knew them by name and reputation and was able to address to each man the taunts that would most deeply sting, just before he sent him to the block.

7

Swerve to the Right ——Nobody's fault (said Caesar to his men); Luck's against us now, my hearties, but never stays so long. Remember how we wiped out Gergovia in the Vale of Tille and after? Heads up! We'll pipe these perfumed dandies yet a tune to make them jig.——

The soldiers' hearts went up high, as men's do who feel themselves unreasonably beaten; they would have fought once more that night, gone growling against Pompey's trenches, but Caesar said no, now we must wait a fairer day, retreat's the word and see whether this Infinite Wisdom will hold himself, as few men do, restrained in victory.

Retreat itself was no easy problem, with two bridgeless rivers to cross and a long train of wounded from the late battle; they went on in the wagon-train at night with a legion for convoy, toward Apollonia. Four legions followed; toward day the signal sounded and Caesar marched out with the rearguard. Pompey might have rumpled up badly during the movement, but his scouts got drunk in celebration and he was so happy he did not care. It was day before he discovered the escape, pushed out the cavalry on Caesar's trail and caught up his rearguard at the Genusus, but there they were received with so rude a shock they were glad to cry quits. The pursuit went on beyond the river; at the Apsus it caught up again and Caesar turned as though to bay, fortifying a camp. Pompey did likewise, but when his men were scattered to hew down timber Caesar packed up, flitted across the river and away to safety by a cleverly stolen march.

The Senatorials though the war was over now; they held wrangling debates in which the offices of the state were assigned for seven years to come and a triple list of proscription prepared—those for death, those for confiscation without death and those who would receive only heavy fines. Everybody wanted to embark for Italy at once and begin the joyful harvest, but Pompey misliked the idea on grounds of first catch your hare, whereat the lords of the fish-ponds raised a terrific hullabaloo against him for prolonging the war and thus his own magnificence. "We'll eat no figs in Tusculum this year," snarled Favonius, Cato's ape, and a standing joke grew up among the young men that after Caesar was put down there must be another war to rid themselves of Caesar's slayer. The Infinite Wisdom only growled and gave out marching orders for Thessaly, where by a quick move and a secret one, he hoped to trap Caesar's legate Domitius Calvinus as he manoeuvred against Metellus Scipio along the banks of the Haliacmon river.

Calvinus had had all the best of the exchange, for Metellus Scipio was an ass—"Since his soldiers would not confer on him the title of Imperator he assumed it for himself and coined money to prove his dignity"—an ass who had been pushed from the north Greek cantons by his opponent without a battle. But now it was early summer, with the young corn unripe and old stores gone, so shortage of victual oppressed Calvinus. He heard there was a depot at Heraclea along the great Egnatian Way, adroitly slipped a march around

See map
facing page 257 Metellus Scipio and made for it. Among the Lyncestian hills his cavalry screen suddenly encountered a Pompeian patrol. It was led by Egus and Roucillus, the traitor-Gauls. They held up their hands to Calvinus' men. ——We have changed lords (they cried) and our new master is a great chief who has lately beaten this Caesar in a battle and is coming to eat your general up. Join now and save your lives.—— Calvinus' men galloped away with the news; he could not know the whole story but saw something was amiss, so spun round on his heel and headed south across the mountain-spurs by forced marches for the great plain of Thessaly.

Near Aeginum he made contact with Caesar, who at news of Pompey's movement (even in defeat his espionage service was working) had swung eastward up the valley of the Aous, a narrow and difficult route, but shorter than that by which Pompey had come.

The news of Dyrrachium had spread like a ripple across a lake, and the Thessalian communes won by Calvinus' good work were all

changing allegiance. When Caesar came before Gomphi the gates
were closed and warders on the wall, with messengers already
riding to beg help from Pompey and Metellus. Caesar tried to parley;
the townsmen shot an arrow at him, and since time pressed (for he
could neither afford to turn back into the mountains nor to leave
an inimical fortress in his rear) he ordered the place be stormed.
The 9th led the onset, blazing fiercely to erase its failure at Dyrrachium, up, up the walls and in after a hard three-hour struggle.
For the inhabitants' changeableness and hardness of heart Caesar
let the town be sacked.

Next day early the army took the march again, arriving toward
night before Metropolis, second of the quadrilateral of strongholds
that held down the Thessalian west; Gomphi-Metropolis-Trieca-
Pelinaeum. Here also the people offered defiance and stout walls
but Caesar sent an embassage forward with prisoners from Gomphi,
whose tale of their woes weaned the Metropolitans from any warlike
humors. The troops marched in. Caesar set guards to keep the
townsfolk safe from plunder or even insult, which clemency, set
against the sack of Gomphi and the Pompeians' steady policy of
plundering every city, friend or foe, insured Caesar complaisance
from other towns within reach of his arm.

This meant all south of the Peneus river, which splits Thessaly
midway, for Pompey was now descending the hills north of that
stream with Metellus Scipio's two legions and his own, harried on
toward battle by senators desirous of playing football with Caesar's
head. Labienus was after the general, too. "Think not," he said,
"that his army before us is the old invincible that brought down
Germany and Gaul. The men of that army have died in battle or
of the autumn fever, or have retired from mere old age. These are
raw Transpadine recruits; a puff will blow them down the wind."

Military judgment bade Pompey caution, but who should know
better than Labienus the quality of Caesar's men? and his own
troops had behaved excellently well in the surprise attack at Dyrrachium; and he did have that overawing force of cavalry which
would bite deep in any action where they had room enough to work
up a charge. He came tramping south and east through Larissa,

turned at a pass south of that city and headed for the Enipeus, a stream small but with harsh banks, behind which a pass led to the Aegean coast.

Caesar was already in the same district, camped just north of the river, waiting with 22,000 infantry, cavalry a few hundred and some light-armed auxiliaries, on the stage of an old theatre of war whose walls were hung with heroic memories. Away behind his camp Pharsalos castle frowned from a mountain spur, the dark keep once named Phthia, where Homeric Achilles ruled; north of it stood the shaggy Cynoscephalae, the Dogs' Heads Mountains among which Flaminius broke the Macedonian phalanx that had ruled a world, back in the old days of Roman glory; beyond them, dim against the sky grim Ossa, Titans' mountain, and Olympus, home of the immortal gods.

It was August first; on the fourth Pompey's legions appeared along the crest to the northwestward with splendor and music, and fell to building a camp, high up. Caesar drew his dusty ironsides forth in line of battle, but the Pompeians only formed on their slope and awaited. The next day it was the same and the next and the next, with each of them marked by little cavalry clashes at the break of the plain. On the evening of the 8th a loud argument rose in Pompey's camp, all the old reasons and many new ones offered for battle.

——Fight now (the leaders begged), have done, have done. We are two to one of this fringed circus fop with his Queen Nicomedes airs, and have beaten him before.—— By sheer violence of debate Pompey's scruples were overborne.

——We'll fight them in the morning, since you wish, he said, and went to bed to dream a dream of a great triumph through the streets of Rome, flowers and cheers and himself hanging trophies before the altars of Venus Victrix.

In the morning he told it to Theophanes the Greek secretary, who was overjoyed, holding it a portent of certain success, but Pompey did not point out what made his heart heavy—that Venus Victorious was Caesar's own goddess, the genetrix and founder of his house, the emblem of his favorite 10th Legion, and if Pompey's trophies were hung in her temple it would be most likely that Caesar placed them there. Nevertheless he put on a cheerful face when he went out to address the officers in the morning council.

"I am aware," he said, "that I am promising a thing almost incredible, yet I say we shall destroy the enemy before the infantry lines even meet. Hear but the nature of my plan: our right and Caesar's left rest on the river. The cavalry will ride on the opposite wing; as soon as the armies draw near they shall come down on Caesar's right and rear, take that army on their shieldless arms and backs, crush and break them before a man is wounded along the main battle-line."

So sound, so simple and so quick a plan that the officers burst into acclamation. Then Titus Labienus spoke, repeating his opinion on the quality of Caesar's forces; and men rode to their places in the army with much courage and very good heart.

The night before Caesar had come to the opinion that Pompey would not accept battle on this spot either, and made plans to begin a new campaign of manoeuvre, dancing around the Senatorial rear with a threat at their communications. Still he set his out as usual on the off chance, in the regular order of battle, with the weakened 9th on the left and black Antonius to lead them. Domitius Calvinus had the center and the main guard. Anyone could see the right was the point of danger; here Caesar placed his favorite 10th, the trusty old legion, under Publius Sulla this day, and here he himself took post in general command. As the troops drew out he could see the Pompeians pouring down from their mountain peak; they came on, they were going to fight, and a few moments later the nature of their arrangement was visible, with the huge block of seven thousand horsemen sweeping menacingly outward toward their left, the Caesarian right, and their big force of archers close behind.

The Consul had only a thousand horse, too few to stop that mass, were they the best troopers in the world. Thinking quickly, acting fast, he drew eight cohorts from his rear line, one from each legion, men of the *triarii,* the choicest veterans. ——You must face the Pompeian cavalry (he told them): Use your spears not as javelins but as pikes; thrust and not throw. Now charge them as you charged the Gauls at the Vale of Tille, and Mars of Rome's battles be your aid.——

The lines swayed forward, paused for a few minutes, two hundred yards apart. ——Stand! (ordered Pompey) Do not meet their charge with charge, let them come in blown and disordered with running.—— The trumpets shrilled, Caesar's men gave an unanimous shout and charged; but when they saw the Pompeians quietly waiting a little above them, came to a spontaneous halt, took breath a moment, and then dashed in. There was a clash of steel, a cloud of dust; the javelins soared over the battle and dipped like level hail and the two forces locked in combat, perfectly equal, numbers in Pompey's ranks balancing skill and old experience in Caesar's. As they clenched Pompey waved to Labienus; Labienus spurred to his place, gave the signal, and the huge cavalry charge came down like a cloudburst on Caesar's flank, Pontus and Cappadocia, shepherds and mounted slaves, Galatia, Syria and Thrace riding boot to boot.

Caesar's thousand horse gave way in front and spread out; from behind dashed the devoted eight cohorts, all in line and spears held high. The heterogeneous mass of cavaliers had never seen such a thing; they rained in, lost momentum, and as they hung stationary, the eight cohorts were upon them, stabbing fiercely at face and breast, just as Caesar's thousand wheeled and struck into their flank at the gallop. The whole mass broke, and when whirling from the field in wildest rout; Caesar's thousand rode down the archers behind, the eight cohorts spun round and fell on the left and rear of Pompey's line. Caesar saw the turn, whooped in his last reserves; under the double shock Pompey's left collapsed, the 10th Legion also wheeled in on the flank of his center, and the whole Pompeian line, caught between two fires, shredded out and dissolved, with the Caesarians shouting behind them, driving the deadly steel into their backs.

Pompey had sat his horse like a man transfixed as he saw the great cavalry charge fail; now he turned from the battle and rode uphill to the camp. "Guard the place," he muttered thickly to an officer at the gate. "Guard the place. I am going round to inspect the gates," and went to his tent, where he took off his golden helm and badges of rank, then sneaked out the back way and rode off on a fast horse, out of his first defeat in forty years of fighting.

Away behind him it was high noon and hot; in the neck of the pass wild Antonius was leading the Caesarian cavalry as they hunted down fugitives (among them Domitius the Red-beard, brought to book at last); on the height Caesar was urging his weary legionaries up the slope to storm the camp, and breaking in, and making slaughter among the tents, and marvelling at the luxury of the senatorial quarters, with their embroidered carpets, carved tables set with silver plate and ivy trailed across the windows to keep out the heat. The Pompeian army was lost, utterly lost, the last had taken refuge on a ridge where they were presently surrounded and captured to the number of 24,000, the rest being dead or fled.

But that was beyond sight or sound of Pompey the Great, riding into Larissa with thirty horsemen, then down the shadowy Vale of Tempe to the mouth of Peneus River, where he slept that night in a straw pallet in a fisherman's hut. In the morning a ship appeared offshore. He went out to it with three friends; Lentulus Crus, the other Lentulus, and Favonius, who ministered to the numbed old man, unlacing his shoes and serving him at table as though these small kindnesses might ease the smart.

Few words were spoken on that voyage; Pompey was like a walking ghost—"They betrayed me. How did I ever make such an error of judgment?" he kept saying over and over. The others did not know what to say, except Theophanes the Greek secretary, whose forced insouciance fell flat. At Mitylene in the isles Pompey's new young wife, Cornelia, was waiting for him to come, laurel-crowned and victorious. She burst into tears when she saw him, regretting her marriage aloud in terms that drew the blanket of gloom still deeper, and so the dolorous argosy put to sea again, with those aboard discussing whether the flight should be to the barbarians of Parthia or to some other shore. Theophanes the Greek held Egypt the fountain-source of power and new strength. Pompey was dubious:

> He that once enters at a tyrant's door
> Becomes a slave though he were free before;

he quoted from Sophocles, but no longer having any volition of his own, let them take him where they would. After all the present King of Egypt was a youth who owed Pompey a debt of gratitude for placing him on the throne; they bore up to the border fortress of Pelusium where the King was in presence.

News of their coming had preceded them. At the shore they were met by young King Ptolemy and his suite, including the Greek vizier Theodotus, and a couple of Roman officers long resident there. It was a magnificent turnout. "Hail, Imperator!" they cried as Pompey stepped out of the boat. He plucked up comfort from the reception, and as he drew from a fold of his toga a little notebook in which he had set down a carefully prepared address in Greek— "Surely, I recognize an old comrade of the Pontic wars?" he said warmly to one of the Romans. The man gave him a nod and a peculiar goggling stare; as Pompey turned and began to read the address, he whipped out a sword and stabbed his old commander in the back.

"Dead men don't bite," remarked Theodotus the vizier, turning the body over with his foot.

Pompey the Great

FANTASIA

Movement in Disgust—A singularly figurative, almost romantic element enters the story of Julius Caesar at this point, surprising after the cloudless rationalism of the preceding passages, for the figure is hyperbole and the romance that of an Arabian night with all the dirt, squalor and cruelty left in and all the glamor left out. About Caesar's previous escapades from reality—the early flight to the isles of Greece with his beloved Cornelia, the young adventure to Spain, the armed exploration of Britain—there had been an atmosphere of freshness and candor, of engaging superficial enthusiasms. Even the blood spilled seemed less the true sanguine fluid than red ink. The adventure always came to a happy end with something of rational, provable benefit achieved for someone beside the author of the enterprise.

The Alexandrian episode that follows Pharsalia violated this convention. It did not end well, it accomplished nothing but to detain Caesar from tasks he held near at heart, the *décor* was compounded in equal parts of blood, intrigue and degeneration. It had neither light nor life, only the ageless existence of the East, where sin was invented. The ensemble is so much out of focus with the man at the heart of it that some special explanation seems demanded.

But the primary condition of Caesar's being was that no special explanation need ever be demanded; that having survived the storms of Julia's and Aurelia's passing, Pompey's desertion, young Crassus' loss and Labienus' treachery (when Cicero went it was less an emotional than an intellectual deprivation, Caesar having evidently read him long ago as a weakling and a trimmer)—having ridden out these tempests, nay more, having sublimated the shock into splendid and enduring achievement, he was impervious to anything that might happen.

The special explanation, therefore, must commence with the admission that the whole incident bears the impress of another and a less utilitarian personality. This in itself furnishes adequate proof that Queen Cleopatra possessed that appeal for which her name has become a byword, but it is also the most astonishing feature of the whole transaction. The age was one in which dogmas of government, religion, social and personal philosophy had been quite thrown into solution. Roman intellect had always possessed prodigious force, but that force had been harnessed to the purposes of the group-mind by the old Roman "morality" (as much social as anything) of which Cato was the last representative. Greek learning, especially the intoxicating hedonism into which the austere doctrine of Epicurus had been translated, had struck off the chains . . . or perhaps it would be more accurate to say that when the Roman state became the world state the chains fell off of their own weight.

It had been easy for Cincinnatus to be loyal to a community of farmers and small traders, most of whom he knew by name. It was extremely difficult for a money-lender of the late Republic to hold any fellow feeling for a mountain shepherd in Cilicia or a fur trapper in outer Gaul. The human mind will not normally accept such large loyalties. The Roman intellect, in losing its old social morality, had been set free from its traditional restraints without losing any of its traditional strength and the result had been a tremendous explosion of individualities, the more violent because the thing had been so long under control.

Caesar's own contemporaries numbered such vivid and varied personalities as Marius, Sulla the Dictator, Cinna the pseudo-dictator and the elder Lepidus; Catullus, Lucretius and Calvus, the poets; Varro, Cicero, Catiline, Lucullus, Pompey, Crassus, Clodius, Caelius, Antonius and Servius Sulpicius Rufus, any one of whom contained individuality enough to be the subject of a rounded biography (as Plutarch, nearly a century and a half later, discovered) and every one of whom left indelible traces on the history of his time and the world. Yet Caesar had not permitted one of these engulfing individ-

ualities to affect him, save in the most indirect way, by adumbrating
the background against which he operated. Indeed he had so high
a valence that he actually absorbed several—Crassus, Clodius, Caelius,
Antonius, Sulpicius Rufus, men most various—and during the
period of his contact with them they have almost no existence except
as expressions of him. Individualities strong enough to fight off his
absorption, though men gigantic in another day—Pompey, Cicero,
Caelius and Clodius in their later stages—were ruthlessly ridden
down.

This is what makes it so astonishing to find Caesar at the height
of his powers playing wax to another personality, above all since
that other was Oriental, feminine, autocratic and lazy, almost his
exact antithesis at every point. It makes a special explanation of the
event and of Cleopatra inevitable.

The special explanation most frequently advanced is that Caesar
was no longer at the height of his powers, or rather that he was no
longer at the height of his self-control; that he was, in fact, the vic-
tim of a malady sometimes observed in men of his age—fifty—a kind
of girl-fever which makes them easy victims for anything female.
It is no more convincing than the alleged evidence that Caesar was
an epilept, on which Suetonius was moved to remark that the sei-
zures of the disease came always at moments when the epilept needed
a few moments to think his way out of some inconvenient corner.

There is also a good plea in rebuttal, to wit, a flat jointure of issue
on the question of fact. Caesar had just come from Pharsalia, where
he had added to his earlier laurels for the first time those of a great
general in the technical military sense. In the Spanish campaign he
had manoeuvred into the ground a general famous for his skill in
manoeuvre in a fashion never seen before and rarely since. At the
beginning of the Dyrrachium operation he was only the Caesar of
Gaul, the expert in supply, espionage and engineering; it would not
do, he took a defeat and realized that Pompey's tactical and strategic
skill was of an order that required skill as great to meet it. Though
he liked war no better than he ever had, he made himself a great
general by sheer thought. Few generals have ever produced such a
campaign as that which moved like a star through the retreat from

Dyrrachium, the march up the Aous, the breaking of the Gomphi quadrilateral, and the dazzling impromptu battlefield tactic that broke through to victory at the point where the enemy felt himself strongest.

It may be protested that the effort, the accentuated pressure under which Caesar had been living ever since the day he set out for Gaul with the frontier in a flame, had left him mentally and neurologically exhausted. But, as has already been shown, he had been living a highly compressed life long before Gaul, and the war there only meant the exchange of an intense private life for an intense public life. If there were any breakdown it must have been a general breakdown, in which the strain of the Pharsalia campaign was only of proximate importance.

And there is no evidence of any decline in Caesar's intellect or energy, no ground for the theory of a girl-fever. The opening moves in the Alexandrian interlude were as crisp, peremptory and effective as any he ever made. The day after the battle at Pharsalia had to be spent on the field handling the captures. The goods were divided, enough of the prisoners persuaded to follow Caesar's fortunes to make up three new legions, a task which included the appointment of officers and organization throughout, and which, we may be sure, the Consul delegated to no one else, as these legions were destined for immediate and serious service.

The next day the pursuit began. By night the Consul was in Larissa with eight hundred horse, where he had news that Pompey had taken ship and the vessel had been seen pointing to the north. North was the Hellespont, beyond it the Euxine and the kingdom of Pontus, whither, in view of Pompey's past, he might reasonably have gone. Caesar set out along the shore with his eight hundred cavalry. At the strait he found Pompey had not gone through. He must have landed somewhere on the Asian shore then; Caesar gathered a few old merchant vessels, loaded his men aboard and began to cross. In the middle of the process a fleet of ten sail of war hove over the horizon. They were Pompeians, with one L. Cassius for commodore; they could have sunk Caesar forever there, where Leander drowned, but Caius Julius coaxed an interview with the commander, gave Cassius and his crews the smooth side of his tongue with such astonishing effect that the ten galleys first surrendered to him, then enlisted under his banners and turned south along the Asiatic shore as convoy for his troopships.

The performance was certainly not that of a man losing his grip. Neither was the next act (undertaken on arrival at Ephesus)—a revision of the whole Asiatic tax system, practically between dawn and sunset during a trip which had to be, and was a military pursuit at hot speed. The new arrangement abolished tax-farming in the Asian province, a step simple and desirable if seen down the telescope of the centuries, but not the least radical of the Caesarian enactments when viewed from a community in which tax-farmers formed a class of vested interest not widely different from the bankers of today.

It also involved finding a new method of taxation, a task which Caesar reduced to perhaps its simplest form by giving most of the communes of the province considerably more autonomy, and allowing them to collect a flat-rate contribution to the treasury by methods of their own choice. Even this involved fixing the flat-rates for a large number of communes in the midst of an unedifying uproar from the horrified tax-farmers on one side, and from communal delegates desirous of further concessions on the other. The interesting thing is not that the task was done (the performance required only that vigorous intemperance with objection to reform which is one of the most familiar Caesarian characteristics) but that it was done so nearly for all time that only minor adjustments in the rates were made, well into imperial times, and the system itself was extended to nearly the whole empire.

The incident also has a certain premonitory importance; in their relief at deliverance from the exactions of the tax-farmers the citizens of Ephesus set up a bronze tablet in their famous temple pronouncing Caesar a god; quite a normal thing in the communes of Asia Minor where kings held their position by virtue of a fiction of royal adultery with members of the Pantheon.

The new god apparently set no great store by this apotheosis; long before the bronze tablet could have been cast a ship came in from south with news that Pompey had been seen in Mitylene and again in Cyprus. This meant Egypt; Caesar sailed at once for Alexandria with the 6th Legion, which had cut across the Aegean to rendezvous with him at Ephesus. At Rhodes he stopped long enough to gather up a few formations of warships under Euphranor, Lord High Admiral of that island republic, then rode down the etesian winds for Egypt.

The opening passes of the business there were also run off in the best Caesarian style. As the fleet hove to off the Pharos, a caparisoned barge put out from the shore toward the Consular flagship. It contained Theodotus the vizier and an object which that worthy thought would entitle him to the most distinguished consideration—the head of a man who could no longer bite, packed in a box with sweet-smelling spices and wine. Caesar turned his face away from the grisly object and burst into tears—what if the man had been seduced from old friendship and mutual ideals in the empoisoned atmosphere of Roman politics? they had been happy together once and had shared the love of little Julia, and now the last link with that golden past was broken.

Theodotus the vizier, a man wise enough according to his lights, which were the flickering beams of an Oriental harem, doubtless concluded that the display of emotion had been made *pro forma*. At all events he made another effort with some remark to the effect that the King of Egypt was holding in bonds all the Pompeians who had fled thither after His Magnificence's glorious victory at Pharsalia; that the King hoped the Magnificence would accept these miserable wretches as a present from him, in evidence of the exalted esteem in which he held the Consul of the Roman people and in settlement of the debt he owed Julius Caesar in person.

. . . We have no means of knowing whether Caesar had originally intended to stop at Alexandria for the collection of that debt or not. The campaign had been very expensive; he needed money badly. Pharsalia, though a won battle, had been a financial liability rather than a relief, for the official share of the salvage was more than offset by bringing onto the military establishment three new legions at the doubled rate of pay Caesar always allowed his soldiers. The concessions to the free cities of Aeolia had had the effect of decreasing the amount of revenue Rome derived from them; many other sources of income were closed off by the existence of the war. In brief, finance was a pressing problem.

The debt itself was a tidy little matter of six thousand talents—say something over $3,000,000—promised by the present king's father, old Ptolemy the Piper, as the price for replacing him on the throne from which he had been driven by a palace revolution, back in the palmy days of the triumvirate, when Pompey and Crassus were consuls. They had made the deal with Ptolemy's representative, seen the work was done, but never collected. The surviving partner to the triumvirate probably held he had a good juridical right to the reversion of the sum.

On the other hand Caesar had never before allowed mere lack of funds to distrain him from anything he wished to do. There is a story about him as a young man, far away in the days when he was running for the office of Pontifex Maximus, and seemed likely to carry the election. One of his old and wealthy rivals, who wanted the office for its title much as a modern millionaire wants to be president of the golf club, offered him a truly generous bribe if he would withdraw from the canvass. "Why, I expect to borrow more than that to buy the election!" laughed the young Caesar, and did borrow and did win it, laying the foundations of the debt that was not discharged till he returned from the governorship of Lusitania. And when he set out for the campaign against Afranius, being in difficulties like the present one for money for his military pay chest, he had borrowed funds from his officers and distributed them among the privates, "thus insuring the loyalty of the one by interest and of the other by gifts" as he remarked.

No, the possibility of mining the golden sands of Nilus would only be attractive to Caesar if there were nothing important to do elsewhere. Just at this moment there were a great many important things to do in many other places. Affairs at Rome were in a terrible mess. Milo the mobster had his gangs out again (having escaped prison) and P. Dolabella, apparently with the object of proving that his failure as a naval officer came not through any lack of the combative spirit, was matching him and more at the game of clubs trumps. The situation had become so anarchic that after Pharsalia Caesar's first step was to send Antonius with full powers, the title of Master of Horse and all the veteran legions but two. The appointment itself was in need of early revision, strictly an emergency measure, as the very qualities that made Antonius useful in such a pinch—his crude swashbuckling energy, intolerance of legalism and delay—made him a liability in any purely civic capacity, where such men translate intolerance of delay into intolerance of independent thought sooner or later and make themselves petty despots.

There was a war brewing in Pontus also, where the young Prince Pharnaces had poisoned his father and was imagining himself another Mithridates. Domitius Calvinus had been sent to the front with the three ex-Pompeian legions (36th, 37th, 38th), but he might need more men and certainly needed direction.

Beside the assignment left Caesar with no troops at all to send to the African province, where the wreckage of the Senatorial party was hardening into a new army around the nucleus provided by King Juba of Numidia. And there was a Pompeian fleet still afloat and active in the Adriatic, become a kind of pirate fleet now, but dangerous nevertheless. And Q. Cassius Longinus was proving a most expensive and uncomfortable governor in the two Spains—latest dispatches said the provinces were most uneasy; and the Parthians were threatening an invasion of Syria, and the Dacians of Illyricum . . . Clearly the public interest demanded the Consul's presence almost anywhere but in Egypt, and there seems no rational reason why he stopped there at all, unless it were the desire to unshackle the corn-supply question by clearing up the mess in which Ptolemy the Piper's will had left the affairs of that country.

That instrument, apparently drawn by some commission of temple priests, was more than ordinarily cryptic, even for a document of its type, and the confusion was not helped by the fact that each of the four minor children of the late king was backed by a camorra of ambitious eunuchs. The representatives of young King Ptolemy XII had made possession their nine points, and driven out the most dangerous rival, Cleopatra, who was entitled to share the throne by normal Egyptian rule of succession, both as Ptolemy's sister and his wife.

There was another sister, Arsinoë, and a younger Ptolemy. Just what their rights were, no one knew, but their dissatisfaction was limited to underground intrigue, whereas Cleopatra had managed to raise an army which was besieging Pelusium in a somewhat languid manner at the date of Caesar's arrival.

It is rather odd that Caesar should have stirred this stew with so vigorous a finger, even for the sake of order. It was not his usual habit with barbaric kingdoms. In Gaul, for instance, it had been his wont to give arbitrament only when asked to do so and to back it with force only when the award was refused. Yet after his interview with Theodotus he had the fleet swung into harbor and he himself landed with his legion marching in battle formation behind and his twenty-four lictors, two and two, before, the axed fasces held high, official sign that he came not as a visitor, but as Consul of Rome, with power of death and summary confiscation and intent to use both.

No—none of the ancillary reasons for the adventure is adequate against the countervailing demands on his time, nor do they seem adequate together. The final determining cause must have been one of those apparently insignificant triggers that lie hidden deep in character, which touched, set off the train of great events in a manner exoterically inexplicable.

In this case the sight of the pickled head, the head of his old friend Pompey, and the assumption of the oily Greek eunuch that it would meet with Caesar's warmest approval. The Consul's entry into Alexandria was just such another explosion of passion as that after the massacre of the 14th Legion or that before the statue of Alexander the Great in Gades. A passionate, irrational action, founded in the angry, unexpressed thought of somehow making these Orientals pay for doing him a service which they had rendered an injury by the manner of its performance.

2

Dance, Little Man—"We do not know whether Cleopatra's nose was
of the right length to change the face of the world"—a modern observation betraying the Latinity of its origin, for it does not appear
that the lady's basic physical equipment was a matter of importance.

Coin of Cleopatra

There is a tradition that she was not beautiful at all. It may be perfectly accurate, although it probably originated with some Roman
connoisseur of loveliness who preferred women in the Italian convention, decently matronly or vivacious and virginal, but strangers
to those tricks of allure taught in the East, where sex rather than
marriage is a woman's career. Cleopatra's beauty, like her intellect,
was certainly of the Oriental type, with the emphasis on artificiality,
on synthesis. There is the curious little detail that she was the first
woman in the western world to own a silk dress, brought at enormous expense across Asia. Her appearance was part of an ensemble
of body, mind, position and money, the whole being treated as
materiel exchangeable for whatever she desired.

In this case the desire was political. It would have to be political or
sensory; Alexandria was the Paris of the Mediterranean world; there
was no aesthetic enjoyment its rulers could not obtain with a wave of
the hand. As for spiritual or philosophical desires, why the Ptolemies
had none. Nine generations of an absurd position as the living deities

of a state religion in which only the least intelligent of their subjects believed, left them with a morality of pure enjoyment of the moment. The endless hair-splitting of the court philosophers had pretty well destroyed philosophy as a vehicle for thought, leaving it only a kind of game, a raw material for fine rhetorical passages. On the purely sensual side it is unlikely that Cleopatra looked forward to a love-affair with Caesar as a pleasant thing for its own sake. He was a retired great lover of fifty and she a reigning beauty of twenty-two.

In this case the desire was political. Cleopatra wanted a favorable probate of her father's will. Theodotus, for her brother, had struck a clever stroke of policy by presenting the Consul with Pompey's head. The Roman was now in residence at the royal palace, from whence he had issued a command that she present her case in person, and the message was so peremptory in tone that it was clear she would have to use all the tricks.

The famous lady-in-the-rug entry may have been dictated by this idea, but only may have, for Cleopatra was too clever to have imagined that the master of the world would lose his head at the sight of a naked woman like a sailor in a bawdy-house. More likely the ostensible reason was the true one. The eunuch Potheinos, who had secured the succession to the viziership when Theodotus was disgraced for blundering with Caesar, had a man waiting behind some door with a dagger to prevent any meeting whatever between Cleopatra and Caesar. Her death might be dangerous but Potheinos knew that alive she would be more dangerous still. Whatever the reason the princess arranged the cooperation of a boatman and a slave and had herself delivered at the conqueror's door in a bale of drygoods, from which she emerged nude and gracious as Aphrodite in Cypris.

Caesar found her a new experience. Not merely that she was intelligently aware of every device of passion, an artist of incomparable brio in the symphony of the senses. Caesar had already known many such and known also the dreadful reaction, the contempt of self, partner and the world that follows when passion has exhausted its little trick. Rather it was that Cleopatra never permitted this reaction to take place. The draining of all her body had to offer stimulated rather than depressed her mind; she passed over easily and naturally from physical delirium to intellectual companionship, from fire to ice.

More particularly it was the quality of her intellect that seems to have fascinated Caesar. Her views differed from his all down the line, which was not a new thing to him, as many people in Rome, notably Cicero, differed. But Cleopatra defended her strange ideas with an agility and consistency he had not encountered since his schooldays in the Greek archipelago, yet without attempting to impose them upon his action. It was all an exercise in philosophic debate, a conversation in a vacuum, like those he used to enjoy so much at the dinner-tables of Rome before his own ascent to power had cut him off from the intellectuals of the city. A recovery, in two directions, of a vanished youth.

It seems worth while to speculate on what the princess' views may have been, and in view of the surroundings and the subsequent actions of both characters in the little dialogues we may claim to recover them with some degree of plausibility, provided only that we do not attempt too much precision of either idea or statement. It would be Caesar's fundamental political philosophy that she attacked, his confidence in radical democracy, in government on the broadest possible basis. One can imagine her demonstrating that by any criterion of civilization the democracy is helpless to provide for its own or others' well-being, dissolving inevitably into faction and internal warrings, its power to destroy always greater and more willingly put to use than its power to create. Her experience and education were of the Hellenistic cities and especially of Alexandria, where this was true. The old Greek civilization that had shattered down under the earthquakes of arrogance and selfishness, the new Hellenistic civilization where the fruits of the spirit were gathered in peace at Alexandria under the shield of the royal power, would be her examples.

And what if a spirit of cooperation exists, a spirit of state patriotism, nullifying the individual selfishness, as at Rome? Why, then your democracy goes corrupt, the better minds cooperate indeed, but to their own pleasures and the state's despite—we of the Greek world have worked out these problems in all their variations long ago, and we pay the cheaper price for our tranquillity and justice by supporting one king instead of many.

Is it too long a stretch to put such arguments into her mouth? I think not; the conversation must have taken some such turn; it must have been something dealing with issues Caesar found essential, to hold his interest. Aesthetics would be too soon run through to interest them long; there was not enough of mutual acquaintance to lend interest to personalities; Caesar always kept his own counsel on details of practical action, and though he might submit to indirect influence, suspicion would leap up, full-armed, at the hint of direct suggestion. She was playing a game for a prize, would consider the matter of whither to turn the conversation coldly and bend it on the subjects most interesting to him. No—politics, abstract politics, political philosophy, would be the staple of the conversational banquet, and as for the tenor of the talk, why the material lay too readily at hand to be ignored. So much we might deduce indeed, even if we did not have the testimony of subsequent events and the change in Caesar that proclaims the influence of Cleopatra's doctrine.

3

Waste—So the conversations and the lover-like exchanges went on in the palace and the soldiers mounted guard and the growl of an angry mob floated in at the windows through the lucid afternoons. The Alexandrines, always turbulent for riot's own sweet sake, had conceived an insult to their dignity by Caesar's entry in arms, and now word ran through the palace by runnels which eunuch Potheinos knew how to use that uproar against the transmarine greedy-guts would please persons high in power. Soldiers of the royal guard sifted through the streets helping matters along; javelins plunged out of the night and legionaries who left the palace precincts never came back.

Potheinos, in fact, was playing position for the ruling on the will, having calculated to a nicety that the trade-winds which blew Caesar to Egypt would keep him there, where he had not force enough to make a fight of it if it came to violence. Caesar had calculated the same; two days after arrival he got off one message to

Domitius Calvinus to take the defensive against King Pharnaces in Pontus and send down the 37th and 38th legions with speed, another message to Fufius Calenus to hurry on with the legion and ships he had at Ephesus.

Before they arrived, before the messengers had even reached their destinations, the Consul announced his judgment: Ptolemy and Cleopatra to rule jointly. Potheinos set up a cry of favor and petticoat sovranty, which had this much truth in it, that joint rule with Cleopatra as a partner was the brotherhood of lioness and lap-dog. But the arbitrament was sound Egyptian law and consonant with the will, so that Potheinos had to have the king's army of twenty thousand men brought into the city to carry the matter further.

They came under the Grand Marshal Achillas. On the morn of their arrival they tried to storm the palace in a regular battle, crying they wanted to rescue their king from the hands of foreigners. The Roman pickets beat them off from windows and barricades. Achillas cleverly slipped the bulk of his strength leftward through back streets and came rushing down the quay-front in serried ranks of spearmen to clip Caesar back from the harbor, which would cut off reinforcement and supplies. The Consul jabbed into the flanks of this attack with little columns flung down alleys at charge speed, but it was a thousand men against twenty thousand, the Egyptians came right along in spite of losses and in desperation Caesar ordered fire to the Alexandrine shipping.

A north wind drifted flame and cinders across the quays, warehouses began to blaze and while the fighting rocked to and fro among the crashing beams a great stock of manuscripts and half the city's corn were destroyed. Still the Egyptians were only checked, not beaten—they gained, they gained, building after building fell. Caesar sent men in boats across the harbor mouth, who seized and fortified the tip of the island making the inlet of supplies secure against anything but a sea blockade. Night closed with the fighting even on technical points, Caesar winner by definition, but only for the day. He could see worse coming soon.

That night he had every man in the palace precincts busy. One after another swift messenger ships ran down the harbor and away into the teeth of the wind—to Domitius and Calenus; Hurry on reinforcements, this has become a full-fledged war—to King Mithridates of Pergamos, alloy of Rome: Come with your armies, take what you like of plunder in Egypt—to Malchos, Sheik of the Nabataean Arabs: Rise on the Sinai border, Egypt's arms are locked here—to Syria, to Cilicia, the free cities, Crete: Send ships and bowmen, artillery and supplies.

There was sporadic skirmishing in the streets during the night, and though the troops were weary, they were too few to take chances, so Caesar kept them working till morning, turning the palace quarter into a fort, beating down walls, making barricades, loopholing buildings. He handled the engineering questions himself and it is a pity we lack the one view of him at this hour we could wish to have, which is Cleopatra's when she saw her lover, calm, active and intelligent, the only sane man amid the hurry and tumult. For Cleopatra had the quality of her defects, a magnificent imperial largeness of outlook, freedom from pettiness and taste for greatness in however strange form it might present itself, the same quality that in old attorney Cicero had made him cry the Alps should sink.

Next day there was more outpost fighting and for several days thereafter. The situation was very odd, with Potheinos and King Ptolemy prisoners of Caesar and their army outside fighting him. Princess Arsinoë was outside, too, but she was fishing in these troubled waters for her own hand, bribing the soldiers with huge sums to proclaim her sole queen. Grand Marshal Achillas dreamed of a new dynasty and counter-bribed, and the siege limped during this debate of the purses, which Potheinos attempted to compose by secret messages that they should settle their difficulties, smother Caesar first and divide the spoils after. He enclosed a plan of the defenses, with the indications where the weak points lay; a silly thing to do, for he was playing lip-loyal to Caesar, Cleopatra, and an honest reading of the will, and the letter was proof positive of treachery. The Consul tracked his messengers, read their scrolls and put the eunuch to death without delay or pity.

On the outside meanwhile, Arsinoë won by the hallowed Orient practice of slipping poison in Achillas' gruel. Her personal eunuch,

Ganymedes, succeeded to the command, a more stirring man than his predecessor, who forthwith invented water-wheels that pumped the conduits to the Roman cisterns full of brine. There was brief panic in the palace, allayed by Caesar himself. He directed the sinking of wells along the shore, so there was plentiful to drink.

The day after the well-digging a scout ship ran in; the 37th had come from Pontus but the transports had made landfall west along the coast and the prevailing wind held them back from Alexandria. Caesar took his warships and ran down the coast to bring them in, but it was slow, heavy labor towing the laden troopships against a headwind and they came to for the night at the promontory Chersonesos, whence word of their numbers and situation was borne to Ganymedes in Alexandria.

He called away the Egyptian battle-fleet and hurried down to attack them, arriving late in the afternoon. Caesar held his ships close along shore where there was no sea-room for ramming, but one of his Rhodian allies anchored too far out and the Egyptians fell on her. For his own credit he had to go to the rescue, taking the Rhodian squadron, small in number, but manned by the master-seamen of the world. They took their ships into action with a skill and resolution marvelous to behold, sank one of the big Egyptian quinquiremes, captured another, and sent the rest reeling back, so shattered and water-logged that they might all have been sunk but for the intervention of night.

Ganymedes had the heart of the matter now. Sea-power would win for him if he could mobilize it. He called up the naval reserve, ships from customs duty and from ordinary, fitted out new vessels in the western harbor of the city. Within a few days he had a powerful navy again, five quinquiremes, twenty-two quadriremes, and any number of triremes and smaller vessels. Caesar had only twenty-seven ships all told, of which but sixteen were heavy rates, but urged on by his own fiery haste and the promptings of the Rhodian Admiral Euphranor, he put to sea, swung round the island of the Pharos and launched at the Egyptians within the lips of the western harbor.

Shoals barred the entry. For a time both fleets hung unwilling to dare the passage through, where they must go in single file. At last

Euphranor cried " 'Tis shame these dogs should mock us!" put out his battle standard and dashed right into the jaws, with the Egyptian giants circling to ram from every side. Behind him the Rhodians piled in; they bore themselves so stoutly Egypt never had a chance to ram, the rest of Caesar's armada followed, laid alongside the enemy and poured a flood of dangerous legionary swordsmen across their decks. The struggle raged briefly with the Rhodians lashing round the flanks like comets at the head of long pennons of foam; three times they rammed Egyptian ships to the bottom, a great quin-quireme and two triremes were cleared up the lashing swords, then the rest of Ganymedes' ships broke for beach and quay, where they could not be followed, because of the heavy artillery protection there provided.

That left the victory partial. Caesar hoped to round it out by seizing the island of the Pharos and the great Heptastadion cause-way that bound it to the mainland, which possession would auto-matically leave Ganymedes' fleet without a base. The first attack was on the island, and double—from the outside in galleys and the harbor in small boats. It succeeded after some fighting that began difficult, but eased up when the Romans got on land where they could swing a broadsword. The island was cleared and the outer end of the Heptastadion gained by night.

Three cohorts were told off for the attack on the southern end of the causeway next day, with the galleys rowing up against it in close support. The plan miscarried. Ganymedes was vigilant; he con-centrated troops and counterattacked sharply down the causeway, giving the three cohorts all they could do, then landed some men of his own at the other end and took the Romans in the rear. There was a panic; the legionaries began to jump into the water, Caesar was carried off the edge with them, and landed with a crash in the midst of a tumult of arrows, stones and spears falling from above, flailing oars and drowning men in armor, clutching for their lives.

Address and athlete's old skill saved him. As he went down he managed to get a shield over his head, which gave him a little room; dived under the buckler and swam a stroke or two from the worst of the press, then appeared on the surface, one arm holding aloft a roll of papers, while he dragged his red commander's paludamentum in his teeth, swimming his way to a shallop. From the slight platform he shouted orders for all the small boats to go in and save the drowning, which they did, but four hundred legionaries were lost and it was a sad check.

Young King Ptolemy, doubtless spurred by whatever eunuch had succeeded Potheinos (we do not know the name), snatched the opportunity to beg Caesar to let him go and bid the army keep peace. He would, he said, throw Princess Arsinoë in a dungeon and cut off Ganymedes' ears. Caesar assented with such alacrity that the puzzled youth began to back water; shed a few tears, said that after all he would prefer to entrust himself to the protection of his good friend Caesar and the Roman people.

"In that case," said Caesar evenly, "you will the sooner be back. Farewell."

He went; and word ran through the town that the lad had diddled Caesar, no mean accomplishment if it were true, but he could, as Caesar and Cleopatra had foreseen, bring nothing to Ganymedes but weak malignance and the dissension of his presence, while he removed from the palace a spy dangerous because impossible to restrain.

The military situation continued bad for Caesar, however; Ganymedes had time to refit his fleet and send it to sea. The ships cruised off the eastern mouths of the Nile to hold back any supply vessels coming for Caesar. The Consul had to send his own navy to break it up, and whether through emergency at the city, where the war had settled down to a daily dingdong battle or whether from love of lying in Cleopatra's white arms, did not go with them himself.

The result was one to punish whichever were the worser reason. Euphranor of Rhodes was the truest sea-captain of the fleet, but as an outlander could not command Roman warships, so the high admiralty went to Legate Tiberius Nero, a man valiant on land, but whose heart turned to jelly when the waves bounced him. The fleets met in a seaway off the Canopic Nile. Tiberius Nero hung back, gallant Euphranor tried to carry it alone and was sent to the bottom for his valor, the only thing saved from the disaster being that Ganymedes' navy was so hurt he could not keep a tight blockade.

That left matters even again and Caesar might have stayed in Alexandria at the same pace till he rotted, but there came a rescue from Asia Minor, King Mithridates of Pergamos took up the offer of the plunder of Egypt, came hurrying down through the Syrian corridors with a big army and laid siege to Pelusium. The castle warden sent messengers to Ptolemy, but by time they reached the capital Mithridates had smothered the defense under his numbers and was marching up the eastern Nile to flank the Delta. Ptolemy dropped the siege of the palace, got his men aboard transports and sailed upstream to meet this new danger. Caesar similarly took ship, speeding east along the coast as though flying from Egypt, but beyond the Chersonese cape put out his lights, ran in to shore, landed the legions and set out on one of his famous speed marches to join Mithridates.

He marched so fast he beat the Egyptian ships. Ptolemy and Ganymedes, as men were wont to do when opposed by Caesar's restless outpouring of force, abandoned the initiative to him and fortified a position on a hill by the Nile bank, covered in its rear by a marsh, on one flank by the river and on the front and other flank by rugged heights. Below, a wide and deep canal defended it like an outwork, with the Egyptian horse patroling the farther bank in a position "where courage had no chance to exert itself and cowardice ran no risks." Caesar sent the few German horse with him down the canal; they swam it and came charging into the Egyptian rear just as the legionaries hewed down tall trees that made a causeway in front. Cowardice and courage alike went down under the slashing double onset. The rout poured in on the Egyptian camp in such disarray that Caesar thought to carry it out of hand, but desisted when he saw the formidable character of the position, for it was late and the soldiers spent.

Next morning he went at it hammer and tongs. The legionaries hammered up the hill in front against the camp, but could make no headway, what with a good defense and the cross-fire from the Egyptian ships in the Nile on their flank. It occupied the defenders' full strength and attention however. Caesar noted the fact. He drew three cohorts from the storming column and sent them round the flank of the camp, where the rocks were steepest. They scrambled up by their fingernails, won a gate and raised a shout. The Egyptian resistance collapsed at this sound from the rear; there was a frightful panic and a rush for the boats, with many of them capsized by overloading. King Ptolemy was in one of those that went down and Ganymedes in another, so that was the end of the war.

Caesar returned to Alexandria in triumph, to find the gates of the city open and the inhabitants coming out to pay to him and Cleopatra the honors due the gods. For himself he declined, naming the young Prince Ptolemy, a lad in his early teens, as king, the thirteenth of his line, with Cleopatra as his official wife and Queen.

That finished the settlement of Alexandria and Egypt on a basis to everyone surviving, but Caesar felt he needed a vacation, so he went on a trip up the Nile with Cleopatra in a gilded barge, a kind of honeymoon in which intellection and passion were mingled for two gorgeous months. When they came back north the queen was pregnant with his child, but Italy was all in riot, the old legions mutinying and the world filled with wars.

4

They Are Hollow—How Marcus Junius Brutus acquired the reputation for virtue that became permanently associated with his name has been a mystery to twenty centuries of scholarship. It is true that as Cato's nephew and the husband of his daughter he might be supposed to have some sort of family lien on virtue. It is also true that when Cicero returned from the governorship of Cilicia, his friend Atticus wrote that if he had gained nothing in that province but the friendship of Brutus the expedition was still worth while, and that this flattering opinion was shared by most of his contemporaries.

In itself this proves no more than that he was well provided with the gifts of social amenity, a thing meaningless without something in support, for any gigolo has qualities as attractive. In fact, his social presence becomes important only when we understand that Brutus' winsomeness was rooted in the thought of the golden Academe. Romans generally were Stoics or Epicureans, gnarling the one into Catonian harshness or pushing the other into rank Clodian extravaganza. Brutus was almost the only living, certainly the only

practising Roman Platonist, a rarely balanced and pleasing plant in
this garden of tumescent growths.

Caesar also, who leaned toward a Stoic persuasion by necessity of
meeting the world with an iron-shielded front, was drawn by this
debonair balance of the spirit to an affection beyond that he might
have bestowed on Servilia's son for her sake. Brutus' viewpoint

Coin of Brutus

chimed so exquisitely with the inner aestheticism, the basic Platonism
of his own nature; he felt that Brutus was the one man he could
trust within the secret garden of his heart. Even when the world split
as he rode across the Rubicon with a sword in his uplifted hand and
this friend of his intimacy joined his enemies the personal affection
never quavered. He met the young man in Larissa after Pharsalia
and welcomed him warmly; Brutus told him which direction Pompey had taken and rode with him on the pursuit.

Caesar felt and many Romans felt and Plutarch afterward declared
(as a historian a hundred years beyond the passions of that age) that
Marcus Brutus could have acted in both these matters as in everything he did, only from the purest of motives, a high unselfish
patriotism, a genuine belief that Pompey's party was defending justice and the Roman constitution, and that when he crashed down
at Pharsalia the one hope was to win Caesar to more constitutional
doctrines. And perhaps this was the secret of Caesar's clemency
throughout the Civl War, that clemency so thoroughly without

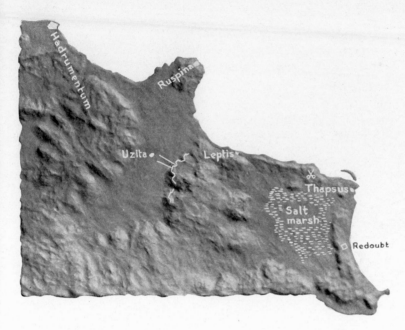

THE AFRICAN CAMPAIGN

Utica, the capital of the province, is off the map, north and slightly west of Hadrumentum, which is shown here. Caesar's lines before Uzita are shown, but not all his complicated manoeuvres across the plains. The redoubt shown is the one constructed to force Metellus Scipio to come north around the salt marsh and attack in a position of Caesar's choosing.

precedent in Rome history—that if he forgave Brutus he must forgive everyone and he could not afford not to forgive Brutus.

Yet the two men were as essentially different as the high priest Caiaphas and Christ Jesus and in the same way. Brutus' famous "virtue" was of a type to appeal only to those pedantic Romans who made Rome a religion, his philosophy a Platonism for local consumption, which he packed away in an air-tight box when not dealing with his social equals. Caesar's gentleness, on the other hand, was extrovert to the world at large, with nothing but his sorrows hidden beneath the carapace of his Stoic pose.

Brutus, for instance, had gone to Cilicia as an under-official during Cicero's governorship, and found the citizens of Salamis considerably in arrears in tax payments. With one hand he remorselessly enforced collections, with the other he lent the Salaminians money to pay their taxes—at forty-eight per cent interest.

There was a law against Romans making such loans in the provinces and another against interest above twelve per cent. Brutus avoided the one by working through a roguish Levantine named Scaptius and the other with a troop of cavalry. The articulate Roman classes could see nothing in the transaction but a good stroke of business, or beyond that an exhibition of Brutus' celebrated "virtue" —in having collected the long-overdue taxes. Humanitarianism, fellow-feeling, was on their definition, something exercised only among Romans of the Optimates. Slaves, foreigners and the lower orders were exterior to their emotions; one does not shed tears over the cock that comes trussed to the table. For a long time Brutus' remark to the Pergamenes (while acting as Pompey's legate) was quoted as an example of epigrammatic wit and nothing more: "I hear you have given Dolabella money; if willingly, you must own that you have injured me and pay accordingly; if unwillingly, show it by giving willingly to me."

The trait in Caesar which Brutus and his fellows could never understand, which indeed, roused their burning indignation, was that he treated these races outside the law as though they were Romans. Pompey the Great had shown the right Roman spirit when he went East to find the Jews quarreling among themselves, stormed

their capital city, threw down its walls, dragged off a percentage of
the citizens as quarry-slaves for the erection of the new theatre at
Rome and laid the rest of the nation under a heavy obligation of
tribute to keep them out of mischief. That was virtue; nearly everyone in the imperial city benefited somehow.

No one there could fathom why Caesar should upset the satisfactory settlement by treating these indigestible factionists as useful
citizens, remove their special disabilities, remit their tribute, grant
them permission to rebuild their city and that Temple whose altar
(said common Roman report) was ornamented with an ass' head.
Worse yet, the eccentric Consul actually granted the Jews the privilege of doing business in Rome itself on a basis that would throw
them into competition with Roman financiers, which gave the Jews
advantages manifestly unfair, since they did not charge forty-eight
per cent.

Brutus, as one of the forty-eight per cent financial men, was doubtless very indignant about this, but bit down his irritabilities, as the
pro-Jewish decrees had just been handed down when he met Caesar
in Syria after the Alexandrian war, and he saw just then exerting all
his celebrated charm to secure the pardon of a particularly ardent
Pompeian. The man was a friend of his, one Caius Cassius, a lantern-
jawed dyspeptic, soured on the world, like a caricature of some old
hawkbeak of the Punic wars.

Had Brutus but known it he might have spared his persuasion.
Caius Cassius was well known as the man whose generalship had
been the one bright spot in Crassus' defeat and death at Carrhae;
he had saved the wreck of the army then. Caesar was just planning
an eastern campaign and the adhesion on any terms of an officer with
a good service record in that type of warfare he regarded as a blessing.
Affairs in the west were urgent, but both for moral and for financial
reasons he could not well leave Syria until matters there had been
placed on a sound and permanent footing. For moral reasons particularly; as the political legatee of Pompey, he must improve upon
the latter's settlement of the eastern question or make the tacit admission that he had pulled down a greater man than himself.

The situation in Asia Minor pressed the analogy, being much as

Pompey had found it, with the poisoner Pharnaces doubling for King Mithridates against the Lucullus of Domitius Calvinus. The Alexandrian necessity had weakened Domitius to a single legion, the 36th, with some regiments of Asiatics; he was heavily defeated at Nicopolis, and Caesar arrived to find him huddled back against the mountain-gates of Cilicia, with Pharnaces doing about as he pleased

Brutus

in the central plateau of Asia Minor. Caesar could bring little rein-forcement but his own presence, for the 6th, the only legion which followed him from Egypt to Syria, was down to a thousand men. Nevertheless he gathered in some barbarian aids, marched boldly into Pharnaces' country and camped on a hill over against the royal army, near Zela.

His easy victory over Domitius' attenuated force had given the King the idea he was another Alexander; he instantly and astonish-ingly attacked, uphill and at twilight. The auxiliaries in Caesar's center gave way under the charge of some scythed chariots, but the little veteran 6th on his right broke down the Pontic wing opposite, turned in on Pharnaces' center and threw that also into disorder, just as Caesar himself, with Cassius and Domitius, swung the 36th forward on the other flank and got the center rallied. Pharnaces was killed and his army wiped out; the monstrous empire he had built up collapsed.

Caesar found to his amazement that there was not the slightest spirit of nationality or resistance in town or countryside; a single deputy with a signet was enough to bring all the threads of government into his hands. It was his first intimation that these Oriental kingdoms, so imposing to an exterior eye, were actually like puff-adders, with all the strength in the head and nothing but wind behind it.

"Veni, vid, vici," he wrote home, "I came, I saw, I conquered them," considering any more lengthy dispatch unbefitting the occasion, but privately he remarked, "Happy Pompey! To have won the name of Great by victories over enemies like these."

This also represented a discovery—that Pompey's greatness required to be viewed from Pompey's angle.

5

Democracy in Action—On the 16th August Caesar was at Nicaea; on September 7th in Athens. He reached Tarentum on the 19th, before anyone expected him, and Brundisium two days later, where he met Cicero, a Cicero now utterly in occlusion, his troubles symptomatic of those he felt in the state, which, when all's said and done, he truly loved. Caesar greeted the old man with much consideration. They talked apart for a while before the conqueror sprang to saddle and rode off for Rome at his usual fiery pace, while the orator returned to his lodgings and wrote his wife that the Tusculan villa should be opened and a new basin provided for the bath, as he had permission to live near the city and was bringing a few friends.

It was the last letter he ever wrote her. A few months later they were quietly divorced and Cicero married a rich young madcap who had conceived the droll idea of appearing at drinking parties with a white-haired consular to play the ape of her jejeune humoresques. The old man hardly seemed to care, numb to an aching misery, not so much that his ideals had died, but warped into forms unrecognizable to himself, and in the procedure twisted askew the axis of his private life.

The old ideal of a nation great in the concord of its parts, unselfishly ruled by an aristocracy of talent who had proved worth by financial success—that went long ago, when the Senate flouted the eastern army's claim to gratitude and Clodius was bribed free of the sacrilege charge, setting the orders at variance and personality free to follow ambition. Corrupt, corrupt. ——There must stand behind right opinion (he had written then) a *rector* or *moderator,* strong and fearless enough to wield the military sword, philosophic enough to use it justly—— . . . but the moderator was not, as he thought, Pompey; he broke in the pinch, first his philosophy when he set the evil example of proscriptions, and then his strength, as though the widening fault had cracked clear across his character. Yet a man might still dispute with himself aphorisms on the relation of the citizen and the state, while hoping for better times, when the young men of the new school would be grown to social consciousness. And so this man Cicero had done till Caelius fell, the pupil whom he had intended as his spiritual legacy to a revived Rome, since his own son was proving less than Ciceronian.

He had cared for and tutored this young Marcus Caelius all his life, been more than a father to him, who was more than a son. The orator from the first had discerned in this favorite disciple a glimmer of his own keen interest in humanity, with some additional vivid spark not quite recognizable, but which he thought might be the flash of genius.

——Well, the boy must sow a few wild oats, he will settle down—— murmured Cicero, when Caelius was drawn into the outer fringes of Catiline's plot, but it was not long later when the orator had to defend him against a deadlier accusation. It came from vixen Clodia; Caelius had fallen into her net and become her lover, but astonished Rome and the lady by dismissing her before she was tired of him. The termagant was furious; it made her feel she was losing her grip, which is the gravest insult that can be offered to a woman who feels her charms becoming a trifle overripe. She retaliated by levelling a charge of attempted poisoning against the faithless lover, complete with evidence obtained from a few tortured slaves.

The shock seemed to sober young Caelius; after his acquittal he settled down to law and politics, spoke like an archangel, shone as a tribune, so that happy Cicero, sure now that the youth had found himself at last, made him his confidential correspondent when he went off to govern Cilicia.

The letters still survive; gay, dazzling, witty and malicious on Caelius' part, serious on Cicero's, with a certain heavy frivolity like an elephant at play, as he strove to fall into the light mood of his gossip; but with augmenting gravity as the realization was gradually borne in upon him through those tell-tale letters of what the unfamiliar streak in the alloy of his pupil's spirit was. Not a presence but a lack, the lack of the one thing that had enabled Cicero to swim safe through the seas of political passion—conscience, integrity, honest faith that a man can find a greater pleasure in acting true to some principle than in consulting immediate self-interest.

——Men (writes Caelius lightly, as the horizon shimmers red with coming civil war) should follow the more honorable part while the struggle remains within civil bounds; but when it comes to war, the stronger. And Caesar's army is incomparable, so that I am become a most hot ardent Caesarian and you had better do the same.——

So Cicero's great gift to the coming age was after all only another Clodius. Yet he could not but shamefacedly glory when the beloved, graceless scamp approved himself so well in his new service that he won appointment as Praetor of the foreign jurisdiction, the second ranking judicial office in Rome. Next would come a province—one of the Gauls? then the consulate—oh, aye, (whispered Cicero to himself, clutching at any straw of hope where he really had none) the young man would steady yet under weight of ambition, which may furnish a driving force equal to principle or pride in work nobly done. (He forgot Catiline.)

The defect in Cicero's hopeful prognostic, as he might have known by the company his disciple kept, was that Caelius' shimmering brilliance hid the mind of another butterfly, like all the Clodius-Clodia-Catullus-Calvus set, ambitious only to drink of whatever sweets lay near. He could play serious, none better, for he had noble parts; but this new industry was only a case of the devil being sick. The crown Caelius had hoped to gain with his transient sainthood was that of Urban Praetor, or high justice. He was fathomless in debt; the post had legislative as well as juridical functions attached. As lawmaker he could offer a stay-law popular with the debtor masses and steer it through the assembly of the people. As law-interpreter, read it to his own benefit, and best of all he would be in a strategic position to make himself a millionaire out of the estates of proscribed Pompeians.

The fine plan foundered. Credit had been destroyed, property sunk to the vanishing point, by the coming of the war, so that old debts were worth six times the values for which they had been contracted. But Caesar himself realized it before Caelius and designed a stay-law of his own, shooting it through between the campaigns of Spain and Dyrrachium. ——Creditors (it read) must accept stocks or property in discharge of old debts at their assessed pre-war valuation.—— Proscriptions, confiscations, fines, he rigorously forbade. Caius Trebonius, a judge advocate out of the military service, tiresome old man who believed laws meant justice, drew the big prize of the Urban Praetorship. Caelius himself got only the foreign jurisdiction, which gave him no control whatever over decisions in matters of debt, but many opportunities for useful service, the last thing he wanted. What was the use of serving a cause which would not enrich the server? and in a civil war, too!

Bah! He pouted; then set up his curule chair beside Trebonius' in the Forum and announced that anyone who wished to appeal from the Urban Praetor's judgment in debt cases would be heard. No one took the offer; Trebonius was satisfying all parties. Caelius tried legislation, offering a bill for a stay in debt payments without interest for six months. It fell flat, the terms of Caesar's law were better, even for those who owed most.

That third failure sent the young man right off his crumpet; he brought in a crazy bill for the abolition of all debt and house rent, had it vetoed and himself removed from office as a public danger. He sat down then and wrote an angry, bitter letter to old friend and preceptor Cicero. ——Well (he wrote), I wish that Curio were on your side; it was my friendship with him that imperceptibly lured me to embark on this accursed cause. As for you, you neglected your duty as a friend; you ought to have warned me about this. Oh, I'd sooner be hanged than endure any longer the sight of these rascals here.——

Nor did he endure them but set off post haste for Bruttium, where T. Annius Milo, the ex-mob-leader and murderer of Clodius, escaped from prison, had set up business as a kind of robber baron. Caelius, full of wonderful ideas for their mutual enrichment, got Milo to break open a couple of *ergastula* and make an army of the chain-gang slaves, and they marched off happily to plunder the city of Thurii, which Caelius proposed to gain by bribing the garrison with a share of the spoil. The garrison were some of Caesar's Gallic horse; for answer they charged into the convict band and killed both its leaders. And that was the end of Marcus Caelius Rufus, with his fine brain and fascinating wit and all the help and schooling Cicero could give him.

In the long run his fall was less of a blow even to Cicero than to Caesar, for he was the most gifted of the recruits from the old governing class to the service of the radical state; if he rotted they were all rotten. There was Servius Sulpicius Rufus, to be sure; after delicate balancings and many a heart-wrench, he had joined Caesar early in the war, declaring the Proconsul had the juster cause. But Servius Sulpicius was a justiciar, not an executive; he would serve any state well where he was permitted to handle those matters of civil and criminal law politicians consider beneath their notice.

Then there was Cornelius Dolabella, the jolly fat man, but he could not compare with Caelius for talent, and he turned out rotten, too. Having failed as a naval officer, he came home for a career of orgaistic debauchery in the Clodian manner, a great sorrow to Cicero, who had married his beloved daughter Tullia to the wretch. Dolabella abused her so shamefully she had to divorce him, a case which made a scandal, but what did the discarded husband care? He shrugged, stole his wife's money, and himself adopted a plebeian (like Clodius), won a tribunate and began a career as gang-leader,

Was downright left-wing Radicalism then the only cure, taking the leaders for the reformed state from the proletariat? The lower orders had given Caesar good sergeants for his armies, among them Antonius, lately named Master of the Horse and Governor of Rome. But how had that experiment turned out? Not well.

Antonius had left the army after Pharsalia when Caesar, disturbed by news of Caelius' uproars in the city, sent him there with the victorious legions, as the best man to bring things to order. Moment and man were ill-met; Antonius was naturally of a vaunting, ostentatious humor, with a passion for cheap glitter that betrayed his origin, now coming home in a tremendous glamor of military renown, with unlimited authority to grind down the men who had despised him as a cheapling. A man of intellect might have held himself aloof; one of philosophy would have been amused at the antic genuflexions of the rich men who had spent the last six months openly predicting Pompey's victory, and now tried to make it all up in a day by feverish adulation of Caesar's representative.

But Antonius had neither intellect nor philosophy, only splendid battle courage and a gasconading charm; he took flattery for fact. His mistress Cytheris met him at Brundisium; they rode to Rome together in a pair of gilded litters, a triumphal pageant with flute-players dancing beside them through the day, and supped from golden dishes, drinking themselves to stupor on precious old vintages every night.

At Rome Antonius' rule was well enough till Dolabella rose, for Caesar had given him strict orders on the conduct of business, and being a soldier, he obeyed them strictly. But outside office hours, he played the wild roue, with night-long carousings and feasts in honor of the marriage of actors and prostitutes, which he forced grave senators to attend with the idea of taking down their pride a bit. His headquarter was the old mansion where Pompey once lived with Julia, Caesar's daughter, in the street Carina; its walls decorated with the beaks of ships captured from Rome's enemies in heroic sea-fights—in those surroundings he drank and shouted.

"It is related that one morning, having to make a speech before the assembly, he came forward all boozy from an overnight debauch and vomited before them all. And it seemed very unreasonable that Caesar, with great fatigue and danger, should pursue the remainder of a hazardous war, while others by favor of his authority should insult the citizens with their impudent luxury."

Nor did his orders say what to do in such a case as Dolabella's, and Caesar could give no advice, being beyond reach of couriers up the Nile with Cleopatra. Antonius fumbled; Dolabella saw his chance, revived Caelius' crazy bill for the abolition of house rent and turned out the scum of the city to swing clubs and give a cheer for it. The landlords got up mobs of their own; there were riots in the streets and fires set to the houses of unpopular owners, while the Governor of Rome wabbled helplessly, afraid to unfriend the multitude who were his party's support, yet wishful to preserve the rights of property. The Senate gave no help; in a panic of fear lest Caesar come back and take off their heads, they spent every session voting him some new and ridiculous honor. He should have a consulship for five years, a dictatorship for as long as he wanted it, a triumph over Pontus, another for the victory he had not yet gained over the King of the Numidians. Matters went to such a pitch that the Vestal Virgins moved the public treasure to a place of safety outside the city. The Senate came to their senses a little then, and begged Antonius to restore order by force.

The next day was that on which Dolabella meant to bring his no-rent proposal to the vote. He had his gangs out the night before, barricaded the streets leading to the Forum and packed the place with his partisans. But the matter was military now and within Antonius' competence. At daybreak he came down from the Capitol in armor at the head of a legion of regulars; the veterans stormed through Dolabella's barricades as though they were paper, slew the boldest of the mob, captured the ringleaders and pitched them off the Tarpeian rock. A week later Caesar rode into the city.

The incident had more than casual importance. As in Caelius' case it had been not the individual but the Senatorial order that stood on trial, so in Antonius' it was the new radicalism, with its leaders raised from nowhere to the top through military merit. Antonius was the best of the legates as Caelius had been the most brilliant of the recruits from the old order, and his failure was more dismaying than that of Caelius, for the latter had merely demonstrated that the Senatorial order was rotten, which everyone knew before—but the former laid bare the defect, the inescapable greed, lack of refinement and carelessness of others' welfare, inherent in a system which brings to the control of wealth and power men who have no special training in the handling of either.

Radicalism not the answer then. The proletariat was as greedy, as selfish, as unproductive of any but imitative abilities as the aristocracy, and less attractive, because its vices were more vulgar. The disease lay too deep to be cured by any change of parties or even of constitution. Corrupt, corrupt; Cicero was right, when all the able individuals of the state campaign for their own hands, when individualism rots out the sense of corporate responsibility, there is no cure but the surgery of the sword. ——There must stand behind right opinion a *rector* or *moderator* . . . whose interest is non-political, who will administer the state as an estate, from the outside and above, with the mind of a soldier or an engineer and in the interest of cold efficiency, subduing all ebullitions of personality under military discipline. Otherwise your state will tear itself to pieces, whatever label its constitution bears. Antonius had done well in everything he did under orders.

. . . But the new organization meant a permanent military establishment and permanent military government.

6

The Unwelcome Gift—Antonius did badly with the veteran legions, too. They had been sent home from Greece to get a rest, but he gave them too much of it, with no drill or other occupation. They spent the long days visiting to and fro or listening to the sea-lawyers found in any idle camp. Mostly they were stirred by Antonius' example to follow his idea of a military man's proper place in a world at peace. ——To the victors belong the spoils; what have y' got to drink? where's our money?—— They could get no satisfaction from the junior officers, so began stoning them out of camp. Antonius was so busy with Dolabella he could spare no time to deal with them and did not know how to, anyway. By time Caesar reached Italy it was a full-fledged mutiny, and for two coppers they would have come to Rome and sacked the city.

Caesar sent Sallust, the literary legate, to talk them round with a promise of four years' pay and land allotments when work was done, but to point out there was a war to be fought in Africa, where the Pompeian refuse had coalesced round the Numidian kingdom. The men stoned Sallust too, and marched on Rome, where they gathered in the Campus Martius, milling around, singing an impromptu marching song whose burden was that they would have cash. Suddenly a wave of silence spread outward from the front ranks; those behind looked up to see their old commander, Caesar himself, standing quietly on the tribune, in the full regalia of a Roman general.

The crowd swayed forward; Caesar's voice cut sharply across their excited whisperings.

"Fellow soldiers," he said, "why are you here? What do you wish?"

"Money!" "Our bounty!" "Discharge—discharge—discharge." The last word rose like a refrain till they were all bellowing it.

Caesar surveyed them icily. "Very well, you are disbanded."

For a moment there was a gasping silence, while he let the import of the sentence sink in, then he spoke again. "I have promised you a bounty at the end of the war. You will receive it after I have conquered with the aid of others." He turned his back on them, every movement expressing scorn, and strode toward the steps leading down from the tribune. A few of the old sergeants, feeling like naughty children sent to Coventry, pressed forward, begging him at least to say a few words of farewell to the men who had served with him for eleven years around the world. For a moment the Consul hesitated, then turned back to the tribune and raised his hand for silence.

"Gentlemen—" he began, but that one word was enough, he got no further. Whatever the rest of the sentence had held, it was drowned in a vast chorus of "No, no! We are not gentlemen, we are soldiers!" The centurions of the 10th, the faithful old legion, pushed through the mob with tears on their cheeks. "Decimate us," they cried, "punish us as you will, but let the survivors go with you, and we will follow you to the end of the world."

Three weeks later the army embarked for Sicily, the base for the African campaign. The delay was caused by the necessity of straightening out the credit situation at Rome, where, after careful investigation, Caesar put through a law reducing excessive house-rents and another remitting all interest that had accrued on debts since he took the field against Pompey.

7

Dust, Elephants and Blood—King Juba had four legions, his own Numidian men, but drilled in civilized fashion. There were eight more of refugees and two of natives, with eighteen thousand horse and all the thousands one might name of light-armed slingers, bow and javelin men. Juba had sixty-four war elephants, Labienus sixteen hundred Gauls who had followed his fortunes across the sea. The leaders were desperate men, mostly breakers of their pledged parole, with that division of counsel and pursuit of queer fantastic ideas that is the stigma of the expatriate, but they achieved a kind of unity and elected Metellus Scipio, who had opposed Domitius Calvinus in Greece, as their commander.

His plan of war was as good as any can be that is pure defense; gather all provisions into the cities, hold them with heavy garrisons and let the navy patrol the shore. Should Caesar land, he must bring every quart of grain or blade of grass his army would eat. It was the edge of winter and there had been no harvest, for the Pompeians had kept the peasants of the African land at labor on the stones of their forts throughout fall and summer, so provision was scant in any case.

Caesar based on Lilybaeum in Sicily, with his tent hard by the shore. He was very short of ships, but on the 25th December sailed See map facing page 288 with six legions, two thousand cavalry from Germany and Gaul and a force of Cretan archers. There was trouble from the start. The fleet met storm, it scattered, and no rallying-point had been given, as Caesar was uncertain on leaving where he might find a landing place. On the 28th, with a few galleys only in attendance, he came to shore near Hadrumentum. As he leaped from the dory that brought him in he tripped, measuring his length on the beach, so evil an omen that the men about him gasped, but he cried aloud in a great voice, "Land of Africa, I have embraced you! You are mine!"—and rose with a face shining with joy, so that the soldiers burst into cheers.

There was little to cheer over in the situation when the troops were landed. Hadrumentum was garrisoned by two Pompeian legions under Considius Longus with 3000 Numidian cavalry, and Caesar had present only 3000 foot and a mere handful, 150 men of Gallic horse. They camped that night where they took shore. The Numidians from Hadrumentum came out to bother them while they were about it, but to balance that, there came word from Ruspina town, fifteen miles down the coast, that the gates would be opened if Caesar came, the folk there being heartily tired of the tyranny and taxations of the Pompeian leaders. The Consul set out for the place in the morning. The Numidians of Hadrumentum rushed after him and began to buzz around the rearguard, but Caesar flung his little force of Gauls at them in a tight charge, rein to rein, and so rumpled up the Moors that they let him alone.

The next day was the first of the new year. Leptis, a city six miles farther down the coast, sent in adhesion, and Caesar marched thither to gain it, a heart-lifting advance, though he still had worries enough to drive a man haggard. The rest of the transports had not come, there were no supplies and rumor of a big force on the march to smother him.

Legate Vatinius went out with ten warships to search for the troopships and convoy them in, or for alternative, to give the Pompeian battlefleet a blow that might sacrifice the ten but leave their enemies too lame to hinder sea-traffic. Messenger ships were hurried to Sardinia for corn and to Sicily for reinforcements and artillery. Two days more brought no news but of the enemy; Caesar took the desperate resolve of going on the search himself with seven cohorts to man the few remaining ships. He slept a night on the plan; at dawn, just as the men were beginning to embark, the missing convoy swept round the promontory and into harbor, giving the Consul his six legions once more.

Even yet things were not near the best; lack of victual nagged like a toothache. The morning after the troops' arrival Caesar set out on a big foraging expedition with three legions and four hundred horse, marching up a valley plain that leads behind the coastal hills. Three miles out the scouts brought word the enemy were at hand. Caesar swung his cohorts into line just as the foe came on, a great host, horse and foot together underneath an arching cloud of dust.

It was Titus Labienus with a good portion of the main Pompeian force, light armed and cavalry. He would not close, but set his cavalry circling, throwing javelins and shafts from a distance. Men were hit in Caesar's cohorts and charges futile, the cavalry were driven in by superior numbers. The sun was hot and as the long day wore the Caesarians were flanked at both extremities of their line, with the legionaries cramped into a narrow circle and things looking worse every minute.

Was there escape? Curio had died in just such a pinch two years before and Crassus in such another before that. But they had covered their faces and wept when the saw the dreadful prospect; Caesar let sound the trumpet, faced round alternate cohorts in a parade-ground manoeuvre that steadied the men by mere performance of orders; then blew again and hurled the tips of his line in a quick charge at the Pompeian ellipse around him. The ellipse tore through, Labienus' men were split in two sections and one of them was hit, hard and sharp, by a charge of the whole Caesarian line, so that many a light-armed Numidian went down in the rush. Caesar's men began to retreat toward their camp, with the Pompeians unwilling to get too close to them again, when up out of the desert came Petreius, the old opponent of Spain, with strong reinforcements for his party. Caesar's legionaries were dog-tired and their horses ready to drop, but now in great heart at having overcome the danger of the desert. They faced round cheerfully and gave one more rousing onset that broke Petreius, then made good their way to Ruspina.

That town Caesar made his headquarter, with a camp outside the place and an officer left at Leptis with three cohorts and the artillery. Metellus Scipio arrived within the week with his full strength, eleven or twelve legions and clouds of horse. He had plenty of provision from the country, while Caesar was so short his horses must be fed on a paste of sea-weed pounded up in water. Labienus with the Pompeian cavalry had a go at Leptis, but it broke down against the artillery, when a catapult nailed a high Numidian sheik to his buckler at three hundred paces, "whereat the rest, terrified, gave a shout and fled, and by this means the town was delivered from any further attempt."

Metellus moved in close and challenged to battle; Caesar stayed in his lines. Metellus sent for labor and began to close him in with trench and wall. But Caesar had a trick worth two of that; he slowed the labor by negotiation. There was a man named Publius Sittius; he had been in Catiline's plot at Rome, fled the city to save his head, and since had been living as a freebooter on the borders of Mauretania, with a gang of bandits. Caesar's agents reached him with a promise of free pardon and reward for aid; he took the offer. Just as Metellus was doing good work on the enclosing trench he broke loose far in the rear, stormed King Juba's capital of Cirta, sacked it, and ravaged the Numidian dominions so that the king turned back from Scipio's camp to face the freebooters and took his men along. The Pompeians were too gentlemanly to soil their hands with digging in a country where slaves would one day do it for them, so they waited, and while they waited a great Sicilian convoy reached Ruspina with the 13th and 14th legions, eight hundred Gallic horse and provisions in abundance. Caesar had the men now to move and fight. He started a campaign of manoeuvre, slipping south from the city along the seashore, then to the crest of a range of hills, and marching along the summit, set out lines facing west.

He was opposite and near the town of Uzita, the Pompeians' only source of water. Labienus, chief of cavalry in that army, pushed forward a few Numidians to break up Caesar's labor parties, but the Caesarians only dug the faster while their archers shot up the interfering cavalry. This made Labienus angry. He threw in his whole wing to retrieve the check and when they were committed, Caesar

THE SPANISH CAMPAIGNS

The two detail maps both cover the campaign against Afranius and Petreius. The numbers (1) and (2) indicate where the Pompeians and Caesar, respectively, camped after the first day of the pursuit from Ilerda. (3) is the neck of the defile to the high mountains where Caesar cut off the Pompeians' escape; (4) is the knoll the Spanish targeteers tried to gain. (5) and (6) are the final camping grounds.

let loose his Gauls into their flank. The attack was a surprise and
Labienus' heavy cavalry were wiped out. He himself escaped with
difficulty, and the Pompeian legions were so shaken that when
Caesar came down from his height to offer battle, they stayed on the
slope with Uzita fortified in their center and a deep wadi across
their front, which was a refusal to fight and gave Caesar the moral
superiority he had been seeking since the beginning of the campaign.

That cracked an egg but made no omelette; nothing happened in
a military sense. Caesar's men went on fortifying, but became very
miserable under continual rain and hail storms, once so heavy the
whole army had to spend the night sitting up with shields overhead
to fend off the beating. Tales began to run through the camp that
King Juba had disposed of Sittius the freebooter and was coming
back to destroy them with a huge army. As four of his legions were
recruits who did not yet know their commander's quality Caesar
judged it prudent to call the army together and make them a speech,
after the following manner:

"In a few days King Juba will be here. He has ten legions, thirty
thousand cavalry, a hundred thousand light-armed men and three
hundred elephants. Now stop spreading rumors and making con-
jectures about his strength. The next man I hear chattering will be
put on board some worn-out vessel and sent off to sail to nowhere."

When Juba did appear he had only three legions and thirty elephants. The Caesarian soldiers watched the parade from their hill-
crest with scorn, vowing they had seen better ones in the circus, and
went back to their business of digging on a new engineering work,
not the least clever of those Caesar undertook in his career.

It was a double line of trench and wall, reaching out from the
hills toward Uzita, which still was the enemy's only source of water.
King Juba's fantastical monarch humor bore hard on the Pompeian
dignitaries opposite as the work went on. He would not let them
wear red, his own royal color, or sit at meat after he had risen; but
without his scouting cavalry they were helpless, so they bore with
his manners. They were rewarded; Caesar's provision failed before
he reached their water-sources. He had to leave the front and
manoeuvre wide across the country for his bread.

The Consul could do this now, if not without risk, at least with a minimum. Early in March the Sicilian convoy had brought him the 9th and 10th legions and a little later the 7th and 8th. The arrivals were accompanied by two incidents, neither without its importance. When the 10th arrived, several of the vessels were loaded with slaves and baggage belonging to subalterns, embarked against orders and with tonnage much in need. The men who had done it were the same who led the mutiny near Rome. Caesar paraded them before a general assembly of the army:

"Tribune Caius Avienus," he said, "you instigated the troops to mutiny, you have plundered the civil population, you have taken slaves and baggage into the ships instead of troops and supplies. You are useless to me and to the service of the Republic. You are dishonorably dismissed from the service. And you, Centurions Aulus Fonteius, Titus Salienus, Marcus Tiro, Caius Clusinas, have shown yourselves unworthy to command by the same faults. You will leave Africa and the army by the first ship."

That purged the last remnants of the movement of disobedience and set the capstone on the structure of morale, already higher than that in the Pompeian army, which was suffering much by desertions. King Juba was a hard master and Metellus Scipio a cruel one; the latter tortured prisoners to death and punished his own soldiers with savage beatings; the former crucified those of his men who were beaten in skirmishes and executed whole townships that showed an infection of Caesarianism.

The other incident was on the sea. Attius Varus had brought the main Pompeian battle-fleet of fifty-five sail down to Hadrumentum, where he heard that Caesar's ships were divided, some at sea with the Sicilian convoys, some lying at anchor off Leptis. He made a sudden raid along the headlands with a favoring wind behind, burned out some transports, captured two warships and turned away. News came to Caesar inland; he would not let the matter rest, but galloped the six miles to Leptis, flung himself aboard a ship and put out into a rocking sea in pursuit. The wind still held from north and west, which slowed Varus, but was as severe against Caesar. Nevertheless the Consul pushed his rowers to so inhuman effort that they overtook the skirts of the Pompeian armada at Ruspina point, rammed one to the bottom, captured another, recovered the ships Varus had taken and harried him right into Hadrumentum. At dawn Caesar followed to that port; he burned or captured everything in the roadstead outside, and then went back, to the great comfort of the recruits in his army who now were sure they had a general who would never be beaten.

Back on land the campaign bogged down again into the old business of dodging here and there to get provisions. It was a long, intricate criss-cross of army movements, with Caesar marching along the ridges and ravines to avoid the Numidian horse which was such an unceasing pest, Scipio, Labienus and Juba trying to trap him into open country. Once they almost made it, but Labienus bungled, throwing his riders against Caesar's rear, which hurried along the retreat of the Caesarians, instead of attacking the head of their column, which would have slowed or stopped it. Once the allies set him an ambush, but the Consul got wind of it through his spies and counter-ambushed them with a loss of five hundred men.

The success was minor. All the successes were minor, they gained nothing but a full bread-bag for the day, and time fought like a giant on the side of the Pompeian allies. The weeks dragged on to April and spring, and Caesar perceived he could never manoeuvre these enemies into a corner while he had Labienus' craft and their huge clouds of cavalry against him.

The basis of the campaign must be changed. To what? The siege of cities, in which his own engineering skill and the hearty labor of the legionaries would give him an advantage over inconstant Moors and shirking Pompeians. It is only necessary to be superior to your enemy at one point in war if you can make that one point essential. To try the new system the army turned toward Thapsus, the great city of the southern coast, next below Leptis.

It stood on a promontory over the sea, with a big salt marsh like a needle's eye inshore and behind it. Caesar stole a march by night to the place and had it shut in with siege-lines before morning. Metellus Scipio and King Juba came pounding after him next day, advised by messengers from the town, whom Caesar had taken very good care to let run through.

Scipio swept round to the south of the marsh, seeking to braise a passage through the lines there, but found Caesar had anticipated that with a strongly held redoubt at the one point where the ground was smooth enough to let an attack gather momentum. He counter-marched then, round to the west face, and on the morning of April 8, drew up in triple line of battle opposite the Caesarian front, the elephants before his infantry wings to break down Caesar's oppos-ing flanks, the cavalry out beyond them to circle round and close a net behind the consular army as its center was allowed to drive for-ward between the shattered wings.

A good plan, but Caesar had foreseen it and arranged to counter with the old tactic of Pharsalia, to turn the enemy's strongest point into the device for his ruin. His line looked flat and ordinary from a distance, but there lay concealed behind each flank five cohorts of the 5th Legion, equipped to deal with the elephants. They were specially armed with sheaves of light javelins and fireballs; they had been specially drilled against elephants brought down from the circuses of Italy for the purpose, at whom they had been pitching cork-tipped spears these seven weeks to improve their marksmanship.

As the Caesarians tramped out into the open ground, cheerful and confident, they noticed signs of disarray among their adver-saries and wavering along their lines. A bugler of the 10th saw it clear; without orders he lifted his instrument to his lips and blew a long, thrilling blast; all down the line the other trumpet-bearers caught up the note and the Consul had just time to shout "*Felicitas* the watchword!" as his army went cheering forward in a charge of its own volition.

Scipio was not ready. The move caught his lines half disordered and his men half helmed. He threw forward the elephants and cavalry to take the shock, but out leaped the nimble legionaries of the 5th with their darts and their fireballs, and gave the elephants such a foretaste of hell that the big beasts turned and fled screaming right through the Pompeian lines. Out beyond the flanks the Gauls charged home, and the Numidians could not bear the weight of that stroke, but blew away like the haze of their own sandstorm, and the lines of infantry slashed in to close with Scipio's flanks bare and torn to tatters by the weapon they had counted on to win.

In proper sense there was no fight, only a moment's check before the dismayed Pompeians broke along the whole line. Their camp went lost as the Caesarians poured through the gates on their heels; the Gallic horse stormed Juba's camp like circus-riders. Flight was no safety in that bare land; the wreckage of the allied armies took refuge on a little hill and made the sign of surrender. Though Caesar rode among his men, crying "Spare them!" the legionaries, raging angry with the pains of this long war and Scipio's cruelties, romped fiercely in and cut them down to the last man. There fell Metellus Scipio and M. Petreius, King Juba and many other notable men. Of all the leaders only Labienus escaped and Cato, because the latter was not in the battle, but back at Utica, the capital of the province.

The news reached him through the arrival of some troops of Pompeian cavalry, who had ridden from the field by way of the little town of Parada, where, being refused admittance, they had forced the gates, and savage to the last, bound the inhabitants and tossed them into a bonfire of their own goods. Afranius and Faustus Sulla, son of the old dictator were their leaders. They wanted Cato to join them, plunder Utica and live the life of free border companions, but he refused and with the aid of Utica's citizens, half repulsed, half bribed them to go away into the desert, where they were presently slain by the natives.

Utica had neither heart nor mind to stand against Caesar's legionaries, though, who came marching into the suburbs a day or so later. The town flung open its gates. Cato retired to the rented house where he was living, read Plato's discourse on immortality and then committed suicide, being a sea-green incorruptible pedant, born into a world where he did not belong. Caesar was much put out at being deprived of the opportunity to show generosity to his most implacable enemy by forgiving him.

8

The Long Year—"A dinner party is my delight," wrote Cicero to his friend. "I have, in fact, just taken my place at table and am scribbling this in my notebook. Where? At the house of Volumnius Eutrapelus. Next above me on the couches is Atticus and below me Verrius, while next below Eutrapelus reclines Cytheris, Antonius' mistress. You will ask me what I am doing in such company. On my honor, I never supposed she would be present, but I can at least reply, like Aristippus the Socratic, who, when his friend reproached him for having a mistress, answered, 'Yes, but I am her master.' It is better in the Greek; translate it for yourself.

"Really, my dear Paetus, I advise you to take my prescription for a happy life; keep around you a group of good fellows and dine often. The government is dead. Do you really think there would be less legislation if I were in Naples? Here I am in Rome and in daily attendance at the Forum, and all the while the bills passed by the Senate are being drafted at the house of our friend Balbus, on whom you made such a good impression. Indeed, whenever it occurs to him, my name is put down as a witness to the drafting, and I am informed that some decree of the Senate passed in accordance with my vote has been published in Syria or Armenia before I ever heard of the matter. Do you think I am exaggerating? I have been receiving letters from petty kings in the uttermost parts of the world, thanking me for voting them titles, when I was not only in ignorance of their deserving the titles, but even of their existence.

"But, my dear Paetus, I am not inquiring into these matters because for the last four years the very fact of being alive has been so much clear gain, if indeed it be a gain, or if it be life at all to be living after the Republic has passed away. Are you surprised that we take our slavery so merrily? What, then, am I to do? Am I to suffer agonies, to torture myself? What good would that do me? Live, you yourself say in your books. And I have rather come to the conclusion that of all things the most beautiful is life, and cannot but regard with affection the man by whose grace I am granted it.

"I am moved to admiration of his solidity of character, fairness and good sense. Why, he never speaks even of Pompey but in terms of compliment! And I must own that he is gifted with an extremely acute literary discernment. I am told that in compiling the collection of witty apothegms which he is publishing, if any spurious witticism is offered to him as coming from my lips, he instantly detects and rejects the fraud. Just now he is keener than ever in the matter, since

Coin of Brutus

his intimates spend all their time with me. In the course of conversation I make a good many remarks which strike them as brilliant, which are reported to Caesar with the other news of the day, for that has been his special instruction.

"Well, then, such is my life; every day something read or written; after, that not to fail in courtesy to my friends, I dine in their company—reflecting that the wisest of men tolerated tyrannies either at Athens or at Syracuse."

Yes, yes, but this particular tyranny was as different from the classical model as Caesar's method of war from that of other commanders, the proof of it being that Cicero could call it tyranny in an open letter and make "certain clever epigrams" against "the Chief" and write a memorial monograph on Cato, flamboyantly admiring his manner of life and death, so ardent in its advocacy that the tyrant himself thought it worth while to write an "Anti-Cato" in reply. For tyranny, which in the beginning meant merely leadership, has acquired its ill name through regimentation of thought, a commodity which this tyrant considered underproduced at Rome.

Any thought whatever, even in opposition, if the opposition were confined to the means and not applied to the incontrovertible end of securing a wider spread through society of power and privilege; or fair government without violence.

Yet it was the end and not the means that the Senate hated their tyrant for, hired violence being in the last analysis, the root of their control of the state for their own benefit. And hating him, they built an image after their own hearts of the empty fierce megalomaniac, a kind of fetish-god who could be propitiated to complaisance by abasements. They would have behaved like that.

The news of the victory at Thapsus was received with ostentatious applause. Let it be celebrated (the Senate decreed) with a jubilation of forty days' length. *Cornelius Scipio got five for crushing great Hannibal and ending the Punic War.* Let Caesar have the dictatorship for ten years; let him be perpetually attended by seventy-two lictors; let him have the office of Prefect of Morals, with such superintendence of matters of daily life as the title might comprehend; let him sit in a gold chair before the Senate; let him take precedence of the consuls in speaking; let his statue be set up in the temple with an inscription beneath—CAESAR IS A DEMIGOD.

They thought he would be pleased by this sort of thing. It would have pleased any of them, the noble lords, strolling through their gardens, watching the butterfly-finned carp at their slow pavannes in the pool below. But Caesar, as usual, kept his thoughts to himself and went in the afternoon to Balbus' house, where a decree was drafted as from the Senate, abolishing "social" clubs of the kind that had been the keystone of Dolabella's riot gangs and Clodius' before him—with a special exception in favor of the Jews, whose clubs were really social. Then it was a decree ordering a return from lodging-house keepers on the number of persons receiving the corn-dole in their buildings; and a decree reducing the number by half and sending the rest out in colonies, with land of their own to work and towns of their own in which to market the produce. Then a decree restricting jury service in cases involving large sums to men rich enough to be beyond bribery; then one to reduce luxurious clothes and eating, which sadly failed of its purpose.

Even the calendar received its decree, which we know more of than any other and is worth dwelling upon as an example of the workings of the mind that made it, peremptory and vigorous. There was a man named Sosigenes, an astronomer of Alexandria, to whom Caesar commented while in that city, on how the times had fallen out of joint with the seasons, so that freezing winter first closed down in March and the dog-days fell in October.

The reason was clear enough to both. Months were reckoned by the moon with 29 or 30 days in each, and failed to meet with the sun's paces. The old Roman, "virtuous" custom had been to have the College of Priests appoint an intercalary month every three years and so bring the moon to meet the sun. But the College of Priests was a college of senators. While Caesar was in Gaul they had refused the intercalary months, being unwilling to prolong his term by even so much.

So the Dictator declared there must be a new calendar entirely, proof against human greed or stupidity; Sosigenes helped him build it, and a decree was issued giving January, August and September two extra days each, April, June, September and November one apiece, setting up the leap-year arrangement which has ever since endured and bringing the old system into adjustment with the new by making the present year one of fifteen months. The Senate helped the work in its usual fashion—viz, by voting that the month Quintilis should thenceforth bear the name of Julius.

So much to do—so few hours! Is it surprising that anyone who would help with the task, even if his previous service were inimical, was welcomed? Caius Cassius, the cadaverous, hard-hating soldier, was Caesar's Legate now, reorganizing the eastern garrison troops for desert campaigning in view of the threat from Parthia. Marcus Junius Brutus was Governor of Cisalpine Gaul, Servius Sulpicius governor of Achaia; the Marcellus who stripped and scourged through the streets one of Caesar's men in the pre-war days, and who had fought like a tiger against the Dictator in Greece and Africa, that Marcellus was restored to the Senate with honor, because he was after all, a sound parliamentarian, who sometimes talked good sense.

Unfortunate that the best men in the Senate, the men with any shadow of public spirit and ability, had to be drained off into the administrative services, and the new members from the lower orders took the pitch from the aristocrats they had always thought their betters, while the strong provincials brought into Rome, men like Balbus, full of happy talent in their own jurisdiction, shriveled

Coin of Cassius

up into ineffectiveness under high-bred ridicule.—"If you meet one of our new Gallic Senators, pray tell him where the government house is and have him pull down his toga far enough to hide the hair on his legs."

So the Senate, in spite of Caesar's efforts, remained the gentleman's club it had been for the last sixty years, debating gustily—Whether Caesar's triumphal car should stand beside that in which Jupiter's statue was borne through the streets on state occasions, or only beside that of Minerva? The vote was Jupiter, and the Dictator-Consul-Demigod was not well pleased.

But we may take it that there was pleasure over the new honor in the villa under Janiculum where Queen Cleopatra now lived with the baby Ptolemy Caesarion, born while his father was on the African campaign.

9

Anger in Iberia—Quintus Cassius Longinus failed in Spain. He suffered from one disease endemic with Romans in power—avarice; and one endemic with proletarians suddenly raised to authority—

the desire to have someone kiss his foot. Overtaxed the provincials, sold justice, drove the troops to mutiny by capricious discipline and tried to wean them back by outrageous privileges, distributing fine clothes and silver bridles. It was the wrong method. They revolted.

Caesar sent Trebonius, who might have stopped the rot had he come earlier, a strong, just and severe man, skilled in law and military matters. But he was not big enough for the emergency he found, which had become complicated by the arrival in southern Spain of the two sons of Pompey, with Labienus, Attius Varus and all who had escaped the wreckage of the African war. Gnaeus Pompey, junior, was made leader for his father's name and his own talent, having shown great energy near Dyrrachium. He enrolled an army which had the standards of thirteen legions but hardly represented that much strength, being made up of the two legions that had revolted under Q. Cassius and a scouring of old soldiers, jail-break criminals, local freebooters, adventurous youths and the assembled roguery of the edge of the world.

Toward the end of the fifteen-month year they gained control of the province of Baetic Spain, in the south. Caesar had to call out the veteran legions and go in person against the revolt, which he did in a very sour temper and the legions, too, for they felt they had earned their rest. So the war was marked for bitterness at the outset, and young Gnaeus Pompey, "who thinks cruelty is courage" was not the man to give it any other character. He considered it amusing to torture prisoners.

Caesar, being in a hurry, struck straight oversea for the mouth of the Sucro river. To protect his flank a new legate, Didius, took the battle-fleet down the Spanish coast. Off the Pillars of Hercules he beat Attius Varus of the rebels in a naval action, hammered the wrecked fleet back into Carteia port and there held it under close blockade. Caesar landed on December 2; old soldiers joined his standard and he went sweeping south on one of his famous fast marches, eight legions strong. Before even the news of his arrival in the country, he was outside Corduba on the Baetis, capital of the rebel movement, where Sextus Pompey, the *See map facing page 305* younger brother, commanded. Curious note—dur-

ing the march, with the clamor of a vicious war about him, the
legions hurrying fast, the Dictator whiled away the hours by writing
a poem, one of the few poems he found good enough to leave in copy
for after ages. Second curious note—his heir did not agree as to the
quality of the poem and had it destroyed.

Corduba lies on the outside arc of a northward bend of the river,
with a stone bridge radiating to the center of the circle. Caesar
closed in the big outer circuit with siege lines, bridged the river on
an original system of his own—with gigantic baskets of stones, like
underwater gabions, as piers for the structure—and planted a redoubt
on the south side against the stone bridge. He was careful not to
make it too close in, as he wanted a loophole through which Sextus
could summon his brother to attack the siege lines, wishing to beat
the rebels there behind forts, as he had the Gauls at Alesia.

It worked that way. Young Gnaeus came up by forced marches,
but had too much sense to attack the lines. Instead he began building
fortified lines to connect up with the bridge. Caesar opened lines to
cut him off, and there was a mole-race. The pairs of trenches met in
a week; there was a clash of battle, very hard fought, with Caesar's
men losing under a double attack from town and relievers, and the
siege was broken.

That spoiled the plan of settling the war at a blow. Caesar passed
over into a campaign of manoeuvre and small sieges that would
hurt by cumulative effect. First step; the army decamped at night,
with watch-fires left burning to blinker the eyes of young Pompey's
scouts, circled swiftly round to the southeast and laid siege to the
hill-stronghold of Ategua, a long day's march away. Gnaeus Pompey
hurried after, but arrived too late to interrupt the work of building
the siege lines and could only make a vanguard action in which he
first drove in some of Caesar's cavalry, then was himself thrown back
by a reinforcement of foot.

In the town they had expected nothing less than a siege and were
short of provision. The population wanted to surrender, but the
hard Pompeian soldiery, men with heads forfeit in any case, drew
and quartered those who spoke for peace and pitched their bodies
over the wall, then tossed the babies of the place on spear-points for

a salad to their other barbarities. That did not ease the temper of Caesar's veterans; they cut the hands off runners trying to break the lines and butchered every prisoner they caught.

Nevertheless, as the siege ran down into its third week, Gnaeus Pompey managed to get a message through to concert action with the garrison. Just at twilight he hurled a column out of ambush against Caesar's lines, while the Ategua people made a simultaneous sally against the same point. They had concentrated a good deal of artillery to cover the attack, and it was well served; in the first burst of firing it brought down one of Caesar's siege-towers with a crash and fired two more by throwing burning brands. But this was an old game for Caius Julius; he counter-attacked crisply into the flanks of both relieving and sallying columns and threw them back. Next day Gnaeus Pompey was so used up he had to retreat and the garrison surrendered at discretion. Marvellous to relate, Caesar spared them all and merely sent them home.

The clemency was due partly to the fact that the Dictator had not time to bother with vengeances, for he was off after the enemy army, swinging dangerously round its flanks and supply-lines with the strong force of Numidian cavalry that had come out of Africa to help him, under King Bogud of Mauretania. There followed a long series of intricate manoeuvres, beyond the power of modern man to understand, since the only man who left an account of this war had no conception of their purpose and treated Spanish geography as an endless procession of hills and flats, all precisely alike. Only this is certain; that the two Pompeys cut the heads off the Caesarian inhabitants they found, and invariably discovered that rich men were engaged in correspondence with Caesar; that the exasperated legionaries of the Dictator's army crucified Pompeian scouts; and that at last the rebels, harried and discouraged, short of provender and with no good line of retreat, swung to a stand across the hill-slope of Munda.

Caesar heard the news at dawn by his Numidian riders. The men were put in order of battle and marched across a low and marshy plain toward where the Pompeian legions waited around their eagles, looming gigantic in the brilliant light and ultramarine shadows of a Spanish March day. They stood quietly on the hill; Caesar halted his own men and made them a speech. ——He disliked (he said) attacking at any time; the part of a good general was to win without wounds. The enemy's position was very strong; you could see how they were placed with an intrenched camp half way up the slope behind them and the town of Munda crowning the hills behind that, so even a victory might fail of being decisive.——

——No, no! (the legionaries cried) Go on, advance, fight them now!——And as they spoke, the Pompeian soldiers, fed fat with lying tales from their commandant that Caesar's men were raw levies who would never dare a battle, swayed a few steps forward. The cries in Caesar's ranks changed to the battle-cry; he gave the signal and charge met counter-charge under a whistling flight of javelins.

They charged and clashed and locked, hacking and stabbing through the dust. The Dictator's men could not gain an inch; he put in his second line. So did the Pompeys with their second line; the third lines were called up and added to the second and still the battle hung. The sun rose to meridian and passed it, and began to descend and the Pompeians, with numbers and the slant of the hill in their favor, gained a pace, then another, then two at once. Caesar, riding along behind his lines, saw them heave and give, the men struck slower and the battle-shout came fainter. Even the 10th, the fighting legion, in its post of honor on the right, seemed about to break up. The Dictator pushed his horse right into their ranks, shouting furiously at them—"Are you not ashamed to deliver your old general into the hands of boys?"—leaped from his mount, snatched up a buckler and a sword and fell into the battle like a private, parry and thrust with such skill and strength that a man went down before every stroke. More stung by his words than by the enemy's swords, the 10th rallied, the rest of the line rallied with them, they checked the Pompeian advance and restored the battle, but still it was only even and the first break on either side would be fatal.

There were those who called it Fortune after, but it was Caesar's own keen eye and sound preparation that made it. He had sent

King Bogud and the Mauretanians, light cavalry, no good in a close battle, around in a circuit to raid the Pompeian camp. At this peak of the conflict they reached it, and Labienus drew off a couple of cohorts to stop them. Caesar caught sight of the standards of these reliefs moving to the rear, and in a roaring voice that caught the attention of half the struggling troops on both sides, shouted "They fly! They fly!" The rebels looked over their shoulders and wavered, just as the Caesarians came driving in with hoarse growls of triumphant fury. In the instant the whole Pompeian line burst like a dam that has too long held back a press of water, the structure shivering to its component atoms.

Labienus was transfixed by a Mauretanian arrow as he fled. Attius Varus, the only man with a heart in all that rapscallion crew, died of a sword-thrust in the back; but the two Pompeys got away south and to sea, where they wandered the world as pirates till they were slain by the ordinary bailiffs of the law.

Enough of their men escaped into Munda to hold the place. They killed the male inhabitants of the town (but kept the women.) Caesar's legions were around the place by night, in a mood so grim that they built the siege parallels of the bodies of their dead foes, pinned together with javelins. Corpses do not pile well that way, so they hacked the heads off and used them for catapult ammunition. The rebels were bad and desperate men but they lacked the inner strength to stand such horrors long and soon gave up.

"I have fought many times for victory," said Caesar, as he was taking ship for Rome, "but that is the first time I ever had to fight for my life."

10

The Demigod—The analytical difficulty of the last, peaceful period of Caesar's life is the same in kind and degree as that of the first, or ante-military period, changing only in incidence. In that earlier Caesar we were dealing in effect, with two men—the cultured aesthete of wealthy family, and the politician, Caius-Jack. The coalition proved impermanent, and not merely because of the demands Caius-Jack made upon the time and attention of his twin, though these demands were certainly serious, isolating him for nine years in Gaul and near four in other parts of the world, with few companions but such rough soldiers as Antonius.

The splitting apart of the two personalities seems rather due to a discarding of aestheticism as a personal solution for the problem of existence. In time it dates from, and in thought is obscurely connected with the deaths of Julia and Aurelia, as though the artistic life of the spirit demanded in some way a home around which to crystallize. When Caesar returned from Gaul and Greece and Spain and all the other wars the old house at Rome can have held few but painful memories for him. Not that he was a man who wasted time over sentimentalities as such, but the loss of these two women somehow forced him out of the intellectual life of his own home into the general intellectual life of Rome.

And in that general intellectual atmosphere can be detected the note of the subtle and painful ostracism to which he was subjected—subtle as Cicero's extravagant praise of Cato for "virtues" which Caesar did not possess, or Lucretius' flight from the Dictator's gospel of action. To put it otherwise, the men in whose companionship Caesar most pleasured were oligarchs (or as they would have it, republicans) in politics and capitalists in economics. The central topic of their discourse was the injury Caesar had done them and the Republic by instrumenting a theory opposed to their basic ideas in both directions. They could not well discuss such topics with Caesar for mere good taste, and if they lacked the taste they would still have shut him out of the discussion for fear he would snip off their heads. The men who agreed with the Dictator politically—Balbus, Oppius, Aulus Hirtius—were hacks, yes-men, subaltern executives in whose contact there was little intellectual satisfaction.

It was doubtless this ostracism which made Caesar cling so to the two Bruti, Decimus and Marcus, and again and again to seek out old Cicero. The Bruti never failed fearlessly to speak out their minds. Marcus showed considerable ability as an executive and as time went on it appears that he took more and more, at least in conversation, the Dictator's point of view. He was the only real disciple from the old aristocracy, the hope of the new state, uniting the old Roman

virtues with an intellectual competence and a philosophic appreciation of the new order.

As for Cicero, he loved a sharp epigram too much to let even
fear bridle his tongue for long. There was a curious and characteristic
dinner which he gave the Dictator at his seaside villa: "Oh, what a
formidable guest! Still, I have no reason to regret his visit, for he
was most agreeable. He ate and drank without scruple and enjoyed
his food. It was a very good dinner and well served; beside the staff
were served right royally in these rooms. The humbler freedmen
and the slaves had everything they could want. In fact, I demonstrated that I was somebody. We didn't discuss politics, though there
was much literary conversation. However, he is not the sort of
guest to whom one would say, 'My dear fellow, come and see me
again.'"

Yes, there you have it—no longer the sort of guest who is invited
back, in spite of that old ineffable charm of manner and converse,
which is always to a certain degree an acquired characteristic. It
takes self-restraint, and an unusual amount of taste for the social
contacts for a man to sit, as Caesar did, at a board where he was
served rancid oil on his salad, to eat of it with apparent relish and
to continue amiable throughout the meal. It takes real effort to lie
outdoors wrapped in a cloak, and let another man have the one bed
available, though the high commander of the world, as Caesar did
for one of his officers who was feeling a trifle under the weather
during the last campaign. Or hark back and think how much effort
he must have put into the art of being socially pleasing in the days
when the women of Rome pleaded with Sulla to spare his life.

And now he was ostracized. How welcome the Dictator must have
found the hour of retirement to the villa under Janiculum, the one
place in the world where he could find someone with both the spirit
and the intellect to conduct an honest political conversation with
him and not grow acrimonious about it.

"*Reginam odi*"—"I loathe the Queen", wrote Cicero briefly of the
companion of that villa, and with very good reason he loathed
Cleopatra, for she represented a culture and a habit of mind opposed
at every point to the ideals he held dearest, and moreover, a habit

which she appeared to be imposing upon her lover with increasing success.

It has been maintained that the mere possession of absolute power over the state was sufficient to rot out Caesar's sense of proportion; that being a leader had made him a royalist. The explanation fails to satisfy for two reasons. First and most important, no idea is born of itself, nor grows of itself; like children they must pass through a process of generation and nourishment, and Caesar was a man sufficiently objective to have perceived what kind of a brat he was bringing up in this personal monarchizing tendency. He never before had shown any taste for power as power. He liked it, but as a tool, for what he could accomplish with it.

Secondly, his power was by no means absolute. The limitations upon it were those that lie upon every extra-legal authoritarianism, and were more severe, if not more visible than those upon strictly temporary dictatorship by the free consent of the masses governed. Caesar had the consent of the lower masses, it is true, but when one speaks of the masses in politics, the general meaning is not the people themselves but their leaders, and the consent of the leaders Caesar certainly did not have.

Under such conditions he could obtain faithful service only at a price, the price of a tangible reward to those who served. Thus, when he arranged that Dolabella and Antonius should be associated in the consulate on his return from Spain, both men were so bitterly displeased that the idea had to be abandoned. Dolabella wanted a consulate, but he did not want Antonius for his colleague, or in other words, wanted to collect all the financial rewards for himself, and Antonius would be sure to want his share. Antonius wanted a consulate but wanted to be sole consul, or at least with only Caesar for a mate.

It was not an extremely serious matter that fat Dolabella should be displeased. After having been suppressed in his frenetic tribunate, he had been carried off to the African war and had given a good account of himself as commander of a legion, but had done nothing to deserve large rewards. But Antonius felt with very good reason

that he was not only the ablest of the lieutenants but the most hardly
used and it was important to conciliate him.

When Caesar left him as Prefect of Rome during the Alexandrian
expedition he had hastily bought up the estates of various Pompeians
who expected them to be confiscated and unloaded them at auction
prices. He did not expect he would ever have to pay even these
prices—after all, the sellers were enemies of the public, since Caesar's
cause had been sanctified by victory as the official one, and to the
victors belong the spoils. This was, indeed, the normal Roman procedure in civil struggles, but it proved not to be Caesar's procedure.
When he returned to Rome he forced the astonished and greedy
lieutenant to pay up to the last sesterce of the prices he had offered
for the estates, and what was still worse, from Antonius' point of
view, had insisted upon bringing these estates under his Pre-war
Valuation law. The business ruined Antonius financially, leaving
him land-poor. It took him years to become solvent once more.

So he must be conciliated with a consulate, and since he asked it,
a consulate with Caesar as a colleague, and the Dictator, not wishing
to leave the man alone in charge of Rome after his previous failure,
had to postpone the journey he had intended to the Syrian frontier.

That frontier had been a sore spot since Crassus' defeat and death
at Carrhae. From the best reports Caesar could gather it would remain
one until Parthia were dealt with as effectively as Gaul, either by
downright conquest or the establishment of an unbreakable chain
of border fortresses. Certainly the problem could never be settled
by maintaining the present frontier, which wavered vaguely across
the desert, somewhere beyond the Transjordan district of Syria. The
powerful Jewish nation, whose strength the Dictator had done so
much to build up and whose friendship he had taken so many pains
to secure, was a considerable help, but Caesar was too much of a
political realist not to know that buffer states always ultimately break
down under the combination of internal and external stresses. When
this one went the trade route through the Syrian corridors, so vital to
the Empire's eastern life, would lie bare to the ceaseless Parthian
raids.

No—there was no solution but a military campaign in that direction. Caius Cassius and the Greek geographers Caesar had consulted in Alexandria both reported there was a great river running through beyond the desert, which might be made the basis of a frontier, like the Rhenus of Gaul. It would . . .

At this point the influence of Cleopatra, the monarchizing, glorifying influence, the drive toward superlatives and splendor for its own

Coin of Cassius

sake becomes discernible. It is characteristic of Caesar all through his career, there is not one violation of the principle up to this point, that he kept his objectives within easy reach. The solidity of his work and its permanence were due to this concentration upon the immediate objective. However he were pressed for time, he always took time to consolidate and root what he had gained. No one else, for instance, would have spent that last year in Gaul, settling matters apparently so petty that he did not even include them in his own account of the conquest. The revolt of the sons of Pompey in Spain represented the only time he had to go back and do a thing over (the arrangement of Spain) and even here one could advance the plea that he had never before been in Baetic Spain, the southern quadrant where that last war took place.

On the other hand, remote, incredible, star-flung plans were typical in the Hellenistic monarchies, and particularly in the house of Ptolemy. Superlatives were a natural concomitant of their rule, descending in an uninterrupted heritage of hyperbole from Alexander the Great, the son of a God and conqueror of the whole world, of whom the Ptolemies claimed to be the only legitimate successors. They had assembled as things quite normal to their status, the largest library and greatest scientific academy of the world; the biggest ship ever built had floated from the largest dockyard ever dug in Egypt; the Pharos was the tallest structure ever set up; and even silly old Ptolemy the Piper, when he went to war, had borne before him a banner on which were mingled the emblems of the ram's horns and the disc, symbols of universal sovereignity.

The point is worth laboring as bearing on the provenance of Caesar's idea for giving Rome an Oriental frontier secure against all possible future attack by subjugating the only remaining dangerous enemy state, Parthia. As much of the plan as comprehended the establishment of a Tigris-Euphrates frontier was assuredly his own. It was concrete, realizable with means at hand. So, undoubtedly, was the care that had placed Caius Cassius, the Parthian expert, as Chief of Staff on the army and enlisted a big force of Numidian cavalry, who could meet the Parthians at their own tactics. The rest of the plan, which was for nothing less than a gigantic march beyond the Euxine and that little known sea we call the Caspian, through the heart of old Persia, back north around the Caspian Sea and a return to Europe by way of Sarmatia, Dacia and Illyricum—that grandiose erection upon the original sound foundation, surely smacks of Cleopatra of Egypt.

Parenthetically, the forces destined for the expedition were sixteen legions, or over 80,000 heavy infantry, the greatest Roman army ever assembled, with over 10,000 cavalry, light Numidians and heavy German and Gallic horse and a prodigious force of archery. We can count on the organization and training being right up to Caesar's standard. Eastern desert warfare is very difficult, but so was Gallic forest warfare before he attempted it and the probability is that he would have accomplished what he set out to do, thus saving the world a great deal of trouble in later centuries.

The huge size and sweep of the project, however, marks the emergence of that new dualism; not the fugal interweaving of Caius and Julius Caesar, but of Caesar and Cleopatra. Of Caesar, in whom the old radical, leveling ideas persist and underlie every particle of the social and economic legislation put through under his dictatorship, and of Cleopatra, whose inherited absolutism was as natural to her as the air she breathed. In the Orient absolutism accomplishes half its purposes by the ostentatious insistence upon its power. When these ideas were grafted onto Caesar's original radicalism there resulted that strange type of benevolent despotism which distinguished the Roman Empire, about which the most curious thing is that all the echoes we can catch from the submerged tenth are in favor of it, while most of the upper classes write as though the existence of the institution were a personal injury to them.

As indeed it was; both its outer insistence upon personal rule and its underlying tenderness for the lower orders were in constant irreconcilable conflict with every ideal of the familied oligarchy of the Senate.

The historical difficulty lies in separating the two influences as they appear in the results and in separating both from the acts which the boot-licking Senate performed of its own volition. There is a strong tendency among the ancient historians who are our only sources to ascribe all centralization to an uninfluenced Caesar. ——Cato was right (is their theme); the man wished to be king from the beginning. His whole life has been a gigantic and careful plot to that end, and only now that he nears it is he throwing down the mask.——

There is a reason for this view; both the Roman and Greek intellectuals of the age had racial prejudices against women in politics and rejected the thought of a woman having political ideas as something quite inconceivable. The intellectuals, moreover, were both sentimentally and philosophically devoted to republicanism—not the broad democracy of today, but the oligarchic republicanism of Sparta or Plato's utopia, in which the citizens are outnumbered by the servile classes who have no more voice in affairs than their own breeding-cattle. It was the only type of democracy they had seen at work or even heard of. Such ideas as universal freedom from servitude and universal suffrage were altogether beyond the range of their minds. When Caesar put through a decree that the great sheep-farms of Italy should employ one free man for every two slaves, they were utterly unable to understand why.

They could see nothing in Caesar but a magnified Clodius or Dolabella, trying to subvert society and erect a personal monarchy on the ruins. It was not a view that made for sound judgments, and their attributions of motives nearly always demand re-examination. Thus, when we are told that Caesar provided for extra praetorships "in order to make places for his followers" it is possible to pronounce at once that the ancients are wrong as to the motive and to say that of the three influences at work on the formation of the new system of government, the old liberalizing Julius Caesar certainly was the author of this feature. The Dictator's care for the honest administration of criminal justice was one of his most striking characteristics. The praetors were judges and he had found the court calendars hopelessly jammed. The proof of his honesty of intent is the result, the same writers who accuse him of making offices for place-men admitting that he permitted no sinecures. Moreover, a modern critic has acutely noticed that the number of the new praetorships was exactly equal to that of the provinces which were assigned to ex-praetors—praetorian provinces.

On the other hand it is possible to trace to Cleopatra, if not directly, at least by influence, such an affair as the announcement from the keeper of the Sybilline books that Parthia could be conquered only by a king. Possibly she even bribed the announcement, though this is all conjecture. And it is possible to trace to the Senate or to Cleopatra (their minds showed a curious convergence of action from opposite poles) such enactments as that which set Caesar's statue in the Capitol with those of the seven legendary kings of early Rome, or placed another statue beside that of Victory, with an inscription—"To the Unconquerable God."

Caesar doubtless regarded these manifestations as curiosa; he gives the impression of having been too busy to bother with such matters. Only once do we find him expressing satisfaction with any of the adulatory honors—on the occasion when the Senate voted to allow him the privilege of wearing in public and on all occasions the laurel wreath of triumph. . . . It concealed the bald places on his head.

Yet there was a real danger, which he seems illy to have apprehended, in such enactments as the one which permitted him to appoint the candidates for praetor and consul, offices which were theoretically purely elective. The bill was no more than a legalization of an accomplished fact; and since the days of the Gracchi, a century before, the elections had been hardly more than a public confirmation of the choices of the ruling oligarchy. But the decree brought Caesar's paramount position into the open, as did the law conferring upon him in permanence the title of Imperator, which had hitherto been granted only by victorious armies and for the period between the victory and the official triumph.

The title, the statues and the statutes were all received with dissatisfaction among the common people who furnished the real basis of Caesar's power. Not a hand was clapped when his image was set beside that of Victory, and when on the Lupercalian festival, Antonius tried to rush matters (and perhaps also to restore himself to the lost favor of the Demigod) by offering him a king's crown, a universal groan went up from the spectators of the scene.

Caesar had the good sense to push aside the dangerous gift, but he could hardly anticipate the absurd genuflexions of the Senate. His normal abhorrence of such displays, his normal good artistic taste, may well have become half blunted by the necessity of constant refusals, and also by that constant intercourse with Cleopatra which in itself formed a scandal at Rome. It was not that he kept a mistress; most of the senators had queues of mistresses. It was not even that Caesar was married (he had married a daughter of Calpurnius Piso on the eve of the Gallic campaign for political reasons, a wedding of which we know only that it took place.) It was rather that social Rome felt the Prefect of Morals owed it to his office to throw a decent veil of hypocrisy around the liaison, whereas he lived with her openly in the Janiculan villa and conducted public business from the place. Her character was not one that endeared her to the average Roman, either; capricious, arbitrary and arrogant, she was probably the best hated person in the city.

But to all these matters the Dictator remained profoundly indifferent. He was too busy with the vast program of reforms which remained the backbone of the nation for years under the name of the *Leges Juliae*. They have a peculiar common characteristic; they are mainly administrative, looking to the foundation of good precedents and vested interest to uphold them. It is as though the man who made them had become conscious suddenly of how much stronger tradition and custom are than written enactments, particularly when defended by a group of public functionaries.

The older method of providing for discharged soldiers, for instance, had been to do something for each group in a special law, as when Caesar himself had cared for the veterans of Pompey's eastern wars in the famous Campanian land act. The Dictator founded a self-perpetuating board of commissioners whose duty it was to place old soldiers out in colonies as fast as their time expired, and he himself gave an impetus to the business by planting several large foundations —at Carthage, at Corinth, in several Spanish towns, the 10th Legion around Narbo in Gaul, the 6th at Arelate, also in Gaul.

The collection of literature and its permanent availability to the public were similarly assured by a permanent commission on libraries, with Caesar's old enemy, Varro, the literary agronomist, as director. Another board was placed in charge of bringing to Rome and placing on the citizenship rolls men of science, wherever they might be found. Still another commission had charge of periodical revisions of municipal charters in small cities, with a pattern municipal constitution written as a model for them to work from, as well as a set of standard police and sanitary regulations. The interesting thing about all these boards is that they had money to spend and therefore developed a lively interest in defending the system of which they formed a part; and all of them covered matters that had been treated in haphazard Senatorial enactments or provincial governors' decrees. It was a thoroughly realistic treatment of the problem.

Physically also Rome was being reformed, with the new Forum and Senate House now far advanced, and half a dozen gigantic public works—the draining of the Pomptine marshes, a breakwater at Ostia to convert it into a true harbor for deep-sea vessels which must now lie in the offing, the canalization of the Tiber to prevent floods and beautify its line, the construction of a great theatre on the Tarpeian rock—were in the stages of projection or design.

Even the public works fell under the disapproval of the old Conservatives, who could find nothing in them but more evidence of that Cleopatra-Caesar element of ostentation and personal aggrandizement which they found so distasteful. Why should they select these matters? There was evidence enough of this trend without reaching it from the sky. It might have been the unaided Senate that passed a law that Caesar should have his portrait stamped on the coins of the Republic with the legend *Pater Patriae*, "Father of His Country", circling round the face. But it was Caesar and Caesar alone who received a delegation from the Senate in the porch of Venus' temple, and received them sitting while they stood, with his fine-cut nostrils spreading in disdain as the lordly nobles expressed in rolled eyes their shocked horror (histrionic, like most of their emotions except greed) at an action which indicated the doer thought himself royal.

That was Caesar in his epileptic fit, said some of his friends like Balbus the Spaniard, apologizing for something they could not understand; actually, it was Caesar under the influence of Cleopatra, doing a strange thing, as a man will when drugged. Yet it is difficult to see her influence or any influence but an honest righteous indignation with stupid officialdom in the famous incident of the Conservative tribunes Flavus and Marullus. It happened thus: the Dictator was out riding with his entourage. "Hail, King!" cried a man in the crowd, cheerfully. "I am not king, but Caesar," answered he, (it is a pun in Latin) reining in with a smile to salute the shouter. Flavus and Marullus, however, slammed their horses into the crowd, seized the man and had him thrown into prison for an offense against the dignity of the Republic. Caesar overrode their authority and let him go. The tribunes published a long, tearful manifesto, saying they had no liberty of action, wherupon he gave them something really to wail about by having them removed from office. The Conservatives insisted that the real reason was to encourage more people to salute him as "king" and so acquire the title by acclamation, but they could do nothing about it but be indignant.

That was the trouble; they could think of nothing but their own indignation, and how sweet it would be to return to the good old days when they had ruled the world by endless conversation from the villas where the carp splashed in the marble-throated pools, heedless of the fact that that old world was breaking down and had suffered four revolutions in half a century. Cicero was indignant because the Dictator was too busy with the commissioners for building the new Forum to exchange bon-mots with him when he called one morning, but he was an old man and took his anger out in writing acidulous letters on how shameful it was that the first orator in the world should be kept cooling his heels in an ante-room. Caius Cassius, the thin gangrened dyspeptic, was indignant because he had only been named second-in-command for the Parthian war and not commander; Marcus Junius Brutus was indignant because he was not allowed to lend money at forty-eight per cent; such men as Ligarius, who had fought under Pompey's standards in Greece, and Metellus Scipio's in Africa and twice been forgiven and paroled, were indignant (they said) because of the death of Cato; young Decimus Brutus was indignant because it was the fashion to be indignant, and Trebonius the lawyer was—

No matter; they all had their reasons which were in essence one reason—that Caesar was different and they feared he was better than they. So they voted in open Senate that the members take an oath to defend the Dictator's life with their own. They marched to the temple of Jupiter Optimus Maximus, greatest and best, in a body to swear, and marched out again through lanes of saluting commoners, with the chant of the priests growing faint behind them and the odor of incense on their garments, and crawled into corners with others of their kind and made a plot to murder the man they hated.

The secret was not too well kept. A soothsayer warned Caesar to stay home on the Ides of March, a man shoved a note into his hand with details of the conspiracy. But the Dictator would not believe. Even after all his experience with their stupidity he would not credit that these men could be so stupid as once more to submit their quarrel to the arbitrament of blood after having so narrowly escaped with their lives. So he went to the Senate as usual on the Ides of March, and meeting the soothsayer on the street, promised to turn his prophecy round on him as he had turned the evil omen of his stumbling on the African shore.

He could not make it. As he took his place before the august body, one Tullius Cimber came forward with a petition for the recall from exile of his brother. Caesar had already considered the case; he refused. Tullius Cimber knelt at his feet in a passion of supplication, then snatched the hem of the Dictator's toga and yanked it down. It was the signal; a man named Casca jerked out a dagger and gave Caesar a glancing cut in the neck, spinning off balance as the Dictator half dodged, half struck aside the weapon, crying "You scoundrel, what's this?"

"Help!" shouted Casca; in a moment they were all around him, a dozen or score of swords and daggers. Caesar parried with the fold of his garment, striking out against them with his naked fists till he saw amid the crowding faces one face, distorted with rage, hatred and fear—the face of the beloved friend and disciple, the son of the woman he had loved, Marcus Junius Brutus.

"You too, Brutus?"—and he fell dead, at the foot of Pompey's statue, in the fifty-sixth year of his age and of the Roman Republic the seven hundred and tenth.

BIBLIOGRAPHY AND NOTES

The sources for the life of Julius Caesar are by this time so well known and have received such elaborate attention from scholars that any discussion of their relative importance and credibility would be impertinent. In compiling this book, the chief ancient sources used were the works of Caesar himself, with those of his commentators, Aulus Hirtius (who wrote the last book of the "Gallic War" and possibly that on the Alexandrian war), the unknown authors of "The African War" and "The Spanish War." Cicero's speeches and letters were a mine of information, particularly for personal impressions and touches. Plutarch's lives of Caesar, Pompey, Cato minor, Cicero, Lucullus, Crassus, Pompey, Marcus Brutus, Sulla and Antony were also laid under contribution. Velleius Paterculus and Dio Cassius supplied a little material, as did the poets, Catullus and Lucretius. Suetonius' biographies of Caesar and Augustus, though ill-tempered and inclined to gossip, also furnished much of value, and there are fragmentary hints of no great value from other ancient authors.

Among modern authorities T. Rice Holmes ("Caesar's Conquest of Gaul," "The Roman Republic," and "Ancient Britain") was used most heavily, and his elaborately documented and finely-argued identifications of localities and decisions on disputed points have been followed as a general rule. The few variations have been noted in their proper place in the notes that follow. Other modern authorities used were the Cambridge Ancient History, vol. IX; Sihler's valuable "Annals of Caesar", especially useful in coordinating dates and events; Froude's "Caesar"; Mommsen's "History of Rome"; Abbott's "Roman Political Institutions"; W. Warde Fowler's "Social Life at Rome" and "Religious Experience of the Roman People"; Delbrück's "Geschichte der Kriegskunst"; Napoleon III and Baron Stoffel's history of Caesar and Dodge's "Caesar" which is largely an English rewrite of the same; and Ferrero's "Greatness and Decline of Rome."

15)—Pompeia's blondness is a matter of inference; however she belonged to a family famous for its ruddy complexions and its red hair, and the family name indicated the quality. It seems reasonable to believe that she partook of the family characteristics.

19)—There is disagreement among the classical authors as to whether or not Clodius escaped the house unscathed. Plutarch says the women gave him a beating; Dio Cassius, that he got away without damage, and so there has been a fine argument among classicists which need not detain us here except for the remark that the most likely version was chosen.

22)—There is no direct statement of a plan to dampen Catiline's candidacy for the consulate in any classical author. Yet one is driven to some conclusion of the kind in view of what did take place. As for Clodius' part in it, he was almost certainly too young to be an active member of Catiline's plot.

41)—Sihler ("Annals of Caesar") thinks the incident of Alexander's statue took place during Caesar's first visit to Spain, on the ground that when Caesar made the second trip there he was already older than Alexander had been at the time of his death. The reason seems inadequate; after all, the classical historians bear generally so good a reputation for truth that there is no reason for distrusting them unless there be strong and direct evidence of error on their part.

46–47)—The information on Spain in ancient times is largely drawn from Dierck's "Geschichte Spaniens", in which there is evidence of much patient and useful German research on the various points considered.

64)—The date of Cornelia's death is uncertain.

68)—The meaning of the Latin word Cicero is "With the Wen."

70 et seq.)—Lange has pointed out that the land bill could not possibly have been introduced before February. Bibulus had the fasces, and thus outranked Caesar, during January; and thus many commentators who have insisted upon the January date must be wrong.

76)—Bibulus' edicts. The "Queen Nicomedes" scandal is never mentioned at any date earlier than these edicts, though frequently afterward. It is not an unreasonable supposition that it began with them.

78)—It will be pointed out, of course, that the *ius gentium* made its appearance in the Roman law of contracts long before this date, especially in the acts of the *praetores peregrini*. But this was a commercial convenience only. The carry-over into a regular form, and its establishment as an integral portion of the criminal law, was made by Caesar;

and this is the only hypothesis on which the accounts of his criminal legislation will make sense.

78)—The quotation beginning "There is a universal law—" is from W. Warde Fowler, epitomizing the viewpoint of Servius Sulpicius Rufus.

99)—"And on this account they were greatly distressed—" quotation from Caesar, "Gallic War."

103)—I do not think it has been noticed before that Liscus' charges against Dumnorix many not all have been true. Caesar does not, indeed, say they were true; he merely reports them as remarks, like the good reporter he was. And Liscus was a small man in a big official position, whose envy of Dumnorix' ability for leadership would undoubtedly sharpen his tongue.

120–121)—The strength of the legions at various times is a subject of endless, futile and unconvincing argument among military authorities. At the beginning of the Belgic campaign, however, there is good reason for believing that Caesar's eight legions were all up to nearly normal field strength, or about 5,000 men apiece.

121)—"Black-faced javelin-men from Numidia." Caesar says repeatedly *Numidias et Cretas saggitarios* which is usually taken to mean "Numidian and Cretan archers." But it may equally well be "Numidians and Cretan archers", a reading which seems vastly preferable to the present writer. The Roman auxiliaries were chosen for their skill in handling some special arm, and the Numidians were not a race of bowmen; the horn-bow had not been invented yet and their country produces no wood that is suitable for either bows or arrows. On the other hand the Numidians were most famous lancers when they rode and javelin-men when they went afoot; they appeared in the Circus in Imperial times always in that guise. Why did not Caesar call them javelin-men specifically, then? Because every Roman had been familiar with the picture of a Numidian in arms as a lancer or javelin-man for a couple of hundred years; the mere mention of the word "Numidian" would call that picture to his mind, and Caesar, always sparing of words, did not bother to explain something with which he knew all his readers were already familiar.

141)—The usual assumption, shared by Rice Holmes, is that Brutus built all his ships during the winter, and was delayed in coming to the coast by foul weather. The failure to put a stop to the Venetan plan of removing the population of beleaguered towns by sea certainly indicates either Roman naval defeats or a total lack of warships to prevent the continuance of the Venetan method. But it is most unlikely that the weather, however bad, would keep all Brutus' ships waiting in the river for a matter of months. It seems more reasonable to believe that Caesar originally planned a land campaign with a slight supporting force accompanying him along the shore, and that it was beaten. It is no objection to the version adopted here to say that the galleys would take time to build, as with the labor available they could be built comparatively quickly, being needed for only one brief campaign, and Decimus Brutus later showed he could build a fleet in very short time during the Civil War.

152)—The quotation beginning on this page is made up of selections from two or three of Cicero's letters to his brother. No great violence has been done in selecting and assembling these extracts, as Cicero wrote a number of letters at almost the same time. Indeed, he himself mentions the delivery of four in one packet.

173)—The banishment of Gobannitio is usually placed after the massacre of Cenabum. All that can be said is that Caesar's account is susceptible of either interpretation, and it seems logical to date the event as in the text; after the Cenabum massacre Vercingetorix had matters more important than petty local politics to think about.

183–184)—Caesar's plan in the assault on Gergovia has caused endless argument among commentators, and this is the first time, so far as I know, that the version given in the text has been suggested. Both Napoleon III and Rice Holmes suggest it was intended as a direct assault on the fortress; but it does not seem reasonable that Caesar, one of the most careful of generals in planning the material furniture of his movements, would have sent his men on in an assault without giving them ladders, axes or any means of attacking walls or gates. Moreover the 10th Legion was in position for nothing but a flank blow against a force debouching from the saddle of Risolles.

189)—The quotation is the final passage in Caesar's "Gallic War."

205)—It does not alter the essential facts of the case, nor the force of the argument, that Caesar treated the prisoners captured at Uxellodonum with great, and to a modern mind, unwarranted severity. They had their hands cut off and were sent to beg their bread. Roman opinion, and even Gallic opinion, recognized the punishment as not too severe, in view of the fact that these men were not rebels, but a sort of highwaymen's association; and the normal Roman or Gallic punishment in such a case would have been even more severe than that which Caesar gave.

209)—"An example to the wise of inconsiderateness . . . etc." The quotation is from Plutarch's "Crassus."

214)—"There are strange whisperings . . . etc." The quotation is from Caelius' letters to Cicero.

215)—"I shiver at every word . . . etc." From Cicero's letters to Atticus.

216)—"How slow and inefficient his is!" From Caelius' letters to Cicero.

217)—"A man of noble birth . . . etc." Quoted from Velleius Paterculus.

218)—"You see the point . . . etc." From Caelius' letters to Cicero.

218)—"What am I to do? . . . etc." From Cicero's letters to Atticus.

222)—"Jacta esto alea!" E. G. Sihler has pointed out that Suetonius incorrectly quoted this phrase as "Jacta est alea," whereas in its correct form the quotation was one common at Rome, being taken from Menander's "Arrephorus", and moreover, it makes much better sense in that form.

226–227)—The quotations on these pages are excerpted from some of Pompey's letters preserved with Cicero's papers.

230 et seq.)—The two letters quoted in this section, as well as Cicero's conversation with Caesar, are quoted from Cicero's letters.

234)—"The country is covered with deep woods" no longer. But it was in Caesar's day.

235)—"Fabius was weaker in numbers—" Caesar had, at this period, the habit of raising entirely new legions instead of recruiting the old up to strength as in the first year of the Gallic war, though the latter procedure was followed in a few isolated cases. The six legions in Spain had suffered by waste of war and retirements; they cannot have numbered more than 3500 men apiece and probably less, while Afranius' legions, having been on garrison duty, were full strength or very nearly.

236 et seq.)—Quotations in this chapter are from Caesar's "Civil War."

261)—"Since his soldiers would not confer on him the title of Imperator . . . etc." Quoted from Caesar's "Civil War."

262)—"Think not that his army . . . etc." Labienus is quoted by Caesar in the "Civil War."

264)—"I am aware . . . etc.," Pompey is quoted in Caesar's "Civil War."

277)—The whole section that follows is based on inference but as it bears internal evidence of the fact no defense will be attempted here.

277)—"We do not know whether Cleopatra's nose . . . etc." Quotation from G. Maspero.

310)—Cicero wrote several letters to Paetus, all within a month or two of each other, and with no essential change in the outlook expressed. Extracts from three or four have been combined as in the case of his letters to his brother in Gaul.

INDEX

The Roman naming system, so different from our own, makes considerable difficulty in an index. In making this index the most commonly known name has been used for a key (as, *Pompey*) with cross-reference from other names.

The Latinized forms of Gallic names have been used both in text and index. It is interesting to recover the original Celtic forms (Cassivellaunus, for instance, is Caswallon) but it was felt that readers familiar with Caesar's "Gallic War" would find the result both puzzling and unsatisfactory. Besides, the Gallic war is related through Roman eyes, and the ancient Romans, like the modern British, paid little attention to local etymology. In this index the modern names of Gallic places and rivers have been given in parentheses in cases where they have been identified with a fair degree of accuracy. Some Gallic towns (notably Bibracte) have no modern counterpart, being built on the summits of high hills, a most uncomfortable situation by modern ideas.

348   INDEX